100 BEST

Surf Spots

IN THE WORLD

Help Us Keep This Guide Up to Date

Every effort has been made by the author and editors to make this guide as accurate and useful as possible. However, many things can change after a guide is published—establishments close, phone numbers change, facilities come under new management, and so on.

We would love to hear from you concerning your experiences with this guide and how you feel it could be made better and kept up to date. While we may not be able to respond to all comments and suggestions, we'll take them to heart and we'll also make certain to share them with the author. Please send your comments and suggestions to the following address:

The Globe Pequot Press
Reader Response/Editorial Department
P. O. Box 480
Guilford, CT 06437

Or you may e-mail us at:

editorial@GlobePequot.com

Thanks for your input, and happy travels!

INSIDERS'GUIDE®

100 BEST RESORTS SERIES

100 BEST
Surf Spots
IN THE WORLD

The World's Best Breaks for Surfers in Search of the Perfect Wave

ROD SUMPTER

INSIDERS'GUIDE®

GUILFORD, CONNECTICUT
AN IMPRINT OF THE GLOBE PEQUOT PRESS

Text design by Nancy Freeborn
Maps by Stefanie Ward © The Globe Pequot Press

ISBN 0-7627-2598-2
ISSN 1547-4585

Manufactured in China
First Edition/First Printing

To Meryon Sumpter

CONTENTS

Photo J. Sumpter

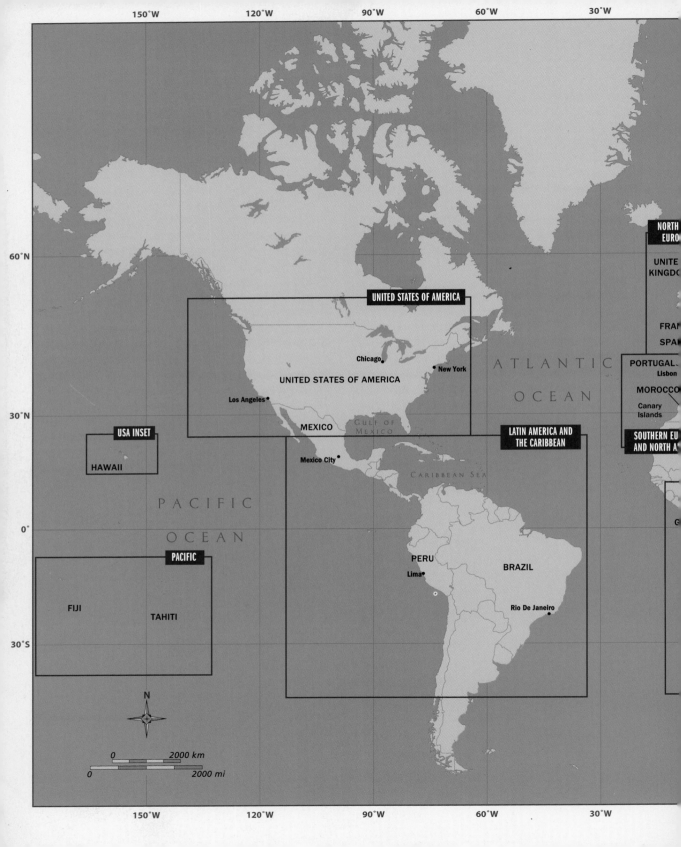

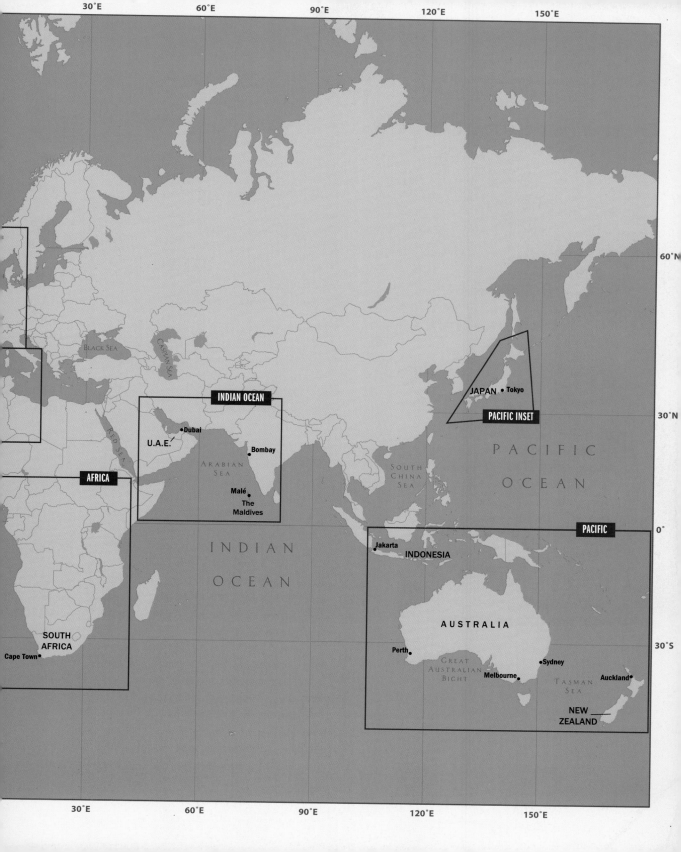

The prices and rates listed in this guidebook were confirmed at press time but under no circumstances are they guaranteed. We recommend that you call establishments before traveling to obtain current information. For international travel, check with the State Department on current travel conditions prior to your departure (www.travel.state.gov/travel_warnings.html).

ACKNOWLEDGMENTS

My sincere thanks go to my wife Valerie, who continually checked and corrected the manuscript, and gave endless support; to my son John, for his adventurous surfing and photography in and out of the water; to my daughter-in-law Sarah and my brother David for photo contributions; and to Mom. A belated thanks to my father Meryon Sumpter, who in 1964, as publicity officer in charge of the Australian Surfing Association, chose Manly for the first World Surfing Championships, which was a great success, and started us out on a surfing life. Also for his encouragement and help researching this book.

Also thanks to the great photographers Don Montgomery, Paul Ferraris, and John McGinty for their classic pictures; to the surfer Colin McPhillips, for his time and insight, as well as Andy Irons, Mark Richards, Joel Parkinson, C. J. Hobgood, Bob McTavish, Mark Occolupo, James Turner, Corey Webber, Bryon DeBoer, Michael Bamp, Al Sehorn, Stephen Maitland, Meg Bernardo, Dave Monnsen, Brian Fredickson, Micky Mabbott, Rob Tanner, Goess Burns, Lee Gerachis, Tony, Kim, Ted, Cath, Bradley and Joe; Anthony Moreby, Davey Jones, Chris Beecham; Simone, Greta, and Jim Renvoize; Steve Mabbot, Tony Holsborn, Eileen and William Warren; Allan Hunt; Ripcurl, *Intense* magazine, Quiksilver, and Billabong; and to Scott Adams for his help and guidance. Thanks to ASP Tostee and the Association of Surfing Professionals at aspworldtour.com.

I'd like to thank R. W. Reynolds, T. M. Smith, and the National Meteorological Center for the production of this data. Thanks also to the Distributed Active Archive Center (Code 902) at Goddard Space Flight Center in Greenbelt, Maryland for putting the data in its present format and distributing them. Goddard's share in these activities was sponsored by NASA's Mission to Planet Earth program.

I'd also like to thank Keone Travel; Terri Gregory, Public Information Coordinator, Space and Engineering Center, University of Wisconsin-Madison; Hawaiian Lifeguard Association; Cape Hatteras National Seashore and the National Park Service; San Clemente Beach Park; Sebastian Inlet State Recreation Area; San Onofre State Beach; Japan Travel/Sport Information; The Australian Surf Life Saving Association; The Newquay Tourism Office; The United Kingdom Hydrographic Office; The Hydrometeorological Information World Data Center (RIHMI-WDC); International Shark Attack File (I.S.A.F.); American Elasmobranch Society; and Florida Museum of Natural History. And finally, to the many people along the way who have helped shape, refine, and make this book possible. Featured surfers pages vii, xv, xviii Rod Sumpter; pages xi, xiii, xix John Sumpter.

INTRODUCTION

On a perfectly sunny day in February, my son John looked out at Waimea Bay on the North Shore of Oahu, Hawaii, and said, "Dad I think you can make the drop." What he meant was that I should join him at one of the world's biggest big-wave spots and ride some of the heaviest waves in the world.

To some, this is extreme surfing. And to others, big-wave surfing is just a walk in the park. Most surfers consider anything above 20 feet as big. Today it was 25 feet plus, and the waves powered in around Waimea Point like steam trains hooting at full throttle. This was my second attempt. The first had ended in disaster ten years earlier, when I wiped out on the drop, broke my leash, lost my board, and was caught in a rip from which I had to be rescued by my surfing buddy Malcolm. Today I was keen and worried at the same time. I was eager to go, more keen to make the takeoff and vertical drop and achieve personal satisfaction than worried by the rips and the thought of going over the falls and wiping out. This was a dream come true, because Waimea does not often break so perfectly—on average, twice a winter. This was a second chance at Waimea Bay.

Waxed up and ready and now facing the awesome shore-break, we waited for our chance to paddle out at a lull. The Waimea Bay Shore Break was awesome, showering us in spray and rainbows. The curling left-hander peeled like poetry in motion toward us and crashed at our feet. Outside at the takeoff it was pumping top to bottom with walling tubes and gnarly barrels; the bay was filled with swell lines of breaking waves going west toward Haleiwa. Light trade winds produced glassy conditions at the point, as sets hung in the air.

John shouted "Go! Go!"—I was already committed to paddling down the face of a monster wave. To make the drop, you need to keep paddling down the wave face to escape the pitching lip. These waves leap into the air when they hit the reef at the point, and the drop becomes a vertical slide down a moving mountain of water. An expert surfer takes the drop, banks a right-hand turn up into the breaking hook, and then heads across the wall to the bay as the whitewater cascades. We did this and had some epic rides, and I recall this for you only because I am frequently asked, *What is the best surf spot in the world?* The answer from me was *Waimea Bay,* because right here, right now, it was. I had just ridden some of the most sensational and exciting waves of my life.

Photo R. Sumpter

But the real answer should have been, *There is no best surf spot in the world,* because it's more to do with best days at best spots with best conditions. This was one of mine. This is when I decided to write *100 Best Surf Spots in the World.* Expert surfers don't always agree on the best spots, but they do have uncanny surf experiences that put surf spots in their favorite ranked order. In the surf world best rides, best days, best spots are just a part of the surfing lifestyle. There's nothing strange about raving about a best spot going off and pumping. The best surf spot today is of vital importance because no one wants to miss out and ride mush when around the corner the perfect wave is pumping. If you're a shortboarder, longboarder, bodyboarder, bodysurfer, or any other wave rider, the best waves at best surf breaks thrill and inspire.

Your home spot tends to become your favorite spot, or the best spot, or both. My dad's favorite spot was Avalon Beach. He used to tell me to ride the shore dump tube, demonstrating the maneuver by bodysurfing and floating on his back in the impact zone. And what a tube he had! Not long after I had surfed all the famous and best spots in Queensland and New South Wales, and shortly after winning the Australian Junior Championships, I decided to ride all the best surf spots of the world.

On a green card, I headed for California, and for two years shaped for Hobie Surfboards and rode the famed Rincon, Trestles, and Malibu. I then won the U.S. Junior Surfing Championships at Huntington Beach (and shot the best pier). Then I surfed the East from Cape Cod to Miami before heading to Europe. After that, I traveled the world two and a half times over continuing my search for the best surf spots.

At this time the idea of the perfect wave took on great importance to me. I surfed the famed Cape St. Francis in South Africa, where the film *Endless Summer* found its perfect wave—the best waves ever seen at that time. I had previously toured Victoria and Western Australia surfing for the film. In retrospect, we realize today many of the best point breaks produce a perfect wave on the right day, and even an ordinary beach might get the perfect wave with the right sand movement topography, when the wind and swell direction are in tune. This book is all about surfing these best breaks around the world.

The final selection is mine alone, and while it may invite controversy, I promise you that every surf spot in this book is capable of giving you a ride of a lifetime. I collected and reviewed data from the world's top surf sources. The criteria I used are speed, shape, quality, size, and length of ride. I was helped by a straw poll I took of surfers, who indicated their favorites and talked to me about many others. This book is about people's best surf spots, the places they like to talk about, the surf locations that have left an impression on them and changed their lives, and the rides they will never forget. I have talked with dozens of surfers the world over to compile *100 Best Surf Spots in the World.* It is a book of destinations to surf, and along the way you'll hear from surfing champions like Andy Irons, Mark Occolupo, Mark Richards, C. J. Hobgood, Joel Parkinson, Colin McPhillips, and others.

Surf Travel

Surfing may be the simplest travel-focused sport on the planet. With only a surfboard and minimum gear, you can go ride the best breaks and, if conditions are favorable, the best waves. Some places are very fickle and seasonal, while others are consistent wave magnets for year-round surf. Checking out a new surf spot you've read about or heard about, riding it for yourself, and putting your own interpretation of it into your memory bank is reward aplenty. But surf travel will also increase your surfing ability fivefold because you're riding different waves and swell strengths. Thicker, steeper, hollower, squarer, stranger, more perfect—because new locations with unique seabeds, landscapes, weather, and marine life make greatly different waves than back home.

A lot of things affect the waves, such as going from cool to hot and from deep to shallow oceans. For example, the

Travel Tip

When you're traveling on aircraft, always go light. Take a backpack, a credit card, and some local currency. Also keep in mind that your board will cost extra on the flight. When you arrive, your backpack will keep things easy, allowing two hands free for the surfboard and any other aircraft carry-on you may have. Whether you're traveling by taxi, bus, or RV, and whether you're staying at campgrounds, guest houses, hostels or hotels, travel light. This will put you in good stead to go surfing quickly and conveniently without a lot of fuss.

shallow kelp beds off many California surf breaks and the region's unique weather systems give regular northwest long-period groundswells, producing the glassiest long waves in the world. The mirror-smooth down-the-line smoking waves at Santa Cruz, Rincon, Malibu, and Trestles are unforgettable. The ultimate big-wave spot of Mavericks breaks ten times overhead, and is probably the scariest travel experience a surfer could ever witness. It's a perhaps lifelong challenge to surf, and one you may never realize.

Surf travel puts you way out in front with more chances to ride big waves and more opportunities to find the perfect wave. A new swell arrives at Burleigh Heads, Queensland. It's from a nearby cyclone. The waves are 15 feet plus. You surf-watch for a while and it's magic just to watch. And then someone takes off on a huge barrel and screams across the bay, pumping turns, getting snagged, and then breaking free of the curl and lining up the barrel. It's enough to get you doing backflips.

It reminds me of the time I saw Peter Drouyn and Keith Paul ride Burleigh at 20 feet maxing out. They had one wave apiece and then headed for Kirra. Kirra is a fickle break that needs to be big with an east swell in order to pass the rock groin and break on the sand point. Thundering sets break in front of you as you paddle out. To the right of you someone takes off and surely wipes out in the barrel, but no, ten seconds on he reappears, and by the time you've paddled four strokes, he's carved two huge turns, thrown a curtain of refreshing water over you, and the same perfect shape swell continues north down the bay. Magic.

Or it may be the heavy peaks of Duranbah that stop you in your tracks, and you hear yourself saying, "I never knew waves could break like this!" Similarly, it could be said at Lennox Head, "amazing," Cabarita, "unreal," and Byron Bay "epic." *100 Best Surf Spots in the World* takes you to places like Uluwatu in Indonesia, one of the best fast left-hand waves a travel surfer could ever wish for. You cannot help but get caught up in the colorful religious festivals, legends of sea monsters, and conversations with friendly people.

100 Best Surf Spots takes you to New Zealand to ride the legendary Raglan Reef and to discover Piha, Maori tradition, and the epic landscapes with mountain peaks soaring above the epic surf at Indicators. To marvel at the best locations in the Pacific, Atlantic, and Indian Oceans, including the Hawaiian Islands, Tahiti, Fiji, and the Maldives, *100 Best Surf Spots* takes you in search of the world's best breaks and the perfect wave.

Safety Tips

Learn to swim and paddle as best you can. This is vital to surfing the best waves.

- Never surf alone—or if you do, have someone watching.
- Check with the lifeguard about any current dangers before entering the water.
- Obey all warnings and posted signs.
- Make sure your board has a nose guard fitted and your fins are not razor sharp—it may save you a trip to the hospital. Check your surf leash regularly, too.
- Before entering the water, see where the rips are flowing. If you wipe out and get caught in a rip, stay calm and relaxed, don't panic; swim across (perpendicular to) the rip.
- Never drop in on another surfer, unless invited to share a wave. This will happen on full-faced waves and fundays. It rarely happens on good days, but on crowded days when there is no other option, surfers do share waves.
- Always carry a first-aid kit in the car and know where the nearest doctor, clinic, or hospital is.
- To avoid a wetsuit and wax rub, use Vaseline sparingly and wear a Lycra rash vest for protection.
- In cold climates wear a wetsuit warm enough to stay warm. If that means boots, gloves, and helmet, so be it.
- In hot climates always bring a pair of reef booties, sunblock, a hat, and mosquito repellent.
- Train. Do five minutes of warm-up exercises, stretching your muscles and relaxing your mind, before every surf. This improves your suppleness and gets your muscles ready for some hard-hitting barrels without injury or strains.

Photo R. Sumpter

Surfing with the Sharks

Sharks are a surfer's worst nightmare. In Florida, many surfers have seen sharks just 5 feet away from them.

These coastal sharks are small (2 to 5 feet) and their bites are not fatal (one death per five years from shark attacks on average). And bites, when they occur, are usually to the hands and legs; most are bite-and-release type incidents (thankfully, humans taste pretty bad, and sharks will usually let us go once they get a mouthful).

So what conditions should you avoid surfing in if you want to avoid sharks? Well, fortunately, it's during the worst possible surf conditions that a shark attack is the most likely—after a heavy rain, during onshore winds, in winter or spring storms that create choppy conditions, when there's muddy water in the surf or winds that whitecap the surf so that it's blown out.

You should be able to surf without fear if you follow some basic principles:

- Stay together. Always surf in a group and don't stray too far from shore. Sharks will attack a solitary individual more often than those in a group. Being a long way from shore further isolates you and makes it hard to contact help and for help to get to you.

- What's on your body matters. Stay out of the water if you have an open wound or are menstruating. Don't wear shiny jewelry that could be mistaken for fish scales, bright clothing, or allow uneven tanning. Sharks perceive the contrast of light and dark very well.

- The time and place are important. Stay out of the water if you know sharks have been sighted. Don't surf at night or at twilight. Sharks are more active at these times and can sense you better than you can see them. You should also stay out of water that is known to have sewage or where there has been a lot of fishing activity. One way to determine if fishing bait is present in the water is to look for diving sea birds. Don't count on the presence of dolphins to be a sign that sharks are not there. They often eat the same things. Be cautious in murky water and around areas between sandbars or close to steep drop offs where sharks like to swim.

- What you do in the water can also make a difference. Avoid excess splashing. Pets should be kept out of the water because they can move erratically. Finally, if you see a shark, don't harass it.

Areas most prone to shark attack include:

- Northern California: the great white shark's home.

- The east coast of South Africa: Ragged-tooth, tiger, Zambezi, and great white sharks.

- South Australia and northern New South Wales: gray nurse, tiger, bull, and great white sharks.

- Florida: bull, blacktip, and bonnethead sharks.

- Hawaiian Islands: sandbar, reef whitetip, tiger, and scalloped hammerhead sharks.

Another vacation-wrecking danger in the oceans of the world are the coral reefs, where razor-sharp coral and spine-covered urchins lurk. These cause surfers the most amount of downtime from injuries. Also, various jellyfish—and especially the Portuguese man-of-war—that blow in during onshore winds can wrap around your leg or arm, causing painful stings.

Surf Schools

The best way to learn to surf is by joining a surf school. You will learn in a group on the beach, practicing paddling and standing up until you're fluid. Then you'll hit the surf on small waves. Your first stand-up ride will be a big thrill, remembered as a best moment. Today's surf schooling is high tech and often includes the best foam boards, wetsuits, surf videos, surf books, and the instructor's wide knowledge and personal experience.

Surf Contests

The Association of Surfing Professionals (ASP) was formed in 1976 to create the World Championship Tour (WCT), a regular yearly surfing tour of the best spots for pro surfers that includes a world qualifying series (WQS) in the Hawaiian Islands of Oahu and Maui, Florida, California, Brazil, the Maldives, Portugal, Spain, Britain, the Canary Islands, South Africa, Japan, and Australia. These contests involve twenty to thirty minutes of man-on-man elimination heats up to the final. The winner is chosen by a panel of experts, who score the best three rides for speed, length, size, and the most radical maneuvers executed in the waves' most critical part. Surfers accumulate points to win the title of World Surfing Champion at the end of the year. Regular sponsors are Rip Curl, Quiksilver, Billabong, Boost Mobile, and Xbox Pipeline. To enter, you need to qualify at your local WQS event. It will help if you're a red-hot surfer and if you have gained national and local championship status, because

the competition level is sky high. If you watch Andy Irons, the world champion at this writing, surfing at one of the best spots on a perfect day, you will be inspired by his performance, best rides, and speed across a range of radical maneuvers, and wave selection. All the pros seem to have a sixth sense as to where a set will be. This puts them into the best waves for the best scores.

For information on the latest ASP World Championship Tour, go to www.aspworldtour.com.

How to Use This Book

There is a lot of information in this book so it may be helpful to have a key to how the information is organized and what it means.

The surf locations are organized into seven geographical regions: the United States, Latin America and the Caribbean, Northern Europe, Southern Europe and North Africa, Africa, the Pacific, and the Indian Ocean. In each of these sections, the spots are further divided by country, or in the case of the United States, Hawaii, California, and the East Coast. There is a brief introduction for each of the geographical regions providing a general overview of the region and a short description of the specific waves and beaches.

For each of the surf spots there are three main parts. The main description of the surf spot is given in the text but there are a couple of features that let you get information more quickly. At the top of the right hand page of each spread are a number of icons. These provide an immediate impression of characteristics of the break, covering the direction of the break, the swell direction, the kinds of boards that work in that spot, and hazards.

Below these icons is an information section to give you the basic information about each spot quickly. There is information on nature of the break, the skill level needed to surf the spot, the commitment it takes to face the wave, the best board to use, if there's a lifeguard, and a few notes on any hazardous conditions you may find.

All of the categories are fairly self-explanatory except Commitment. This is a rating for the amount of skill, guts, and power it takes to surf a certain spot. The rating is based on a scale from one to ten, in which one represents the least amount of commitment and ten the most. The rating is expressed as a number out of ten, such as 7-10 meaning seven out of the scale of ten.

There is also a chart with monthly statistical information on the average size of the swell, air temperature, water temperature, what kind of wetsuit you need to wear, average amount of sunshine and rain, and the average number of days you can surf. These figures are all averages so the actual numbers for a certain month or year may be different.

Finally there is travel information, including the kind of currency you'll use, what documents you will need, where you can stay, how to find the surf spot, selected surfing schools in the area, and other important things you might want to think about or know beforehand.

Photo R. Sumpter

Photo R. Sumpter

UNITED STATES
OF AMERICA

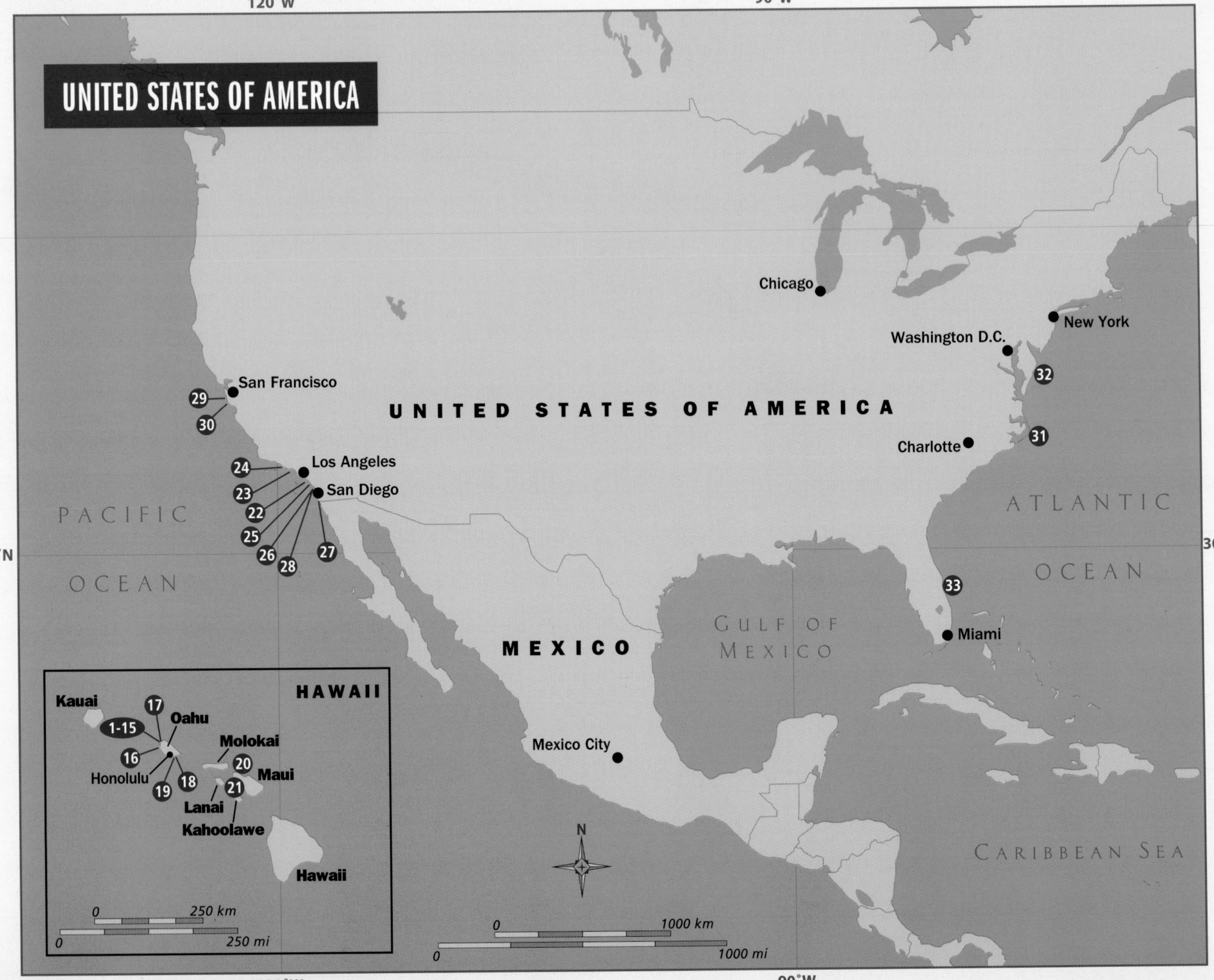

UNITED STATES OF AMERICA

120°W

90°W

30°N

ATLANTIC OCEAN

CARIBBEAN SEA

PACIFIC OCEAN

GULF OF MEXICO

UNITED STATES OF AMERICA

MEXICO

- Chicago
- New York
- Washington D.C.
- Charlotte
- 32
- 31
- 33
- Miami
- San Francisco
- Los Angeles
- San Diego
- Mexico City

24 23 22 25 26 28 27

29 30

N

1000 km
1000 mi
0

HAWAII

- Kauai
- Oahu 17
- 1-15
- 16 Honolulu
- Molokai
- 20 Maui
- 18 Lanai
- 21 Kahoolawe
- 19
- Hawaii

120°W

30°N

250 km
250 mi
0

The United States is blessed with waves of all kinds, from the best in the world to the world's most difficult. To find these waves, you need only to go to Hawaii, California, or the Southeast Coast, where some of the world's leading waves thunder in for prime surfing.

Comprising eight major islands in the Central Pacific Ocean, Hawaii stands alone as the world's first and foremost surfing mecca. This is the place where modern surfing began and where today's best surfers come to test their skills against nature's toughest waves. Among these islands, Oahu and Maui stand apart from the rest, offering up some of the Aloha State's finest surf. Warm waters, blue-turquoise seas, and mountainous groundswells from four directions in the South Pacific give Hawaii its legendary surf.

It is the North Shore of Oahu where surfing is at its peak. From December to March you can see 30-foot-plus surf at Waimea Bay and Keana Point. Maui does quite well on its own, with places like Jaws, which may break at 40 feet, and Honolua Bay, often offering surfers the perfect wave. Overall, what's on offer at most of Hawaii's breaks are short, fast, vertical, and powerful waves with hard sand or sharp coral waiting to break a leg. Hawaii is not for the fainthearted. Many a surfer has grown up, grown older, and grown wiser at the hands of the most gripping waves in the world—places like Sunset Beach, with its bigger-than-life peak, Banzai Pipeline ready to maim, Chuns Reef ready to give longboards the best fun of an entire trip. And there's so much more. Sandy Beach pounds out bodyboards like it's a stamp machine. Waikiki throws outrigger canoes into the mix. And Hawaiian surfing legend Buffalo Keaulana's Big Board Surfing Contest is held at Makaha every year.

California holds its own next to the Hawaiian paradise—home of the Beach Boys, *Endless Summer*, Malibu, Santa Cruz, and the mighty Mavericks at Half Moon Bay. But California is a big place, and weather plays a leading role in the Golden State's wave machine. What makes Southern California small, clean, and perfectly shaped makes Northern California big, heavy, and gnarly. The isobars off Northern California are much tighter, its waters much colder than Southern California. This helps produce such phenomena as Mavericks in Half Moon Bay, home of the biggest waves in the world ridden to date—a reported 80 to 90 feet at their peak. But these waves come along in the winter. Head south and you'll be surfing consistently year-round.

All the Santa Cruz breaks, and especially Steamer Lane, can keep the hottest of world-champion surfers raising the performance bar yearly. Southern California picks up the warm, dry Santa Ana winds off the deserts and a southerly Pacific swell from Mexico and Baja caused by a *chubascos* (a wind that blows from the coast of California) to produce a long-distance swell traveling to places like Newport, where the huge shorebreak wedge will break for the first time in months. But it's the northwest swell for Central and Southern California that is so special, producing the longest clean lines in the world at places like Malibu, Trestles, and Sunset Cliffs, to name but a few. Nowhere else in the world can claim a swell machine so far back from the coast, where tight low-pressure systems form regularly to provide surfers with waves of consistency and quality.

While not often considered home to the world's greatest surf, the eastern seaboard of the United States has unique waves like nowhere else, primarily because it's got hurricane surf. And this kind of surf can be a hair-raiser if ever there was one. From Cape Cod to the Outer Banks and down to Sebastian Inlet in Florida (and sometimes even on the Gulf Coast), there are good waves to be found. One of the best is in Florida at Sebastian Inlet. The human-made pier at Sebastian Inlet is just right for wave consistency. Its fantastic double-thick wedge shape at First Peak is an A-frame barrel, and the warm turquoise waters of Florida make for a no-wetsuit surf experience. A time of total freedom. The Gulf's panhandle is often underestimated; with its paradise beaches, the whole Gulf Coast waits for swells often associated with the most fearsome hurricanes. The mind-boggling roulette wheel of chance plays out with waves such as these, and a long-distance swell might be the best and last wave of your life. This is true of all of the East Coast, including one of the East's best spots at Cape Hatteras, which has its fair share of 4- to 6-foot offshore days. In fact, all the breaks north—from New Jersey to Long Island's Montauk Point and as far north as Cape Cod—can have difficult waves to ride. These waves can have an edge of quick, thick, short, gnarly faces that puts the level of the surfing way up.

Whatever the season in the United States, winter, spring, summer, or fall, there's always someplace where the surf is up.

1. BACKDOOR

North Shore, Oahu, Hawaii

This is by far the world's most dangerous right-hand reef break, so awesome it defies most surfers who attempt to ride it. Backdoor Pipeline goes ballistic on a northeast groundswell from overhead to 15 feet, and then breaks in a thousandth of a second. Kelly Slater, the six-time Association of Surfing Professionals World Surfing Champion, is known as Mr. Backdoor for surfing it so well. "I'm at the peak of my ability to surf Backdoor," he says of this awesome surf. Major ASP sponsors like Rip Curl, Quiksilver, and Billabong consider this spot a slam-dunk as a world-class surf venue, with not only the heaviest but also the fastest, deepest, and longest barrel rides on Planet Earth.

Riding it is all a question of positioning yourself in the wedgy side of Backdoor, finding the right drifting peak in your face, where the whole coral reef world below you moves as the swell draws up water into the mass of the face of the wave. Then it's tension-splitting, life-or-death decisions. And in a blink of the eye you're here or you're gone. It's that fast.

Backdoor is so named for being behind the Banzai Pipeline peak (also known as Frontdoor). The Frontdoor peaks and slams shut, shaking the water around you just yards away from Backdoor, and the sound of its blast echoes across the sea's surface right next to the right reef of Backdoor. The scrambling is insane as sets go wide, break out, or close. Surfers get jumped by howling, crushing Niagara Falls-type waves that wind down to powder-blown spray as they exit the barrel. Backdoor's barrel is like an air ticket to somewhere unknown, but holds the promise of a deep experience. The wave accelerates into a pipedream right-hand tunnel, and all the time just underneath you, inches away, is the meanest, nastiest rough coral.

Backdoor is situated 200 yards west of Banzai Pipeline (Spot 2) and 7 miles east of Haleiwa (Spot 5) on the North Shore of Oahu. This is a right-hand barrel, a wave with one of the best thick curling tubes in the world, breaking over shallow lava and coral. The takeoff is located just 100 yards from shore and looms up quickly, having a vertical drop followed by a curtain lip you'd be well advised to watch out for. The wave turns into a perfect breaking wave and races close to the shoreline, making this a photographer's dream spot for close-ups. In Hawaiian it's called *lauloa,* meaning "a long wave that crests and breaks from one end of the beach to the other," or *Nala ha`i lala,* "a wave that breaks diagonally."

Quickly becoming one of the most famous breaks on the North Shore, Backdoor is likely to be flat during the summer months, but it picks up plenty of groundswells from November to March. This is a great surf spot for the expert surfer if it's 6 to 8 feet, and ideal for the advanced to experienced big wave surfer if it's over 8 or 10 feet, January to February.

Photo R. Sumpter

The surfboard has evolved over the years to suit the waves and the wishes of the rider, especially out here on the North Shore. In the early nineteenth century, the top-rated surfboards of the time were used by the kings of Hawaii, and were a massive 16 feet long. To make them, the wiliwili tree, koa tree, and other premium woods were used. After the craftsman chipped the board into rough shape, he then fine-tuned it with coral stone and covered it with black stain from the ti plant. The completed board was then dedicated to the sea. In comparison, Backdoor waves today are ridden on board lengths averaging between 6 feet, 8 inches, and 7 feet, 10 inches.

Backdoor is one of my favorite waves in the world. It's an incredible wave. It's really heavy, not such a long barrel. It's just really thick. The barrel is really big itself, tubes about five to eight seconds long. When it closes out it's pretty much all reaction.

Andy Irons,
2002–2003 World Surfing Champion

Photo R. Sumpter

 Rights
 N Swell

 Shallow Reef

Break: Right-hand reef break

Skill Level: Expert

Commitment: 10–10

Best Boards: Shortboards up to 7 feet, 10 inches

Lifeguard: None

Hazards: Almost impossible drop-ins to a bottomless right barrel makes for epic rides, when double overhead. Wintertime: frequent big waves, dangerous rip currents, shallow coral reef.

Currency: U.S. dollar.

Going There: Visa required except by U.S. citizens. Vaccinations required except by U.S. citizens—tetanus, typhoid. Check with your doctor, health clinic, and embassy for up-to-date info.

Where to Stay: Rent a house opposite at Backdoor from Sunset Homes, LLC. Call (808) 637–2400, (808) 638–7299. It's easy to find rooms to rent, and apartments are close by. See the notice boards at Foodland at Waimea Bay; Kammies Market at Sunset Beach; and other locations in Haleiwa town.

For cheap laid-back accommodations right in the middle of the North Shore, try Vacation Inn and Plantation Village. Rates start at $15 a night for a hostel bunk, and go up to $100 to $135 for an oceanview cabin that sleeps eight. Don't expect luxury here, but if you're young or young at heart, what's to worry about a few pieces of furniture that have seen better days? Vacation Inn overlooks Waimea Bay. Telephone for reservations or information: (808) 638–7838. The Turtle Bay Resort at Kahuku, a few minutes east of Sunset Beach, is a five-star resort and is the best; call (808) 293–8811 for reservations.

Finding the Break: Easy to find. From Sunset Beach head west on the Kam Highway for 1 mile. Turn right onto Ke Nui Road, continue until you reach Ehukai Beach Park, walk through the park and face the sea, and go left along the beach for 200 yards.

Keep in Mind: Crowded on smaller days.

Month	JF	MA	MJ	JA	SO	ND
Average Swell (feet)	8–10	6–8	3–4	2	5–6	8–10
Air Temp (C/F)	26/79	27/81	29/84	30/86	29/84	27/81
Water Temp (C/F)	23/73	24/75	25/77	26/79	27/81	24/75
Wetsuit	shorty	vest	none	none	none	vest
Average Sunshine p/d (hours)	7	9	10	11	9	6–7
Average Rain p/m (inches)	3	1	0	1	2	3
Average Surfable Days p/m	20	14	8	2	6	17

2. BANZAI PIPELINE
North Shore, Oahu, Hawaii

You haven't really surfed Hawaii until you've surfed the Banzai Pipeline. It is the jewel in the crown, the one spot that always looks magic, beckoning you to come and ride. It is so tantalizing that many who have ridden its 12- to 15-foot waves consider it to be the highlight of their surfing career.

To make it down the face of a huge wave into a barreling wall of pent-up Pacific power takes commitment. And those successful in harnessing this power make it by paddling down the wave's face on takeoff and getting up before their ankles go above their head. When you make the first drop, it's an awesome feeling. It's simple: Don't wipe out. Make the drop. Get in the barrel. Keep charging. If you do it right, you're golden. It is here that the world's best bodyboarders put on an amazing display, while disobeying the laws of gravity and humbling surfers who can't keep their ankles south of their shoulders.

Oahu is the third largest island in the Hawaiian chain. And Ehukai Beach Park, on the North Shore of Oahu, is the home of the Banzai Pipeline, one of earth's most famous surf spots. It is situated just 500 yards east of Off the Wall (Spot 8) and 800 yards west of Rocky Point (Spot 11).

This is the all-time great left-hand reef break that forms close to the shore in the winter from November to March, and has some of the biggest A-frame waves in the world. When the surf's up at the "Pipe," it's the mother of all dangerous surf spots, boasting a huge tubing wave, a cracking, spine-chilling coral reef, and rip currents as fast

The Lifeguard Association of Hawaii is a great institution, protecting the public at beaches on Oahu. Lifeguards patrol the Ehukai Beach Park area, and it's interesting and worth remembering some of their signs:

- **Hazardous Conditions. These are posted when a potential for severe bodily harm exists:** DANGEROUS SHOREBREAK, SHARP CORAL, SUDDEN DROP OFF, SLIPPERY ROCKS, MAN-OF-WAR-JELLYFISH.

- **Dangerous Conditions. These are posted when a potential for loss of life or limb exists:** HIGH SURF, WAVES BREAK ON LEDGE, STRONG CURRENT, SHARK SIGHTED.

- **Prohibited Activity.** NO SWIMMING, NO DIVING, NO SAIL BOARDING, NO BOARD SURFING, BEACH CLOSED.

as rivers. The wave can stack up a couple of stories high, throwing out a white lip over itself and making a perfect *Hawaii Five-0* circle. The Pipe has killed, injured, badly bruised, and made grown men weep. This brutal wave accelerates into a howling tube big enough to drive a truck through, and then crushes down into spray like an imploding concrete building as it nears the shore. The reef beneath is hard and lethal, covered with spiked coral and deadly little caves, waiting to capture or trap the unfortunate surfer who bails prematurely.

Historically this is Hawaii's shortest, hollowest, steepest, and closest-to-shore wave, next to Waimea Bay Shore Break (Spot 15). It is the ultimate challenge to surf. For those unwilling to sacrifice life, limb, and pride, this is the best place in the world for watching others risk everything on spectacular, monster waves. The rarely surfed outer reef called Second Reef Pipeline can double the height of the reforming sets at Banzai Pipeline, making a pounding crack and hiss of breaking waves as you watch one of the most spectacular sights on earth. No other surf spot quite matches the power of the Pipe, the all-time great surf spot—for experts only.

Photo R. Sumpter

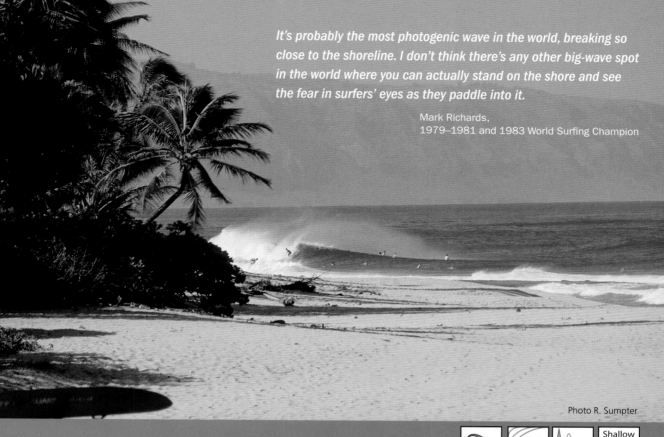

It's probably the most photogenic wave in the world, breaking so close to the shoreline. I don't think there's any other big-wave spot in the world where you can actually stand on the shore and see the fear in surfers' eyes as they paddle into it.

Mark Richards,
1979–1981 and 1983 World Surfing Champion

Photo R. Sumpter

 Lefts NW Swell   Shallow Reef

Break: Left-hand reef break
Skill Level: Expert
Commitment: 10–10
Best Boards: Shortboards, big-wave gun, bodyboards on some days
Lifeguard: Year-round
Hazards: Vertical drop, heavy lip, big waves, dangerous rip currents, shallow coral reef

Currency: U.S. dollar.
Going There: Visa required except by U.S. citizens. Vaccinations required except by U.S. citizens—tetanus, typhoid. Check with your doctor, health clinic, and embassy for up-to-date info.
Where to Stay: Rent a house opposite Banzai from Sunset Homes, LLC. Call (808) 637–2400 or 638–7299, or fax

637–4200. It's easy to find rooms to rent, and apartments are close by. See the notice boards at Foodland at Waimea Bay; Kammies Market at Sunset Beach; and other locations in Haleiwa town. The Turtle Bay Resort at Kahuku, near Sunset Beach is a five-star resort and is the best; (808) 293–8811 for reservations.
Finding the Break: Easy to find. From Sunset Beach head west on Kam Highway for 1 mile. Turn right, on Ke Nui Road, continue until you reach Ehukai Beach Park, walk through the park and face the sea, and go left along the beach for 250 yards.
Contest: X-Box Masters (WCT), December.
Keep in Mind: Crowds on weekends in winter season; packed on good days.

Months	JF	MA	MJ	JA	SO	ND
Average Swell (feet)	8–10	6–8	3–4	2	5–6	8–10
Air Temp (C/F)	26/79	27/81	29/84	30/86	29/84	27/81
Water Temp (C/F)	23/73	24/75	25/77	26/79	27/81	24/75
Wetsuit	shorty	vest	none	none	none	vest
Average Sunshine p/d (hours)	7	9	10	11	9	6–7
Average Rain p/m (inches)	3	1	0	1	2	3
Average Surfable Days p/m	21	14	8	3	7	14

3. CHUNS REEF

North Shore, Oahu, Hawaii

Take a longboard, rub some wax on the rails, on the deck, and a lot on the nose, and go get some of the best nose riding the world has to offer. Grab the rail and turn turtle on the outside sets, then paddle hard for the shoulder. The next wave you catch is going to have you running all over the board. By the time you've surfed four to five sets, the wax will be gone and you'll have had a ride of a lifetime.

Chuns Reef is the ideal performance right-hand reef break—for longboards in particular—and has good days for bodyboards and shortboards alike. Situated off the Kamehameha Highway on the North Shore of Oahu, just 0.5 mile west of Laniakea (Spot 6) and 4 miles east of Banzai Pipeline (Spot 2), Chuns Reef is famous for its classic surf lineup of waves. Seen from the gap in the highway or from the small parking area nearby, the view reveals the wave perfection awaiting you. The waves are soft compared to the heavy, gnarly barrels of other North Shore

He`e nalu

It is believed that a form of surfing originated somewhere in the Pacific around 2000 B.C. It is likely the first Polynesians migrated to Hawaii around A.D. 400, and they were already well versed in the sport. Early Hawaiians called surfing *he`e nalu*, which means "wave sliding." Hawaiian chants dating back from the fifteenth century recount surfing exploits, including competitions against famous surfers of the day.

breaks. This is a perfect, laid-back classic longboarders' wave, set in a tropical coastline of reefs and surrounding coral lagoons. Its best surf conditions are in a northerly groundswell of 4 to 6 feet, with a light offshore southerly wind. Mr. Chun, a local who, lore suggests, built his home here many years ago, surfed and fished the reef in his spare time, and must have been spoiled to the core at his good fortune and prime real estate.

Chuns Reef is best known for its high quality waves that wall and hold up seemingly forever ideal for maximum maneuverability and performance surfing. Chuns Reef has a lot to offer and, on most days, a choice of three takeoff areas. There's the outer takeoff peak, which forms farthest out especially on set waves, a good peak left and right. This then fades into the "Main Peak," which re-forms as a classic takeoff into the best peak you could ever wish for. Like a mountain in the horizon slowly rising into view, the right-hand wall is a performance wave for the first 50 yards, and is ideal for either nose riding or big bottom turns and roundhouse cutbacks, then through to the inside section. The shorebreak, the third of the three takeoff areas, breaks when a swell misses the outer takeoff areas, forming a hard right and peeling off into a shallow coral reef and boulders. Which of these three takeoff areas is best depends on the swell direction and conditions of the day. This is the ideal surf spot for intermediate surfers when it's 3 to 4 feet, and great for experts when it's in the 6- to 8-foot range. In nearly all conditions, however, it is a classic longboarding wave.

Photo R. Sumpter

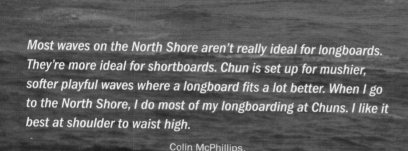

Most waves on the North Shore aren't really ideal for longboards. They're more ideal for shortboards. Chun is set up for mushier, softer playful waves where a longboard fits a lot better. When I go to the North Shore, I do most of my longboarding at Chuns. I like it best at shoulder to waist high.

Colin McPhillips,
2000–2002 World Longboard Surfing Champion

Photo R. Sumpter

Rights | NW Swell | | Shallow Reef

Break: Right-hand reef break

Skill Level: Intermediate to expert

Commitment: 3–10

Best Boards: Longboard; maybe a shortboard if it's big

Lifeguard: None

Hazards: Dangerous rip currents, shallow sand bottom, sneaker sets, closeouts

Currency: U.S. dollar.

Going There: Visa required except by U.S. citizens. Vaccinations required except by U.S. citizens—tetanus, typhoid. Check with your doctor, health clinic, and embassy for up-to-date info.

Where to Stay: Chuns Reef Vacation Rentals, (949) 212–0968. It's easy to find rooms to rent, and apartments are close by. See the notice boards at Foodland at Waimea Bay; Kammies Market at Sunset Beach; and other locations in Haleiwa town. The Turtle Bay Resort at Kahuku near Sunset Beach is a five-star resort and is the best. Call (808) 293–8811 for reservations.

Finding the Break: Not that easy to find. From Waimea Bay head west for 1 mile and look for the second small gap in the road with parking. Chuns is just a tiny cove fanning out to a big reef. If it has any good waves on that day, there will be someone out.

Keep in Mind: Mostly a longboarders' wave. Crowds on weekends.

Months	JF	MA	MJ	JA	SO	ND
Average Swell (feet)	5–6	3–4	2–3	2	3–4	5
Air Temp (C/F)	26/79	27/81	29/84	30/86	29/84	27/81
Water Temp (C/F)	23/73	24/75	25/77	26/79	27/81	24/75
Wetsuit	shorty	vest	none	none	none	vest
Average Sunshine p/d (hours)	7	9	10	11	9	6–7
Average Rain p/m (inches)	3	1	0	1	2	3
Average Surfable Days p/m	18	16	10	5	6	19

4. GAS CHAMBERS
North Shore, Oahu, Hawaii

Peter Drouyn, a former Australian champion, was so stunned on his first trip to Hawaii when surfing at Gas Chambers that he likened it to a steamroller exploding. That's how crushing the curl is.

On big days this is the mother of all waves—big, hollow, and fast. On smaller days it's sweet perfection, a clean hot-dogging fun wave. One of the greatest facts about Gas Chambers is that the drop is straight off until you clear the trough. It's do-or-die at the impact zone, requiring respect, luck, and skill not to get smashed.

This excellent right- and left-hand wave is a medium-to-big-wave spot that lets you know right off the bat who's in charge. It's known for its heavy and aggressive takeoff, giving nothing away easily. If you're on the North Shore, the swell is up, and the conditions have the potential, Gas Chamber is not to be missed.

Working in most swell directions, there is a good chance of some ace waves. Situated between Rocky Point and Pupukea, 0.5 mile west of Sunset Beach (Spot 12) and 0.25 mile east of Banzai Pipeline (Spot 2), this is the ultimate peak-takeoff and drop-down-the-face type of wave, very quick and very fast. The tube can be one of the widest in the world, pitching out a massive curl on close-outs; the takeoff has a mean lip and explosive power. When the Pacific Ocean delivers a swell and the lineup is on the increase to high seas, Gas Chambers forms a breathtaking wave on a shallow lava reef just beyond the sandbars. And the swell that has traveled some 500 miles or more completes its underwater rotation and pitches out a curl. This is a great spot for beating the crowds and having a fun day riding demanding waves and improving your surfing beyond its current limits. It's good from 3 or 4 feet with a first-class performance, but at 10 feet it's a challenging wave to make from takeoff to kick-out. Gas Chambers is for the expert surfer on all but the smallest of swells.

Photo R. Sumpter

If you met your maker on a huge swell at Gas Chambers and you need a board, or if you're just looking to make a deal, the best place to find out where to buy or sell a surfboard on the North Shore is from the notice board at Kammies Market, less than a mile away toward Sunset Beach. Another good source of information on accommodations, surfboards, and a good set of wheels (or just about anything, for that matter) is the notice board at Foodland near Waimea Bay.

The North Shore isn't all always about surfing. When it's flat people listen to a lot of music and enjoy playing other sports. "Jawaiian" music is drawn from soul, reggae, and Hawaiian ukuleles; it's laid back and fits the mood perfectly when there's no surf. Quite a lot of surfers pick up golf at the Kahuku Golf Club, or fix and modify bikes and cars. Some dive, snorkel, or fish, and others keep fit by swimming Waimea Bay or Gas Chambers.

Gas Chambers is powerful, fast, and gets pretty darn hollow; it's a right with a short left. A good barrel.

Colin McPhillips,
2000–2002 World Longboard
Surfing Champion

Photo R. Sumpter

Peak | N Swell

Break: Beach and reef break

Skill Level: Beginner to expert

Commitment: 8–10

Best Boards: Shortboard

Lifeguard: None

Hazards: Strong undertow mid-tide, shallow sand and coral bottom

Currency: U.S. dollar.

Going There: Visa required except by U.S. citizens. Vaccinations required except by U.S. citizens—tetanus, typhoid. Check with your doctor, health clinic, and embassy for up-to-date info.

Where to Stay: Rent a house at Gas Chambers, Oceanfront Vacation Rentals; call (808) 637–2568 or (800) 442–6901, or fax (808) 637–2569. It's easy to find rooms to rent, and apartments are close by. See the notice boards at Foodland at Waimea Bay; Kammies Market at Sunset Beach; and other locations in Haleiwa town. The Turtle Bay Resort at Kahuku near Sunset Beach is a five-star resort and is the best. Call (808) 293–8811 for reservations.

Finding the Break: Not easy to find. From Sunset Beach on the Kam Highway, go 0.5 mile west, turn right onto Ke Nui Road, and take the coastal track out to Rocky Point. Gas Chambers is 300 yards to the west. Gas Chambers is between Pupukea and Rocky Point.

Keep in Mind: Crowded on small days on weekends.

Months	JF	MA	MJ	JA	SO	ND
Average Swell (feet)	8	4–5	2–3	1–2	2	4–6
Air Temp (C/F)	26/79	27/81	29/84	30/86	29/84	27/81
Water Temp (C/F)	23/73	24/75	25/77	26/79	27/81	24/75
Wetsuit	shorty	vest	none	none	none	vest
Average Sunshine p/d (hours)	7	9	10	11	9	6–7
Average Rain p/m (inches)	3	1	0	1	2	3
Average Surfable Days p/m	14	12	5	3	7	10

5. HALEIWA
North Shore, Oahu, Hawaii

A mighty fine swell is running and the scales are tipping 10 to 12 feet. Haleiwa is honking and hooting on the rights. The surfer on the horizon strokes into a left peak, a pitch-black takeoff monster, and zooms right across the bay. Everyone onshore stands and cheers. This is a taste of Haleiwa.

The town of Haleiwa was established in 1899, and was known then as the Home of the Frigate Bird. Today it is known as Haleiwa the Surf Town and has world-class surfing and more surf shops than any other place on Oahu.

Situated 30 miles north of Waikiki (Spot 19) and 7 miles west of Sunset Beach (Spot 12) on the Kamehameha Highway, Haleiwa is within the strip of coastline known as the North Shore. This quaint country town boasts surf clothing shops, arts and crafts, and a remarkable surf museum. But most relevant to you and me—it produces some of the finest surfing anywhere in the world. This right-hand sand and coral reef break is a long ride—up to 250 yards on a good day. Both shortboarders and longboarders excel in this paradise of optimum waves.

Haleiwa's Ali`i Beach Park is one of the finest parks on Oahu, complete with showers, changing rooms, picnic area, restroom, parking, and lifeguard. Many national and international surfing championships are also held here, including the Vans Triple Crown of Surfing Pro, the Roxy Pro women's event, and the Bear longboard contest.

From a surfer's point of view, this is the trickiest surf spot on the North Shore, and for this reason it's the most sought after, especially on medium-sized days. It is here at Haleiwa that the ocean puts on a disguise of soft, sweet, perfect waves. From the shore, this ruse may fool even the sharpest tack. But behind its crafty subterfuge, the waves are heavy, hard hitting, hollow, and break hard in shallow water over coral reefs. The difference between watching from shore and tasting your first gnarly wave, up close and personal, can be shocking. The paddle out is also difficult, avoiding the sets while still on the shallow reef. Judging the length of the lulls can be very tricky, and getting caught inside is the norm until you learn to use the rip. But then there are the small-wave

Hawaii has the dubious distinction of claiming more extinct and endangered animal species than all of the North American continent. The Hawaiian crow or *alala* now totals fifteen birds; the *io* or Hawaiian hawk is still protected, although it's making a comeback; and the *nene* goose, Hawaii's state bird, now roams freely in parts of Hawaii and can be seen at the Hawaiian Volcanoes National Park. The Bishop Museum houses the world's best display of the early Hawaiian period, including the original surfboards used by the early Hawaiian kings and ranging on through the great Duke Kahanamoku era. There is also Captain James Cook's first reported sighting and etchings of surfing in 1779.

days perfect for all the family. On a sunny day, with a light offshore wind, it can be a dream location for fun waves.

There are three different takeoff areas here at Haleiwa. The first is the farthest out. Only set waves break on 8-foot-plus days, and the rights are the most fantastic walling, tubing, and nose-riding performance waves of all time. Rides that will be long remembered happen here, but not before ending 250 yards down the surf line in an ultrashallow tubing closeout—a place to kick out and get huge air! The next takeoff is the inside section, which picks all the swell that the outside passes up, breaking as a right and sometimes a left, fast and furiously, hollowing out and ending up in the rip or channel. The third area is farther on the east side of the beach. A left and right from a northwest swell direction makes this happen.

In 1899 Haleiwa opened the island's first hotel. The Haleiwa Hotel is now long gone, but the town has become a tourist haven, with fine alternative clothing and many health food shops. It leads the way in the Hawaiian lifestyle—simple quality living, fresh food, and karma. The surroundings are of lush vegetation, with banana and sugarcane fields backed by the Wai`anae Mountains. These slope down to the Haleiwa marina, where diving, whale-watching, and snorkeling in the clear water make this a paradise town.

Photo R. Sumpter

It's so rippable. It has everything. It has a really good drop, and off the lip section, it barrels. It's close to the beach. It's not like Sunset where you can be dragged underwater for 150 yards.

Eddie Crawford,
former U.S. East Coast Champion

Photo R. Sumpter

Rights   Peak   N Swell   Shallow Reef

Break: Left- and right-hand reef break

Skill Level: Intermediate to expert

Commitment: 4–10 in small surf; 10–10 when it's 8 to 10 feet

Best Boards: Longboards, shortboards, bodyboards

Lifeguard: Year-round

Hazards: Mammoth paddle out if waves are overhead; avalanche and cloud-break outer reefs herald increasing size of swell; big waves, dangerous rip currents, shallow coral reef; pounding final shorebreak lineup closes out on inside reef.

Currency: U.S. dollar.

Going There: Visa required except by U.S. citizens. Vaccinations required except by U.S. citizens—tetanus, typhoid. Check with your doctor, health clinic, and embassy for up-to-date info.

Where to Stay: See the notice board at Haleiwa Super Market for rent accommodations. Or go 3 miles west to Mokuleia, where The Hawaii Polo Inn's Polo Beach Cottage is a five-acre beachfront equestrian estate adjacent to the Mokuleia polo grounds. The Mokuleia peninsula extends from the old plantation town of Waialua to Kaena Point. Laie Inn, a twenty-minute drive from the North Shore on the windward side of the island; 55-109 Laniloa Street, Laie; (808) 293–2982, (800) 526–4562.

Finding the Break: Easy to find, and just 0.5 mile from the center of Haleiwa. Head north and, just before leaving the outskirts of town, turn left toward the marina. Take a right when you see Ali`i Beach Park.

Contest: WQS November.

Keep in Mind: Crowded on weekends.

Months	JF	MA	MJ	JA	SO	ND
Average Swell (feet)	6	5	3	2	3	4-5
Air Temp (C/F)	26/79	27/81	29/84	30/86	29/84	27/81
Water Temp (C/F)	24/75	24/75	25/77	26/79	27/81	24/75
Wetsuit	shorty	shorty	none	none	none	vest
Average Sunshine p/d (hours)	8	9	12	14	13	8
Average Rain p/m (inches)	3	1	0	1	2	3
Average Surfable Days p/m	28	20	15	5	7	24

6. LANIAKEA
North Shore, Oahu, Hawaii

When the ancient sea gods planned the North Shore, it's clear they wanted to make one spot very different. Set way out on a triangular coral reef, Laniakea, the great break, has a freight-train right-hander that grinds its wheels, then barrel-rolls along a massive channel. Blowing like a stoked furnace, these waves actually roar. This is a unique wave.

Laniakea is a big-wave spot, and there can be a horrendous paddle out to mammoth 20-foot-high right-hand walls when the trade winds are really blowing. Located 2 miles east of Haleiwa (Spot 5) and 4 miles west of Sunset Beach (Spot 12), Laniakea can be seen clearly from the road as a broad reef break. Known as the Gateway to the North Shore, it is the first surf spot you reach when you leave Haleiwa. A fabulous sight on first arrival, the surf lineup is amazing. If the swell is up and the sun's out, looking out to the horizon the heavens appear to crash in as sets pile up, in a mounting succession of waves.

The waves are a long way out, then suddenly a surfer drops in and disappears in the tube and reappears hugging the wall. More waves break closer in, looking inviting, and this is a typically awesome big day at Laniakea. You can feel alone (but never lonely) surfing here. This compared with surfing Waimea Bay, a dangerously crowded spot on biggish days. At Laniakea there may be only a handful of surfers in the water, savoring the adventure, alone in their own world of spiritual glee. The length of ride is 300 to 500 yards on a good 6-to-8-foot day, and 400 to 600 yards on a bigger day. Small waves of quality are also offered by the sea gods here, and most people regard it as a fine performance wave on the smaller days. This is an ace surf spot for the intermediate-to-big-wave rider, depending on the surf size.

Photo R. Sumpter

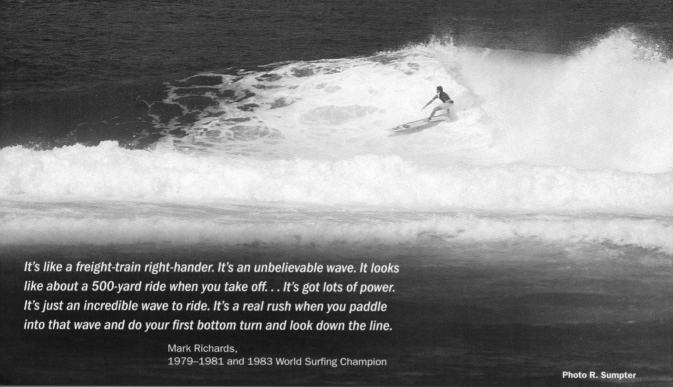

It's like a freight-train right-hander. It's an unbelievable wave. It looks like about a 500-yard ride when you take off. . . It's got lots of power. It's just an incredible wave to ride. It's a real rush when you paddle into that wave and do your first bottom turn and look down the line.

Mark Richards,
1979–1981 and 1983 World Surfing Champion

Photo R. Sumpter

Rights	NW Swell		Shallow Reef

Break: Right-hand reef break
Skill Level: Expert
Commitment: 7–10
Best Boards: Shortboards, longboards on small days and on big days over 15 feet, rhino guns for waves 11 feet or more
Lifeguard: None
Hazards: Long paddle out through coral gullies and pools over coral spikes, into and against a channel rip that doubles the distance out to the takeoff area.

After high tide an outgoing undertow and an offshore wind aids paddling. On big days, more than double or triple overhead, heavy set waves clean up and break all but the toughest leg ropes. The swim in is a nightmare.
Currency: U.S. dollar.
Getting There: Visa required except by U.S. citizens. Vaccinations required except by U.S. citizens—tetanus, typhoid. Check with your doctor, health clinic,

and embassy for up-to-date info.
Where to Stay: It's easy to find rooms to rent, and apartments are close by. See the notice boards at Foodland at Waimea Bay; Kammies Market at Sunset Beach; and other locations in Haleiwa town. Laie Inn, a twenty-minute drive from the North Shore on the windward side of the island; 55-109 Laniloa Street, Laie; (808) 293–2982, (800) 526–4562.
Finding the Break: From Haleiwa head eastward along the Kamehameha Highway and over the famous arched bridge leading out to the country. The road widens as you reach a magically white sandy beach, trimmed with black lava boulders and a few wooden houses.
Keep in Mind: Roadside parking fills quickly so get there early.

Months	JF	MA	MJ	JA	SO	ND
Average Swell (feet)	6–8	6–8	3–4	2	5–6	6
Air Temp (C/F)	26/79	27/81	29/84	30/86	29/84	27/81
Water Temp (C/F)	24/75	24/75	25/77	26/79	27/81	24/75
Wetsuit	short	short	none	none	none	vest
Average Sunshine p/d (hours)	8	9	12	14	13	8
Average Rain p/m (inches)	3	1	0	1	2	3
Average Surfable Days p/m	14	11	4	2	5	10

7. LOG CABINS
North Shore, Oahu, Hawaii

Through the leaves of lush greenery, you stare out at a blue-white reef on the North Shore. It's not just any reef, though. It's Outer Log Cabins, where the Pacific is rolling in waves the size of dinosaurs. These beauties will re-form on the inside at Log Cabins, one of the finest surf breaks in Oahu.

Situated 1 mile east of Waimea Bay (Spots 14 and 15) and 3 miles west of Sunset Beach (Spot 12), Log Cabins got its name from surfers in the 1960s who found that when they tried to line up the surf from the water, they had no obvious reference point on land to use. So they named the reef and surf spot for the first log cabin built on the side of the hill, because this was the most visible landmark from the takeoff area. Once you're out behind the waves, the view of the surf and the mountains is magical. This is a right-hand reef break, with the occasional left, and the right is straight out from the log cabins, which are now almost obscured by vegetation. When you're in the right spot you can take off and ride for 200 yards. It's a fast drop-in, and a fast wall with off-the-lip sections, a tube, as well as a hotdog tail end to the wave if it doesn't close out too soon. It's better to kick out early than be trapped on the inside during sets, because breaking waves over a sharp coral bottom make for dangerous wipe-outs that could be nasty. Log Cabins is for the expert surfer on most days and the big-wave rider on huge days.

Outer Log Cabins, where monster waves thunder in like the three-headed beast before re-forming at Log Cabins, is also called Revelations. This is one of the biggest, most awesome surfable wave spots in the world. On January 28, 1998, monster-wave surfer Ken Bradshaw was reported surfing Outer Log Cabins with waves up to 70 to 80 feet—wave face height!

Set below the topography of craggy tropical volcanic peaks, this largely deserted stretch of coastline has a small community of folks who pride themselves on the ways of Hawaiian tradition, and who cherish their spectacular views of mountains and surf. Coral lagoons form rock pools and shallow fishing reefs for nearly a mile. Early-morning mist regularly forms up in the tropical canopy, making for an almost prehistoric scene. The Hawaiian sun soon comes along, however, and the wave-watching resumes.

Photo R. Sumpter

It's really a fun wave. When it's small, it's high performance for floaters to big airs and big snaps. When it gets bigger, there's some big barrels to be found.

Andy Irons,
2002–2003 World Surfing Champion

Photo R. Sumpter

Peak | N Swell | | Shallow Reef

Type of Break: Right- and left-hand reef break

Skill Level: Expert

Commitment: 7–10

Best Boards: 6-foot, 9-inch, to 7-foot, 6-inch, swallowtail

Lifeguard: None

Hazards: Difficult access paddle out through narrow coral gaps in the reef, then out a middle section past a heavy shorebreak to big waves; rips and currents, shallow coral reef most of the way, worst at low tide.

Currency: U.S. dollar.

Going There: Visa required except by U.S. citizens. Vaccinations required except by U.S. citizens—tetanus, typhoid. Check with your doctor, health clinic, and embassy for up-to-date info.

Where to Stay: It's easy to find rooms to rent, and apartments are close by. See the notice boards at Foodland at Waimea Bay; Kammies Market at Sunset Beach; and other locations in Haleiwa town. Malaekahana Campground, a twenty-minute drive west of Sunset Beach on the windward side of the island; P.O. Box 305, Laie 96762; (808) 293–1736.

Finding the Break: Not easy to find. From Waimea Bay head east on the Kam Highway past Three Steps until you reach a small gap in the road; turn left onto Ke Waena Road. There is parking for a few cars, as well as other public access paths off Ke Waena. The lifeguard tower is just to the east under the palm trees on the sand.

Surf School: Stan Van Voorhis Surf Instruction, P.O. Box 1174, Halweiwa 96712, (808) 638-9503.

Keep in Mind: Rarely overcrowded.

Months	JF	MA	MJ	JA	SO	ND
Average Swell (feet)	6-8	4-6	2-3	2	2-3	6
Air Temp (C/F)	26/79	27/81	29/84	30/86	29/84	27/81
Water Temp (C/F)	24/75	24/75	25/77	26/79	27/81	24/75
Wetsuit	short	short	none	none	none	vest
Average Sunshine p/d (hours)	8	9	12	14	13	8
Average Rain p/m (inches)	3	1	0	1	2	3
Average Surfable Days p/m	12	8	3	2	2	9

8. OFF THE WALL North Shore, Oahu, Hawaii

One long-walling swell hits the reef and jacks up, then breaks fast, almost closing out. Your angled takeoff is a nail-biting moment—pure adrenaline. To choose a board for Off the Wall, it's wise to have a quiver of them, this being the best insurance policy to escape its jaws. Don't worry when your ride is hooked in deep, it's getting dark, and the only way out is forward. Keep going. Of course, praying helps.

Off the Wall is situated at KeWa`ena Beach between Log Cabins (Spot 7) and Backdoor (Spot 1), and is one of Hawaii's best surfing locations. This famous right-hand reef break is a classic barreling tube ride. Off the Wall has surely one of the best tubes in the world, if judged by the amount of Kodak film used by the lineup of photographers who sit on the nearby wall snapping print after print after print.

The name is derived from the long lava wall that runs along the beachfront. The wave's first section looks as if it's going to close out, but it doesn't; instead it gets faster, tighter, and hollower. The waves then peel off in the flicker of an eye. The Hawaiians have a name for it: *lala,* meaning "diagonal surf" or "surfing diagonally to the front of a wave."

With a northeast swell of 6 to 8 feet and a light trade wind, Off the Wall will turn into the fabulous barreling wave it's best known for. This spot is not for the fainthearted; it can be as dangerous a surf spot as there is. If it's over 10 feet, it's so heavy, fast, and hard that surfboards get snapped like toothpicks. Sets can double up and you get *ahua,* "a place close to shore where the broken waves rise and break again." This is an all-time great surf spot, ideal for the expert surfer.

Local surfer Larry Bertlemann became famous worldwide for riding Off the Wall better than any other in his time. He perfected the 360 turns on small days at Off the Wall, making this stunt look like a smooth and relaxed circular flip between tubes. In many ways his approach gave birth to the ripping performance approach of most of today's surfers. On big days at Off the Wall, Bertlemann's performance was nothing short of outstanding.

Photo R. Sumpter

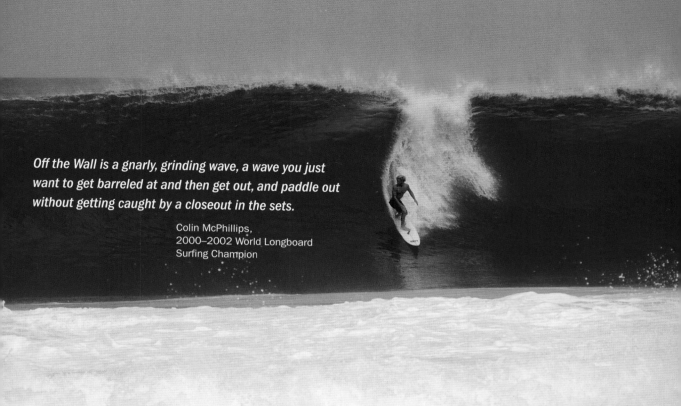

Off the Wall is a gnarly, grinding wave, a wave you just want to get barreled at and then get out, and paddle out without getting caught by a closeout in the sets.

Colin McPhillips,
2000–2002 World Longboard
Surfing Champion

Photo R. Sumpter

| Rights | N Swell | | Shallow Reef |

Break: Right-hand reef break

Skill Level: Expert

Commitment: 10–10

Best Boards: Shortboards

Lifeguard: None

Hazards: Nice entry into clean barrels, which turn heavy in big waves; watch out for dangerous rip currents and shallow coral.

Currency: U.S. dollar.

Going There: Visa required except by U.S. citizens. Vaccinations required except by U.S. citizens—tetanus, typhoid. Check with your doctor, health clinic, and embassy for up-to-date info.

Where to Stay: Sunset Homes, LLC. Call (808) 637–2400 or 638–7299, or fax 637–4200. See the notice board at Haleiwa Super Market for rental accommodations, and see the Foodland at Waimea Bay and Kammies Market at Sunset Beach notice boards for apartments and rooms. Laie Inn, a twenty-minute drive from the North Shore on the windward side of the island; 55-109 Laniloa Street, Laie; (808) 293–2982, (800) 526–4562.

Finding the Break: Located 0.5 mile west of Ehukai Beach Park, Off the Wall (Ehukai Beach) offers a little parking space on the Kam Highway and more on the beach road of Ke Nui Road. A sand track leads you out to the beach, and a 100-foot coral wall on the beach facing the surf tells you you're at Off the Wall.

Keep in Mind: Expect crowds on weekends in winter season.

Month	JF	MA	MJ	JA	SO	ND
Average Swell (feet)	8	6–7	4	3	4	6–8
Air Temp (C/F)	26/79	27/81	29/84	30/86	29/84	27/81
Water Temp (C/F)	24/75	24/75	25/77	26/79	27/81	24/75
Wetsuit	shorty	shorty	none	none	none	vest
Average Sunshine p/d (hours)	8	9	12	14	13	8
Average Rain p/m (inches)	3	1	0	1	2	3
Average Surfable Days p/m	21	18	12	2	4	20

9. PUPUKEA

North Shore, Oahu, Hawaii

This is one of the North Shore's most unique waves, a crescent-shaped shorebreak with a heavy dump when you wipe out, or a clean tube if you don't. The takeoff is yet another do-or-die North Shore epic semi-closeout with a bowling barrel. You take off, drive down the face, turn right, and there are only split seconds to make the bowl, turn left a little, and thread through a gap. Straighten up and shoot for the sun and down onto the shore dump, or be crushed like another puka shell.

Pupukea is located 600 yards west of Rocky Point (Spot 11) and 0.5 mile east of Banzai Pipeline (Spot 2); it has a steeply sloping horseshoe-shaped beach with pearly white sands and palm trees, and is the quintessential tropical beach break. Pupukea is famous for two reasons: the puka shells that wash up on every high tide (those tiny white shells with the hole in the middle, perfect for making into necklaces), and the world-class waves on this superb length of coastline from Haleiwa (Spot 5) to Sunset Beach (Spot 12).

This is one of the great fun beach breaks of the North Shore, with challenging waves for the expert if it's over 6 feet, and fun small performance waves at 3 feet. Best between September and April, it's also superb during the overlapping months in the spring and fall. During the summer months it can often be flat, at which time its clear, warm waters are ideal for snorkeling. In the winter season when the short barrels start to pump, it's a magnet for hot surfers attracted by fast and challenging waves. Here it's mostly a right-hander, but with some lefts.

The shifting sand bottom and lava rock beach break picks up strong currents and undertows quickly, creating dangerous conditions on an increasing swell. An early-morning surf session at sunrise in light trade winds is probably the best time; the waves can have an eerie glassy-smooth face to them. For such a short length of ride—about 50 yards—the waves have impact, and it's just a short paddle out to the takeoff. In fact, takeoff is so close to shore that you can sit on the beach and almost have enough time to see a set arriving, then paddle out for it without missing the wave. This is an ideal wave for both beginners and experts on the right day.

When distant swells are increasing, the shifting, wandering peaks of waves are a feature at Pupukea as swells roam in from outer reefs. Each one moves a little to break either east or west of the last, making positioning a challenge with each breaking set, depending on the tide, swell, and wave height. Considered a classic wave when it's pumping 6 to 8 feet, with a steep shorebreak *huia* or "especially high wave formed by the meeting of two crests."

Photo R. Sumpter

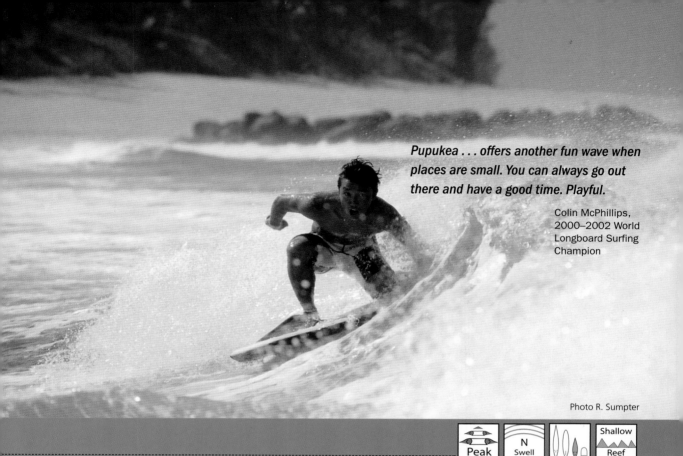

Pupukea . . . offers another fun wave when places are small. You can always go out there and have a good time. Playful.

Colin McPhillips,
2000–2002 World
Longboard Surfing
Champion

Photo R. Sumpter

Peak	N Swell		Shallow Reef

Break: Beach break
Skill Level: Intermediate to expert
Commitment: 5–10
Best Boards: Shortboards
Lifeguard: None
Hazards: Shallow shore dump if under 6 feet; rip currents, shallow coral and sand bottom make heavy waves close out if waves are double overhead.
Currency: U.S. dollar.

Going There: Visa required except by U.S. citizens. Vaccinations required except by U.S. citizens—tetanus, typhoid. Check with your doctor, health clinic, and embassy for up-to-date info.
Where to Stay: Sunset Homes, LLC. Call (808) 637–2400 or 638–7299, or fax 637–4200. See the notice board at Haleiwa Super Market for rental accommodations. See the Foodland at Waimea Bay and Kammies Market at Sunset Beach notice boards for apartments and rooms. Laie Inn, a twenty-minute drive from the North Shore on the windward side of the island; 55-109 Laniloa Street, Laie; (808) 293–2982, (800) 526–4562.
Finding the Break: A quarter mile past Sunset Beach on the Kam Highway going toward Haleiwa, you will see a big Indian head totem pole carved out of wood on the left, about 20 feet high. Turn into the small street on the right across from the statue. Then take a quick left and you're on Ke Nui Road. Go down to the second public right-of-way between the houses, and you have found Pupukea.
Keep in Mind: When it's 4 to 6 feet in the winter, it will be popular on weekends.

Month	JF	MA	MJ	JA	SO	ND
Average Swell (feet)	8–10	6–8	3–4	2	5–6	8–10
Air Temp (C/F)	26/79	27/81	29/84	30/86	29/84	27/81
Water Temp (C/F)	23/73	24/75	25/77	26/79	27/81	24/75
Wetsuit	shorty	vest	none	none	none	vest
Average Sunshine p/d (hours)	7	9	10	11	9	6–7
Average Rain p/m (inches)	3	1	0	1	2	3
Average Surfable Days p/m	21	18	12	2	4	20

10. ROCKPILE
North Shore, Oahu, Hawaii

First surfed in the 1970s and then on a more regular basis in the 1990s, Rockpile is a gruesome spot that few surfers can ride. It's one of the truly big, deep ocean breaks in Hawaii, an awesomely steep hooking wave that defies gravity. It takes guts and skill to surf Rockpile, and maybe a touch of madness.

This is the spot on the North Shore where clean, clear swells approach this mighty reef break then twist like muscles in a spasm around jagged rocks and turquoise seas. When the big, long sloping waves hoist up, you must drive hard to make the drop.

This left-hand big-wave spot is seemingly impossible to ride when, on big days, surfers' eyes scan up and down the beach from Backdoor (Spot 1) or Off the Wall (Spot 8), attempting to find a peak. Only a few will tackle these savage, hollow, left-hand hooking waves because of the pinnacles of lava rock formations that have piled into the sea. This is the ultimate left big-wave spot on the North Shore when most other places are starting to close out, including Rocky Point (Spot 11), and Chuns Reef (Spot 3).

Rockpile is situated 6 miles east of Haleiwa (Spot 5) and 1 mile west of Banzai Pipeline (Spot 2). If you aren't content with Off the Wall and don't mind a strong rip current to paddle against, you can surf this gigantic left.

Rockpile starts breaking when the swell gets over 10 feet and holds waves up to 18 feet high. Viewed from the mountain road, it's impressive to see the huge swells peak and break among the many surfing lineups of the North Shore. Sometimes called Gap in the Road, because it can be seen from the Kamehameha Highway through a break in the fence, this wave is at its best at 10 to 15 feet, and has a length of ride of about 50 to 150 yards. There is a lifeguard tower with seasonal lifesavers on duty who can ride Rockpile better than most, especially when on their specially made big-wave guns. Expect them to close the beach with the red flag as soon as it becomes too dangerous and when a High Sea Alert warning is announced. You can also expect the North Shore to be closed at least two or three times each winter when massive swells arrive, coming off deep low-pressure systems and traveling east across the Pacific Ocean. This surf spot is for the expert and big-wave surfer only.

Photo R. Sumpter

Yeah, I surf Rockpile plenty. Rockpile is a heavy wave. It's really fun when it's 4 or 5 feet. When it gets to 10 to 12 feet, there's a big boil on it, supergnarly, deep water to shallow water, a real open-ocean wave.

Andy Irons,
2002–2003 World Surfing Champion

Photo R. Sumpter

 Peak N Swell   Shallow Reef

Break: Reef break
Skill Level: Expert
Commitment: 9–10
Best Boards: Shortboards
Lifeguard: None
Hazards: Deep water waves hit hard; dangerous rip currents, shallow coral, rocky outcrops
Currency: U.S. dollar.

Going There: Visa required except by U.S. citizens. Vaccinations required except by U.S. citizens—tetanus, typhoid. Check with your doctor, health clinic, and embassy for up-to-date info.
Where to Stay: Sunset Homes, LLC. Call (808) 637–2400 or 638–7299, or fax: 637–4200. See the notice board at Haleiwa Super Market for rental accommodations. See the Foodland at Waimea Bay and Kammies Market at Sunset Beach notice boards for rented apartments and rooms. Malaekahana Campground, a twenty-minute drive west of Sunset Beach on the windward side of the island; P. O. Box 305, Laie 96762; (808) 293–1736.

Finding the Break: From Waimea Bay head east on the Kam Highway past Three Steps until you spot a small gap in the road; turn left onto Ke Waena Road. There is parking for a few cars, as well as other public access paths, off Ke Waena. The lifeguard tower is just to the east under the palm trees on the sand.

Keep in Mind: When it's 4 to 6 feet in the winter, it will be popular on weekends.

Months	JF	MA	MJ	JA	SO	ND
Average Swell (feet)	8	4–5	2–3	1–2	4	6
Air Temp (C/F)	26/79	27/81	29/84	30/86	29/84	27/81
Water Temp (C/F)	23/73	24/75	25/77	26/79	27/81	24/75
Wetsuit	shorty	vest	none	none	none	vest
Average Sunshine p/d (hours)	7	9	10	11	9	6–7
Average Rain p/m (inches)	3	1	0	1	2	3
Average Surfable Days p/m	21	18	12	2	4	20

11. ROCKY POINT

North Shore, Oahu, Hawaii

No one walks the fine line between closeout and freight-train barrels more than Rocky Point surfers. They know that the deceptively strong lefts and rights are like falling over a mountain pass, where jackknifing turns and hitting the anchors to go all out is the only way to survive. But when the trade winds are blowing a hooley and the swell is out of the northeast, you can be sure they will be here.

Rocky Point surf has a reputation for quality lefts and rights when the other major surf spots on the North Shore are missing out on the swell or just not lined up well. Situated 0.75 mile east of Banzai Pipeline (Spot 2), and 0.5 mile west of Sunset Beach (Spot 12), this rock-ledge point produces ace surf when it's 4 to 8 feet or a bit bigger.

Rock pools and half-submerged boulders pepper the beach, while palm trees fringe the point and coastline. Rocky Point derives its name from its location and is aptly named, because most other North Shore locations are usually much sandier. It's a well-lined-up performance wave, hitting hard at times, but softer compared to some of the more heavyweight, famous surf spots, such as Banzai. Access to

those long peeling lefts is across the beach and point, through a sandy cove, to a channel in the coral that makes an easy entry and a fair paddle out. Along the way there are good views of the tube twisting past the shore.

The left is far longer than the right, and is the preferred direction if both are breaking well on the same day. Getting to the right involves a harder paddle out, through sets that often break wide. In addition, there is no channel, just gaps in the reef. It's a fast walling wave with hollow sections that are doable, but the shorebreak that closes out or peels off to the coral slab shore is often the hairiest part of the wave. The shorebreak section may continue toward Pupukea Beach if the swell has a lot of northeast direction to it.

When the North Shore's other major breaks are not at their best, then "Rocky" seems to light up its fire and beckon to be ridden. It's renowned for high-performance surfing waves in 4-to-8-foot swells, often some of the best in the world. But if the swell gets too big too quickly—usually over 12 feet—it will blow out. This is a must-surf spot, on the right day, for intermediate and above-average surfers.

Photo R. Sumpter

Rocky Point, always fun.

Bob McTavish,
former Australian Surfing Champion

Photo R. Sumpter

Rights	Lefts	NW Swell		Shallow Reef	Shallow Sand

Break: Point break

Skill Level: Intermediate to expert

Commitment: 6–10

Best Boards: Shortboards up to 7 feet, 6 inches, round pin

Lifeguard: None

Hazards: Can be the sweetest paddle out and section of surf you could wish for, or a nightmare challenge when a new swell brings triple-overhead waves in a matter of hours; rip currents, shallow coral and sand bottom, rocky outcrops

Currency: U.S. dollar.

Going There: Visa required except by U.S. citizens. Vaccinations required except by U.S. citizens—tetanus, typhoid. Check with your doctor, health clinic, and embassy for up-to-date info.

Where to Stay: Sunset Homes, LLC. Call (808) 637–2400 or 638–7299, or fax 637–4200. See the notice board at Haleiwa Super Market for rental accommodations. See the Foodland at Waimea Bay and Kammies Market at Sunset Beach notice boards for apartments and rooms. Laie Inn, a twenty-minute drive from the North Shore on the windward side of the island; 55-109 Laniloa Street, Laie; (808) 293–2982, (800) 526–4562.

Finding the Break: From Sunset Beach drive east on the Kam Highway and turn right after 0.5 mile onto Soundview Drive. Follow the coast to a dead end with parking.

Keep in Mind: Early mornings are best.

Months	JF	MA	MJ	JA	SO	ND
Average Swell (feet)	8	5	3-4	1-2	2	4-6
Air Temp (C/F)	26/79	27/81	29/84	30/86	29/84	27/81
Water Temp (C/F)	23/73	24/75	25/77	26/79	27/81	24/75
Wetsuit	shorty	vest	none	none	none	vest
Average Sunshine p/d (hours)	7	9	10	11	9	6-7
Average Rain p/m (inches)	3	1	0	1	2	3
Average Surfable Days p/m	18	14	9	5	4	17

12. SUNSET BEACH
North Shore, Oahu, Hawaii

Paddling out hard and looking up under the shadow of the West Peak, a gap 20 feet wide appears beside the loop of the curl, just enough to escape and paddle to safety. There's now the outer reef bearing down on you, and the whole breathtaking view of ocean swells is overwhelming. You could die. Like marching soldiers advancing on your position, you hear them stir your blood and pull the trigger. It's time to go. You push yourself over the edge and down the face, paddling hard. It's steep to vertical before your heart, brain, and body get it together and your first turn is made.

Here, on the famous strip of coastline known as the North Shore, lies Sunset Beach. Situated 30 miles north of Waikiki (Spot 19), 2 miles east of Banzai Pipeline (Spot 2), and a forty-minute drive from the Honolulu airport on the Kamehameha Highway, this world-class surf spot is a long right with the occasional left at takeoff, as the wave peels off to a bowl section, hollow and very hard to make. The famous West Peak may break if the swell switches to a northwest.

The Pacific Ocean's deep-water swells arrive at Sunset and break from 4 to 30 feet in the winter. On big days Sunset Beach is famous for its incredibly steep peaks that seem, at first, to simply fade out, luring you into a false sense of security, only to re-form and jack up on the inside bowl. Surfers from all over the world flock to Sunset Beach to test their skills on these giant waves. And best of all,

when you're done getting pounded, you can stop and enjoy the aloha spirit of beautiful sunsets.

For most surfers, the magic of Hawaii is taking off on a ride of a lifetime. This is what can happen at Sunset Beach, making it one of the most exciting places on earth to surf. Sunset is also a place of extreme variety where, on small days, you can surf on fun longboard waves, riding the nose till the sun goes down. On bigger days you can surf the main peak and get tubed in the bowl. On really huge days you can fly down the drop on takeoff and feel the roar of the wind enveloping you as you bottom-turn into a crystal wall of water. But be careful or you'll get caught in the rip and get pounded by the shorebreak while attempting to leave the water. The sheer power of the ocean is very evident here.

Every year the winter season (November to April) transforms average waves at Sunset Beach into the best and biggest in the world. This famous spot is located on a curved horseshoe-shaped beach with pearly white sand fringed by palm trees, lush vegetation, and tropical wooden houses, making it the quintessential tropical paradise. And those lucky enough to surf Sunset well leave with the same adrenaline rush that you got after riding on your first wave upright.

Towering peaks, strong offshore wind, and grinding, barreling walls make Sunset Beach the all-time great surf break, a shining star on the global surf map.

Photo R. Sumpter

Sunset Beach—it's like a coliseum of big-wave surf spots, . . . You can't compare it to anything. Sunset is just Sunset, and it sort of deserves its own category.

Mark Richards,
1979–1981 and 1983
World Surfing Champion

Photo R. Sumpter

Rights	Peak	NW Swell	

Break: Right-hand reef break

Skill Level: Expert

Commitment: 10–10 if over 8 feet

Best Boards: Shortboards up to 7 feet, 11 inches, pin tails, and big-wave guns

Lifeguard: Year-round

Hazards: When the point and outer reef waves start to break, the main reef rights take on a range of characteristics from hot-dog waves to those with crushing bowls and vertical peaks.

Currency: U.S. dollar.

Going There: Visa required except by U.S. citizens. Vaccinations required except by U.S. citizens—tetanus, typhoid. Check with your doctor, health clinic, and embassy for up-to-date info.

Where to Stay: It's easy to find rooms to rent, and apartments are close by. For Sunset Homes, LLC, call (808) 637–2400 or 638–7299, or fax 637–4200. See the notice boards at Foodland at Waimea Bay; Kammies Market at Sunset Beach; and other locations in Haleiwa town. Malaekahana Campground, a twenty-minute drive west of Sunset Beach on the windward side of the island; P.O. Box 305, Laie 96762; (808) 293–1736.

Finding the Break: Easy to find. Whichever way you drive to the North Shore, Sunset Beach is 6 miles east of Waimea Bay on the Kam Highway, with roadside parking and views of the waves.

Surf Schools: Hans Hedemann Surf School, (808) 924–7778. Nancy Emerson School of Surf, (808) 244–7873.

Contests: Ripcurl Cup (WCT), December.

Keep in Mind: A popular spot in all conditions.

Month	JF	MA	MJ	JA	SO	ND
Average Swell (feet)	6–8	6	3–4	2	5–6	6
Air Temp (C/F)	26/79	27/81	29/84	30/86	29/84	27/81
Water Temp (C/F)	24/75	24/75	25/77	26/79	27/81	24/75
Wetsuit	shorty	shorty	none	none	none	vest
Average Sunshine p/d (hours)	8	9	12	14	13	8
Average Rain p/m (inches)	3	1	0	1	2	3
Average Surfable Days p/m	25	14	6	2	9	22

13. VELZYLAND
North Shore, Oahu, Hawaii

Fear of flying? Heart rate up? Quickening breath and trembling hands? Chances are you're about to surf one of the most wedge-shaped breaking waves in the world, and if you mess it up you'll land on the reef, racked out like a landed fish to dry in the hot sun.

Along the North Shore from Haleiwa, there exists what is known as the "7-mile surf miracle zone," containing most of the best surf spots and waves in the world. This miracle zone ends at Velzyland.

Situated 1.5 miles east of Sunset Beach (Spot 12) and 1 mile west of Kahuku, Velzyland is otherwise known as V-Land, its name derived from a surfer named Daly Velzy who first surfed here in the 1950s. This is one of the world's best right-hand small-wave spots, which works in surf heights of 2 to 8 feet. When it gets any bigger, the surf on the outside reef churns into a boil of whitewater and closes out with no shape. It's then that sailboarders, who descend like buzzards on a fresh kill, flock here and are able to put in a fantastic display, carving up strong trade winds as the swells blow out. Velzyland is also a sought-after spot for shortboards in 4-to-8-foot surf and for expert bodyboarders in even smaller wave conditions, giving them perfect rides.

Besides the two main takeoff areas, there is a third area on the left side of the main takeoff peak. This works on a northwest swell and is a left-hand wave running into a tube section. Over the shallow reef it can be as little as a foot deep, with no channels or gullies through which to paddle back out. It is hard-core. So the left is only chosen

> The Hawaiian Islands are at the root of surfing history, the sport being practiced for possibly centuries before Captain James Cook first recorded it in 1778. The North Shore of Oahu remains at the heart of modern-day surfing, and is the championship surf capital of the Hawaiian Islands.

over a right on rare occasions, and usually only by goofy-foot surfers. The right is a challenging wave to ride from the peak, having a sucky takeoff that is insanely steep. From the shoulder there is little time to drop in beside the pitching lip. Once you've dropped in, you must then trim hard across a tubing wall to a hollow outside wall and over the shallow coral reef. A flattish section that resembles a longboarder's hotdog wave continues to an ultratubey inside section that finishes things off. On average the length of ride is 100 to 150 yards. The walk and paddle out is over sharp coral at first; then a small alleyway cuts out of the coral reef and is filled with sand. This is straight out from the takeoff area and aids entry to a channel and out to the takeoff area. Velzyland is the North Shore's easternmost surf break and is likely to be crowded with top-class surfers. This is a superb surf break for the expert.

Photo R. Sumpter

Velzyland, unreal, one of the better waves in the world. It's just a very perfect wave where you can do everything and get barreled on it. It's not a frightening scary wave but a very good wave.

Colin McPhillips,
2000–2002 World Longboard Surfing Champion

Photo R. Sumpter

Rights | Peak | N Swell

Break: Beach break
Skill Level: Intermediate to expert
Commitment: 7–10
Best Boards: Shortboards
Lifeguard: None
Hazards: Difficult access and dangerous rip currents; shallow coral bottom; solid lines of top-to-bottom breaking waves over coral ledges. The smaller the easier, but watch the reef.

Currency: U.S. dollar.
Going There: Visa required except by U.S. citizens. Vaccinations required except by U.S. citizens—tetanus, typhoid. Check with your doctor, health clinic, and embassy for up-to-date info.
Where to Stay: It's easy to find rooms to rent, and apartments are close by. For Sunset Homes, LLC, call (808) 637–2400 or 638–7299, or fax

637–4200. See the notice boards at Foodland at Waimea Bay; Kammies Market at Sunset Beach; and other locations in Haleiwa town. Laie Inn, a twenty-minute drive from the North Shore on the windward side of the island; 55-109 Laniloa Street, Laie; (808) 293–2982, (800) 526–4562.
Finding the Break: Coming from Sunset Beach head east for about a five-minute drive and turn right after the little bridge over Kaunala Stream, which is after Ted's Bakery. Park somewhere on this street, around the cul-de-sac of Mamao Place. Then walk down Mamao Street to Kaunala Bay (Velzyland).
Keep in Mind: This is a popular spot in all conditions.

Months	JF	MA	MJ	JA	SO	ND
Average Swell (feet)	6	3	2	2–3	4–5	5
Air Temp (C/F)	26/79	27/81	29/84	30/86	29/84	27/81
Water Temp (C/F)	23/73	24/75	25/77	26/79	27/81	24/75
Wetsuit	shorty	vest	none	none	none	vest
Average Sunshine p/d (hours)	7	9	10	11	9	6–7
Average Rain p/m (inches)	3	1	0	1	2	3
Average Surfable Days p/m	23	18	14	4	4	17

14. WAIMEA BAY POINT
North Shore, Oahu, Hawaii

For most of the year, Waimea Bay is as soft and placid as a pond. Then winter storms deep in the Arctic send waves pulsing across the blue Pacific. Waimea Bay becomes a mesmerizing fury of gigantic roaring waves. Surfing Waimea Bay is like launching off a skyscraper and into a pond—bombs away on a vertical takeoff into a steep walling wave face. This is surfing at its most extreme. This is the North Shore of Oahu, where some of the biggest ridable waves in the world are found.

Situated off the Kamehameha Highway just 4 miles east of Haleiwa (Spot 5) and 2 miles west of the Banzai Pipeline (Spot 2), next to Waimea Bay Beach Park and Waimea Bay Falls, is the famous Waimea Bay Point. Every winter viewers watch on the local news breathtaking rides and dramatic rescues at Waimea Bay. From the roadside, December through February, you can look on in amazement as the best big-wave surfers on Planet Earth ride 30-foot monsters. From vantage points around Waimea Bay and on the beach, without ever getting your feet wet, you can witness terrific rides and scary wipeouts on supermonster waves that'll leave you breathless and gawking.

At takeoff the drop will suck the breath from your lungs, and in a moment its massive wall lines up and breaks, throwing out its curl. The steep face falls away to the wave's trough. If you make it this far, there is only the crashing right lip to avoid, and then it's out for the shoulder and the safety of the channel. If you hang on and stay trimmed, you could outrun the roaring avalanche and make it all the way. Waimea is so exciting to watch that, on every wave, it's debatable if a surfer will wipe out on takeoff, go over the falls, or not survive the chase across the wall to the safety of the channel.

A great place to watch the waves of Waimea Bay is from up at the Pu`uomahuka Heiau State Monument, on a 250-foot bluff above the St. Peter and Paul Church. The bay, with its stunningly huge waves, pearly white beach, and tropical surroundings, forms a view to die for.

Nestling in the gorge behind Waimea Bay is Waimea Falls Park, an 1,800-acre botanical garden offering historical and cultural exhibits. The highlight is a breathtaking diving exhibition from the falls, starting 55 feet above the garden. In the early 1970s the waterfall's free-fall experience was used by top wave riders as a training exercise for big-wave surfing. The bay is surrounded by thick tropical vegetation that covers the volcanic mountains.

Photo R. Sumpter

Until they discovered Mavericks and all these other spots, Waimea was the premier death-defying, risk-your-life wave. A lot of people think of Waimea as a bit of a hoax . . . but when you actually paddle out . . . you very quickly realize that it is not a hoax.

Mark Richards,
1979–1981 and 1983 World Surfing Champion

Photo R. Sumpter

R.Point NW Swell

Break: Point break
Skill Level: Expert
Commitment: 10–10
Best Boards: Bodyboard
Lifeguard: In season
Hazards: Every big-wave surfer's testing ground. Currents pour around the point to make the most dramatic takeoffs and amazing wipeouts that do kill.
Currency: U.S. dollar.
Going There: Visa required except by U.S. citizens. Vaccinations required except by U.S. citizens—tetanus, typhoid. Check with your doctor, health clinic, and embassy for up-to-date info.
Where to Stay: Back Packers-Vacation Inn and Plantation Village Waimea Bay. Call (808) 638–7838, or fax (808) 638–7515. Free shuttle from airport. Easy-to-find apartments to rent at Waimea Point, and rooms to rent close by. Go to Foodland at Waimea Bay and Kammies Market at Sunset Beach and other notice boards in Haleiwa town. The Turtle Bay Resort at Kahuku, near Sunset Beach is a five-star resort. Call (808) 293–8811 for reservations. North Shore Vacation Rentals. Call (808) 637–3507 or (800) 982–8602, fax (808) 637–8881.
Finding the Break: By car from the airport, take the Hawaii Highway 1 west towards Waianae, and then take Hawaii Highway 2 north towards North Shore or Wahiawa. Follow signs to Haleiwa. From Haleiwa head east for 4 miles on the Kam Highway. You cannot miss the Waimea Park sign as you wind around Waimea Bay. Parking is free. See the lifeguard and ask about current surfing conditions.
Keep in Mind: When the swell's cranking it's more than busy, it's packed.

Months	JF	MA	MJ	JA	SO	ND
Average Swell (feet)	4	3	1	1	2	3
Air Temp (C/F)	26/79	27/81	29/84	30/86	29/84	27/81
Water Temp (C/F)	23/73	24/75	25/77	26/79	27/81	24/75
Wetsuit	shorty	vest	none	none	none	vest
Average Sunshine p/d (hours)	7	9	10	11	9	6-7
Average Rain p/m (inches)	3	1	0	1	2	3
Average Surfable Days p/m	10	7	1	1	1	9

15. WAIMEA BAY SHORE BREAK

North Shore, Oahu, Hawaii

This wave throws, it doesn't crumble, and there are no mushy sections, just enormous artistic curves. To ride here you need to take off with a big grin on your face and the determination of a downhill racer. It's almost impossible to make the drop, vaulting past double-up sections and vast echoing hollow tubes. So you might as well smile now. Because this wave will do its best to wipe that grin right off your face.

The tropical beach park and beauty spot of Waimea Bay Shore Break is located right next to Waimea Falls, just 4 miles east of Haleiwa (Spot 5) and 2 miles west of the Banzai Pipeline (Spot 2). This is an epic left-hander, a surf destination for advanced-expert bodyboarders, with its multi-breaking gnarly shorebreak packed with extreme power.

Surfers and big-wave riders who come here consider the destination-seeking bodyboarders crazy to surf Waimea Shore Break, when they might tube just 30 yards from shore or end in a hideous wipeout. This tubing wave is a photo call for all who love the very close-up sights and sounds of waves at their best. For the bodyboarder it is the ultimate test of courage (or madness), with its heavy barrels that are only makable on the right day. Waimea produces some classic rides when it's 6 to 8 feet or bigger. But watch out, because the shorebreak has a strong undertow pulling you back into the dangerous

> The Waimea Bay Shore break waves are featured in many famous photographs, including those seen on the TV series *Hawaii Five-0* opening titles.

lineup. Lifeguards will close the beach when these powerful waves, caused by storms sometimes thousands of miles from the Hawaiian Islands, get too big. Expect seasonal High Surf Alerts to occur during the winter months, from December to March, when trade winds blow in from the northeast.

From the winding road circling this beautiful bay, the view of the huge shorebreak is breathtaking. And if you're lucky, you may also see whales breaching near the point. Waimea is a dangerous shorebreak, but for a few expert bodyboarders and big-wave surfers, it's ideal. And for those not willing to risk life and limb, it's a must-watch surf spot.

As if the waves weren't enough, watch out for the Portuguese man-of-war (a stinging blue jellyfish) from June to September. And on the leeward side of the island, the box jellyfish shows up ten days after a full moon. Warning signs are posted by the lifeguards.

Photo R. Sumpter

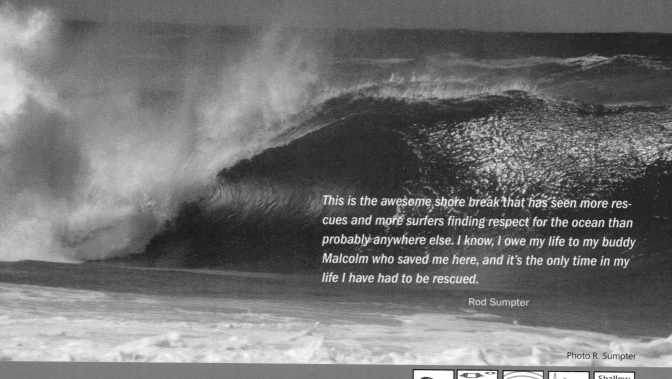

This is the awesome shore break that has seen more rescues and more surfers finding respect for the ocean than probably anywhere else. I know, I owe my life to my buddy Malcolm who saved me here, and it's the only time in my life I have had to be rescued.

Rod Sumpter

Photo R. Sumpter

 Lefts Beachbreak N Swell Shallow Sand

Type of Break: Beach break

Skill Level: Expert

Commitment: 10–10

Best Boards: Bodyboard

Lifeguard: In season

Hazards: Big waves, rips and currents, pounding shorebreak. Heavy shorebreak defies gravity. Waves pile up on top of each other. Double and triple layers are common. Even ten-decker breaking waves occur here.

Currency: U.S. dollar.

Going There: Visa required except by U.S. citizens. Vaccinations required except by U.S. citizens—tetanus, typhoid. Check with your doctor, health clinic, and embassy for up-to-date info.

Where to Stay: Back Packers-Vacation Inn and Plantation Village Waimea Bay. Call (808) 638–7838, or fax (808) 638–7515. Free shuttle from airport. Easy-to-find apartments to rent at Waimea Point, and rooms to rent close by. Go to Foodland at Waimea Bay, Kammies Market at Sunset Beach, and other notice boards in Haleiwa town.

Laie Inn, a twenty-minute drive from the North Shore on the windward side of the island; 55-109 Laniloa Street, Laie; (808) 293–2982, (800) 526–4562. North Shore Vacation Rentals. Call (808) 637–3507 or (800) 982–8602; fax (808) 637–8881.

Finding the Break: By car from the airport, take Hawaii Highway 1 west toward Waianae, and then take Hawaii Highway 2 north toward North Shore or Wahiawa. Follow signs to Haleiwa. From Haleiwa head east for 4 miles on the Kam Highway. You cannot miss the Waimea Park sign as you wind around Waimea Bay. Parking is free. See the lifeguard and ask for current surfing conditions.

Keep in Mind: The parking lot is crowded when the swell's up.

For More Information: Surf Alert recorded message, (808) 596–7873.

Months	JF	MA	MJ	JA	SO	ND
Average Swell (feet)	4	3	1	1	2	3
Air Temp (C/F)	26/79	27/81	29/84	30/86	29/84	27/81
Water Temp (C/F)	24/75	24/75	25/77	26/79	27/81	24/75
Wetsuit	shorty	shorty	none	none	none	vest
Average Sunshine p/d (hours)	8	9	12	14	13	8
Average Rain p/m (inches)	3	1	0	1	2	3
Average Surfable Days p/m	10	7	1	1	1	9

16. MAKAHA BEACH
Oahu, Hawaii

If the swell's up, take out your biggest wave gun, load up, and fire. This is Makaha and you'll need it.

Makaha is the mecca of surfing on Oahu's West Coast, boasting a wave range of 3 to 30 feet. It's a spectacular half-moon bay, and the fantastic point surf wave lines up and peels off over a coral reef into a bowl area, where the wave springs up and curves in a half circle. Then the beach break, with one of the biggest backwashes in the world.

Situated 20 miles northwest of Waikiki (Spot 19) and 10 miles southwest of Haleiwa (Spot 5), this famous surf spot has a long surfing history. The word *makaha* in ancient Hawaiian means "fierce "or "savage," appropriately naming the area that surrounds it.

Makaha is famous for its big right, called Makaha Point Surf, at Kepuhi Point, holding surf up to 30 feet at the outer end of the bay. The ride on a big day includes the famous "Bowl" area halfway into the ride, which curves around to face you in a tight escape tube. Then there's the infamous Makaha Backwash just before the shorebreak, with a reputation for sending surfers sailing 15 feet into the air. This hooligan wave action is caused by one wave washing up the steeply sloping beach, and then rolling quickly back down and out to sea to meet the oncoming wave. The resulting wave confrontation catches unsuspecting riders off guard,

Oahu is the third largest island in the Hawaiian chain, between Molakai and Kauai, and has two parallel mountain ranges, the Waianea and Koolau. Heading northwards up the West Coast, you'll find the superb left break of Ala Moana, which is for experts only. Farther up the coast are the famous waves of Makaha Beach.

catapulting them sky high. If they're clever enough, they can turn it into a huge cutback or aerial maneuver, becoming heroes instead of victims.

Makaha is nearly the complete surfer's playground, because it breaks year-round. Its best waves, however, roll in from April to September in northwest to southwest swells. At the week's end, local Hawaiian families set up their barbecues and stay all day, taking advantage of all this beautiful beach has to offer. There's surf for just about everyone, and on small days children and beginners can ride the shorebreak while the hotdoggers get to surf the waves farther out. On bigger days longboards rule, with nose rides and bottom turns taking the day. Shortboarders aren't left out, spending the day tackling the outside and inside parts of each wave and shredding the Makaha Backwash if they dare.

Hawaiian surfing legend Buffalo Keaulana lifeguarded at Makaha for seventeen years and held the popular Buffalo's Big Board Contest every year since 1978. Considered the world's greatest switch-foot surfer, his performance during the original Makaha International Surfing Championships of 1964 impressed even the great Duke Kahanamoku. Today he's retired from lifeguarding. But you may still find him shredding the Makaha Backwash.

Makaha and much of the west side of Oahu are about the closest thing to an unspoiled Hawaiian paradise as they come. Rising high above the shoreline, the dry, rugged slopes of the Waiane Mountains stretch up to the sky, while pineapple plantations sit farther inland. Ideally positioned on the leeward side of the island where the prevailing winds are offshore, Makaha is located just off the Farrington Highway on the West Shore of Oahu, next to Kaena Point. If you're on the island, you must surf here.

Photo R. Sumpter

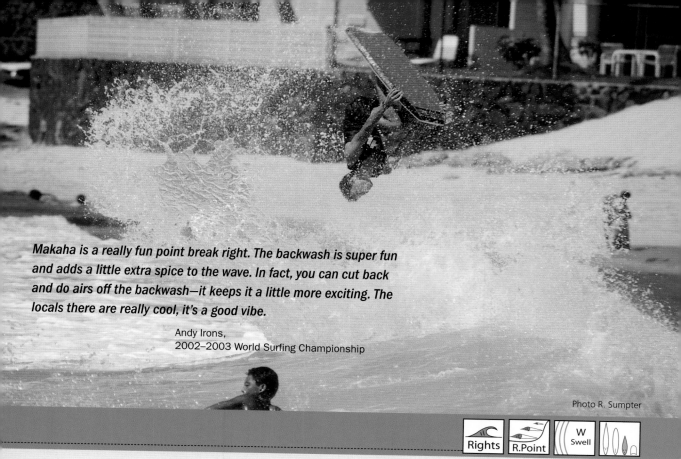

Makaha is a really fun point break right. The backwash is super fun and adds a little extra spice to the wave. In fact, you can cut back and do airs off the backwash—it keeps it a little more exciting. The locals there are really cool, it's a good vibe.

Andy Irons,
2002–2003 World Surfing Championship

Photo R. Sumpter

Rights	R.Point	W Swell	

Break: Beach break and right-hand point break

Skill Level: Beginner to expert

Commitment: 1–10

Best Boards: Longboards, shortboards, bodyboards

Lifeguard: Year-round

Hazards: When it's over 6 to 8 feet chances are the outgoing backwash will be throwing surfers 15 feet high.

Wipeouts are standard on big days. The point surf will break at swell sizes over 15 feet, then watch big-wave carving.

Currency: U.S. dollar.

Going There: Visa required except by U.S. citizens. Vaccinations required except by U.S. citizens—tetanus, typhoid. Check with your doctor, health clinic, and embassy for up-to-date info.

Where to Stay: Hawaiian Princess Resort, (214) 357–5522. Oceanfront Condos, Hawaiian Hatfield Realtor, (808) 696–4499. Makaha Valley Towers, (781) 444–1113. There is basic camping at Kahe Point Beach Park, which is the first beach north of Ko Olina on the Farrington Highway. The campsite is located a few hundred yards up the highway, opposite the rusted Hawaiian Electric Kahe Power Plant. Camping is allowed with a permit.

Finding the Break: From Honolulu take Highway 1 and follow it to Highway 93 going west. After going through the town of Waianae, you will come to Makaha surfing beach.

Keep in Mind: At times crowded.

Month	JF	MA	MJ	JA	SO	ND
Average Swell (feet)	3–4	3	2	1–2	2–3	3
Air Temp (C/F)	26/79	27/81	29/84	30/86	29/84	27/81
Water Temp (C/F)	24/75	24/75	25/77	26/79	27/81	24/75
Wetsuit	short	short	none	none	none	vest
Average Sunshine p/d (hours)	8	9	12	14	13	8
Average Rain p/m (inches)	3	1	0	1	2	3
Average Surfable Days p/m	18	16	10	5	6	12

17. MOKULEIA BEACH PARK
North Shore, Oahu, Hawaii

Like a bolt of lightning, waves rise up from the deep water and head for shore. Mokuleia picks these lightning waves up, then garnishes and grooms the swell into perfect peaks across the bay. The waves are wedged, and the green walls push hard. The bold forms, powerful drops, and steaming tunnels of Mokuleia are heady fun.

The amazing breaks of Mokuleia Beach Park are situated just 2 miles west of Haleiwa (Spot 5) and 1 mile east of Kaena Point at the northwestern corner of the North Shore. For many years this was a secret spot, and it's still relatively uncrowded thanks to the vast choice of breaks and its demanding waves.

On the smaller days when the ocean enjoys light offshore conditions and calm, even swells, this is the ideal place to spend a day of surfing. At Mokuleia Beach Park everything seems easy; you roll up, look out, and make some decisions on whether to surf this peak or that. After a few minutes of watching, you'll know the set patterns and will have timed the lulls. Then you're ready to go. This is the quiet part of the island, the bit that's been left as nature intended: untouched, beautiful, and with plenty of waves.

Mokuleia Beach Park parallels Dillingham airfield, off the Farrington Highway, and there are three main breaks to consider. The reef break off Army Beach is a tough paddle out on a 4-to-6-foot day, unless you judge the lulls right, take advantage of the rips and currents, and paddle out through gullies and channels in the coral to the deep-water peak.

A mile west of Mokuleia and 0.5 mile out to sea off Kaena Point is a rare winter big-wave spot for specialist wave riders only. It was here in the 1980s that a helicopter was first used to get out past the breaking waves. The Point Surf is the location of some of Hawaii's biggest waves, and some of the highest in the world at more than 60 feet.

Then there's the western end of Mokuleia, with slabs of lava rock covering the ocean floor and A-frame peaks providing a perfect left on the inside of Kaena Point. Mokuleia Beach Park also has breaks in the eastward directions from Dillingham. The reef toward the town of Waialua breaks farther out and peaks as a right-hand barrel with a very steep takeoff, but with good reentry, floater, and air possibilities. On most days there are few people in the lineup. You can park and picnic in paradise surroundings, waiting for just the right surf to suit you. The ocean seems to pump out magic waves one after another as soon as the light southerly offshore winds blow. That's when all the breaks start to turn to perfection. This is an ideal surf spot for shortboards and longboards, and occasionally, in strong trade winds, there are good wave conditions for sailboarders as well.

Photo R. Sumpter

Mokuleia Beach Park is a fun wave . . . more conducive to a longboard. You can do everything on the wave.

Colin McPhillips,
2000–2002 World Longboard
Surfing Champion

Photo R. Sumpter

Peak

NW Swell

Shallow Reef

Break: Beach break and reef breaks

Skill Level: Intermediate to expert

Commitment: 4–10

Best Boards: Shortboards up to 7 feet, 4 inches, round tail pins, and big-wave guns

Lifeguard: In season

Hazards: Sharks, rip currents, shallow coral and sand bottom, rocky outcrops. Big waves wander in off the horizon as peaks that flow bottom contours; this makes judging your position in relation to takeoff difficult and dangerous.

Currency: U.S. dollar.

Going There: Visa required except by U.S. citizens. Vaccinations required except by U.S. citizens—tetanus, typhoid. Check with your doctor, health clinic, and embassy for up-to-date info.

Where to Stay: See the notice board at Haleiwa Super Market for rental accommodations. Or go 5 miles west to Mokuleia Beach Colony. The Hawaii Polo Inn's Polo Beach Cottage is a five-acre beachfront equestrian estate, adjacent to the Mokuleia polo grounds. The Mokuleia peninsula extends from the old plantation town of Waialua to Kaena Point. See the Foodland at Waimea Bay and Kammies Market at Sunset Beach notice boards for rental apartments and rooms. Malaekahana Campground, a twenty-minute drive west of Sunset Beach on the windward side of the island; P.O. Box 305, Laie 96762; (808) 293–1736.

Finding the Break: Easy to find. Mokuleia is 5 miles west from rustic Haleiwa town on the North Shore.

Keep in Mind: Rarely crowded.

Months	JF	MA	MJ	JA	SO	ND
Average Swell (feet)	6	5	4	1	1–2	4–5
Air Temp (C/F)	26/79	27/81	29/84	30/86	29/84	27/81
Water Temp (C/F)	23/73	24/75	25/77	26/79	27/81	24/75
Wetsuit	shorty	vest	none	none	none	vest
Average Sunshine p/d (hours)	7	9	10	11	9	6–7
Average Rain p/m (inches)	3	1	0	1	2	3
Average Surfable Days p/m	20	14	8	2	6	17

18. SANDY BEACH

South Shore, Oahu, Hawaii

There are few places in the world where the waves actually make a *crack* sound as they break on the beach. Sandy Beach is one of them. The waves slam down on the shore in an incredible display of Pacific power. Amazingly, there's still room enough for vertical pocket turns, rolls, loops, and disappearing tunnel rides.

A locals' favorite, this seriously hard-core surf spot is one of the ultimate beach breaks for bodysurfing and bodyboarding in the world. Sandy Beach is situated southeast of Waikiki (Spot 19) and 2 miles east of Hanauma Bay on the Kalaniana`ole Highway. It's the ultimate left and right beach break spot, with some of the hardest, angriest small waves on the planet. It's an extreme shorebreak second to none, with more neck injuries and broken arms occurring here than anywhere else in Hawaii. This is where short, fast, hollow tube rides might last only seconds, and might run only 20 yards on a good wave, but they could still be the most exciting bodysurfing or bodyboarding rides of your life.

Nestled below volcanic mountains and lava hills, this is the first out-of-town spot on the South Shore. It's a very powerful short wave that breaks very quickly and doubles up on occasions; the drag of the water as it sucks back into the ocean, after the wave has broken, helps create an even more powerful wave. All waves are close to shore, very short, and fast, in knee-deep water. It's a tourist beach, and the local surfers and international experts make bodysurfing look easy, so many tourists give it a try, which results in some accidents. There is a left-hand reef point 100 yards on the left side of the beach, and this is good for shortboards. The best surf is in the summertime when the south swells arrive consistently from April to September, and with wave heights from 2 to 8 feet. Sandy Beach is for the experienced bodyboarder and bodysurfer, and the expert surfer, only.

Although the waves are lovely to watch, even the most experienced surfers can be tricked on takeoff, on what becomes a closeout from top to bottom or an over-the-falls wipeout. There are lifeguards on duty on weekends and during Surf Alert—High Sea Warnings. And on the far right side of the beach there is the much-photographed Blow Hole, which signals the arrival of swell with a jet of spray forced 20 feet in the air from a hole in the lava rock.

Photo R. Sumpter

I surfed there a bit when I was young . . . they used to have a lot of championships out there. It's a really wedgy wave, super high performance.

Andy Irons,
2002–2003 World Surfing Champion

Photo R. Sumpter

Rights | **Lefts** | **Beachbreak** | **S Swell** | **Shallow Sand**

Break: Beach break
Skill Level: Expert
Commitment: 8–10 if you survive
Best Boards: Bodyboard

Lifeguard: Seasonal
Hazards: Pounding waves slam riders to the floor.
Currency: U.S. dollar.

Going There: Visa required except by U.S. citizens. Vaccinations required except by U.S. citizens—tetanus, typhoid. Check with your doctor, health clinic, and embassy for up-to-date info.

Where to Stay: There are some condos and apartments at Hawaii Kai and Aina Haina, but it's best to go to Waikiki Beach with its huge choice.

Finding the Break. From Diamond Head go west on the Kalaniana`ole Highway past East Hanauma Bay. On the right will be Sandy Beach Park.

Keep in Mind: Weekends can be crowded.

Months	JF	MA	MJ	JA	SO	ND
Average Swell (feet)	2	3	2	1–2	2–3	3
Air Temp (C/F)	26/79	27/81	29/84	30/86	29/84	27/81
Water Temp (C/F)	23/73	24/75	25/77	26/79	27/81	24/75
Wetsuit	shorty	vest	none	none	none	vest
Average Sunshine p/d (hours)	7	9	10	11	9	6–7
Average Rain p/m (inches)	3	1	0	1	2	3
Average Surfable Days p/m	15	7	12	10	9	14

19. WAIKIKI
Honolulu, Oahu, Hawaii

There's no better place to learn to surf the Hawaiian way than at Waikiki. This is where the great Duke Kahanamoku mastered the surf. Paddle into the beautiful lines of swell out on the reefs, under the awe-inspiring view of Diamond Head. Slide into waves that lift, rise, and break gracefully, ride with style, and carve off spinning curls toward the most famous beachfront in the world.

Waikiki, the beachfront of Honolulu, the capital city of Oahu, is one of the most famous surf beaches in Hawaii. The Waikiki surf locations starting from the southeast sector are all outer reef breaks, which provide the wave action for the bay.

The first break, called Rice Bowls, is in front of the Outrigger Canoe Club and is good for shortboarding, longboarding, and bodyboarding. Both intermediate and expert surfers will find a good wave that suits them. This break works best in a southeast to southwest swell and is best between 3 and 8 feet.

Then there's Publics near Kapiolani Park. This is a superb left, best from May to September.

The next break is Queens, the surfing spot most featured in journals about Hawaiian surf and the Waikiki beach boys. It's the best canoe, beginner, and longboarding wave, and the view from shore, of shimmering swell lines marching in against blue and white cresting waves, is simply fabulous.

Canoes, a wonderful surf spot where the waves feather endlessly and the curl is easy, is next in line. This break is ideal for beginners and surfers looking for a fun performance wave.

Just across on the opposite reef is the break called Populars. A long paddle from the beach out over a lagoon will bring you out and around to the takeoff area for this break, which is mostly right-hander waves with some lefts. Populars, as the name implies, is a very popular spot with hollow, steep waves with more power that peel all the way to the lagoon channel.

Last in line, Paradise Reef is straight out from the Royal Hawaiian Hotel. A long paddle from the beach, it's the outermost reef at Waikiki, providing some superb longboarding. Waikiki is ideal for the beginner to intermediate surfer.

There's no wave in the world that has taught more surfers to surf, seen more surfers stand up for the first time, or symbolized the idea of surfing to more people than Waikiki. Its fantastic soft, feathering, reef break waves offer some of the longest rides in the Hawaiian Islands.

I took this picture of Duke in 1964.   Photo R. Sumpter

Duke Kahanamoku

Nelson Mandela, John F. Kennedy, and Duke Kahanamoku. Folks new to surfing may not be familiar with the last name, but "The Duke" is as famous among surfers as the others are to the wider world. A five-time Olympic medal winner in swimming, he became an unofficial ambassador of Hawaii with his gentle nature, good humor, and skill as a surfer.

I first saw the great Duke Kahanamoku Team in Australia in 1957 giving a display of surfing that changed my life forever. I began following his surfing equipment and style.

I later met him in Makaha at the 1964 International Surfing Championships. He gave the kind of speech great people make, seemingly off the cuff with words that moved and inspired. I was directly below the podium hanging on every word.

Waikiki is a classic. It's a really good beginners' wave, really soft and rolly; you catch waves that have come for 200 yards. . . . Kind of hard to ride a shortboard, but it's great for longboarding.

Andy Irons,
2002–2003 World Surfing Champion

Photo R. Sumpter

Rights	Lefts	Peak	S Swell		Shallow Reef

Break: Reef break
Skill Level: Beginner to expert
Commitment: 1–10
Best Boards: Longboard
Lifeguard: Year-round
Hazards: Some breaks require a lot longer paddle out to avoid the shallow coral reef and sand bottom at low tide.

No hazard at high tide except beach shore edge in places.
Currency: U.S. dollar.
Going There: Visa required except by U.S. citizens. Vaccinations required except by U.S. citizens—tetanus, typhoid. Check with your doctor, health clinic, and embassy for up-to-date info.

Where to Stay: You're spoiled for choice here. The Royal Hawaiian Hotel (The Pink Palace), (808) 923–7311; fax (808) 931–7098. The Ohana Waikiki Hotel, (800) 655–6055 or (808) 923–4402. The Waikiki Beachside Hostel, (808) 923–9566, or fax (808) 923–7525.

Finding the Break: From Honolulu follow signs for Waikiki Beach. Ask directions from the lifeguards in front of the police station on the beach.

Surf Schools: Hans Hedemann Surf School, (808) 924–7778. Nancy Emerson School of Surfing, (808) 244–7873.

Keep in Mind: Always busy.

Months	JF	MA	MJ	JA	SO	ND
Average Swell (feet)	2–3	3	3	1	1–2	2
Air Temp (C/F)	26/79	27/81	29/84	30/86	29/84	27/81
Water Temp (C/F)	23/73	24/75	25/77	26/79	27/81	24/75
Wetsuit	shorty	vest	none	none	none	vest
Average Sunshine p/d (hours)	7	9	10	11	9	6–7
Average Rain p/m (inches)	3	1	0	1	2	3
Average Surfable Days p/m	26	25	19	16	17	21

20. HONOLUA BAY
Maui, Hawaii

When push comes to shove, there's no better place to be than Honolua Bay waiting for the wave with your name on it. Then off you go, and the ride of a lifetime begins. This fast, awesome point wave is so long and neat that the swell lines are like dark blue flecks of marble in a light blue sea. The curling barrel is like a white-green cavern. So hang on in there and bite the bullet. On takeoff the explosion behind you hammers your tail. The oncoming wall curls, and then gracefully breaks clean over your head. You feel your feet lift up and fly.

Honolua Bay is situated 5 miles from Lahaina on the northwest coast of Maui, the second largest Hawaiian island, and is famous for its perfect point surf breaking off the headland. Honolua Bay, one of the most scenic bays in the Hawaiian chain, is well known for its world-class surfing from November to March. The waves march in around Lipoa Point, building up to a takeoff that is near vertical. The wave breaks fast, hollowing out and pitching a curl next to a long shoulder, which curves around to face you as the "Bowl" nears. The focus of this wave is unique to Honolua Bay: The wave's outer swell bends inward into a horseshoe shape, forcing you left toward the cliff and a steepening fast section. While the wave stretches out in front of you, it doubles in height. This is what locals call the Bowl. And it's amazing.

Honolua Bay is a symbol of surf perfection, a bay steeped in wave-riding tradition since the time of the Hawaiian kings. The island of Maui is just twenty minutes' flying time from Honolulu International Airport, and just five hours from the U.S. mainland. The local Kahului airport is named for the capital of Maui. The lush vegetation, trees, and vines make this an exceptional beauty spot.

When summer brings flat water, the snorkeling is very good here. But leave the fishing spear at home—this is one of Hawaii's Fish Conservation Areas. Since there are no lifeguards here on Honolua Bay, you'll be surfing entirely at your own risk. Some beach breaks do, however, have lifeguards, so check notice boards before surfing on these beaches and follow the warnings. Surf Alerts will be announced on the radio station's weather bulletins.

Perhaps Maui's most famous landmark is the mighty Haleakala to the east of the island. This massive dormant volcano is 10,023 feet high and capped with thick snow in the winter. The central spine connecting Haleakala with the West Maui Mountains is Maui's prime agricultural region. It was created when lava flows from the Haleakala volcano filled in the gap between the much older West Maui volcano above Honolua Bay. The West Maui Mountain Range is 5,788 feet high, and is surrounded by prime farming land, cattle ranches, and sugar and pineapple plantations.

Photo © ASP Tostee

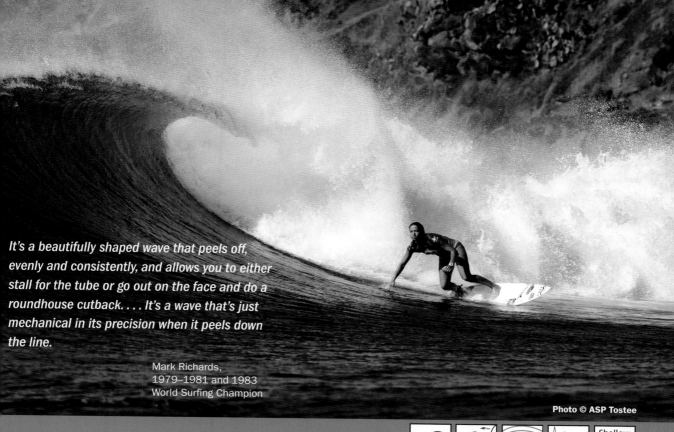

It's a beautifully shaped wave that peels off, evenly and consistently, and allows you to either stall for the tube or go out on the face and do a roundhouse cutback.... It's a wave that's just mechanical in its precision when it peels down the line.

Mark Richards,
1979–1981 and 1983
World Surfing Champion

Photo © ASP Tostee

Rights | R. Point | N Swell | | Shallow Reef

Break: Right-hand point break

Skill Level: Intermediate to expert

Commitment: 7–10

Best Boards: Shortboards up to 7 feet, 10 inches; pin tails

Lifeguard: None

Hazards: Big waves, dangerous rip currents, shallow reef. Steep walk to small rock and coral beach area. Inside section closes out hard on all size waves.

Currency: U.S. dollar.

Going There: Visa required except by U.S. citizens. Vaccinations required except by U.S. citizens—tetanus, typhoid. Check with your doctor, health clinic, and embassy for up-to-date info.

Where to Stay: It's easy to find many top-class name resorts, like Marriott Hotel, along with motels. For rooms to rent, apartments, and condos close by, see the notice boards at Farmers Market, Kaahumanu Shopping Center, Lahaina Cannery Mall.

Finding the Break: Easy to find. Go north of Lahaina on Route 30, the Honoapi`ilani Highway. Honolua Bay is 5 miles north, past Kapalua. Park on Route 30 unless you have four-wheel drive. The bay is 200 yards down the small roadway.

Surf School: Nancy Emerson School of Surfing, (808) 244–7873.

Contest: Women's WCT, December.

Keep in Mind: Crowded much of the time, when surf is good. Early mornings are best.

Months	JF	MA	MJ	JA	SO	ND
Average Swell (feet)	6	5	3	1–2	2	4–5
Air Temp (C/F)	26/79	27/81	29/84	30/86	29/84	27/81
Water Temp (C/F)	23/73	24/75	25/77	26/79	27/81	24/75
Wetsuit	shorty	vest	none	none	none	vest
Average Sunshine p/d (hours)	7	9	10	11	9	6–7
Average Rain p/m (inches)	3	1	0	1	2	3
Average Surfable Days p/m	14	11	7	2	8	9

21. MA`ALAEA PIPELINE

Lahaina, Maui, Hawaii

Take a big chance and paddle out, look at the speed, the fall line of the curl, the thickness of the lip, and the reverse curve in the wave face. Then tell yourself, *Go for it!* That's the attitude you need to ride one of the fastest waves in the world. Just sit back, watch, wait, and wax up until the first signs of the reef turn to a boiling white. This signals the start of an epic voyage.

Situated 15 miles south of Lahaina near Kihai, the Ma`alaea Pipeline in Ma`alaea Bay on the west coast of Maui is known for its superfine, very fast surf. Here the seabed is made of sharp coral and lava rock, angled at just the right degree to produce fine waves. When it's a 6-foot day and the surf is really pumping, lots of experience is needed to handle the takeoff. Once off, you need even more experience to handle the speed of the Racetrack. The Racetrack, just about halfway through the ride, is so called for being the fastest section of Ma`alaea Pipeline. The length of ride can be between 150 and 300 yards on a good day. Ma`alaea requires a swell from 3 to 5 feet before it will work. It can, however, hold waves of 12 feet or higher when a south swell and a southeast wind create the ideal conditions.

Crowded surf conditions will prevail when the surf's up—and the word will spread quickly. Therefore, surfing by yourself is very unlikely when the waves are incoming.

Other breaks to surf on Maui are at Lahaina Harbor. One is called Shark Pit; the other, Breakwall. These two reef breaks are great for the intermediate to experienced surfer. Farther north, there's Honolua Bay (Spot 20), a classic break, Palm Point for expert surfers, and Baldwin Beach, on the north side of the island, for intermediate surfers.

Lahaina is the center of surfing on the island, and has some of the best surf shops and alternative-style shopping in the islands; the marina is ideal for booking whale-watching tours and seafood restaurants.

Maui possesses an amazing array of natural beauty. On the east side of the island is Haleakala Mountain, House of the Sun. Below this you can see the endless white ribbons of beaches. Included in this view is Ho`okipa Beach, one of the world's finest sailboarding destinations, which holds the international championships each year.

When you're resting your gams in between surf sessions, head over to the Maui Ocean Center, home of the largest tropical reef aquarium in the Western Hemisphere. If the surf's flat, then capture this piece of underwater Hawaiian splendor while you wait.

Photo R. Sumpter

Once committed here there is no turning back or pulling out through a change of mind.

Rod Sumpter

Photo R. Sumpter

Rights | W Swell | | Shallow Reef

Break: Right-hand reef break
Skill Level: Expert
Commitment: 7–10
Best Boards: Shortboards to 7 feet, 6 inches; pin tails
Lifeguard: None
Hazards: Paddle out over shallow razor sharp coral reef; hollow waves, which seem impossible to get into; rip currents.

Currency: U.S. dollar.
Going There: Visa required except by U.S. citizens. Vaccinations required except by U.S. citizens—tetanus, typhoid. Check with your doctor, health clinic, and embassy for up-to-date info.
Where to Stay: Oceanfront apartments overlooking Ma`alaea, Hawaii Vacation (808) 244–7554. Hono Kai condos on Ma`alaea Bay, (800) 207–3565.

Wailuku Hostel, (808) 244–5090 or (800) 846–7835.
Finding the Break: From the Kahului airport take Route 380 toward Lahaina. After 6 miles there is a traffic light; turn left onto Route 30. Stay on Route 30 and drive toward Lahaina. One mile after the traffic light, turn left onto Ma`alaea Road at the MA`ALAEA VILLAGE sign. Turn left again onto Hauoli Street. Ma`alaea Banyans, 190 Hauoli Street, is on the right. Driving time is about fifteen minutes. Public access to the break is from the Maui Ocean Center; it's a short walk to the east side of the harbor.
Keep in Mind: Crowded surf conditions will prevail when the surf's up.

Months	JF	MA	MJ	JA	SO	ND
Average Swell (feet)	4–5	3–4	2	1–2	2	3–4
Air Temp (C/F)	26/79	27/81	29/84	30/86	29/84	27/81
Water Temp (C/F)	23/73	24/75	25/77	26/79	27/81	24/75
Wetsuit	shorty	vest	none	none	none	vest
Average Sunshine p/d (hours)	7	9	10	11	9	6–7
Average Rain p/m (inches)	3	1	0	1	2	3
Average Surfable Days p/m	4	1	1	1	1	4

22. HUNTINGTON BEACH
Southern California

Hold up the nose, sink the tail deep, and launch yourself into a flying left hook heading straight at the pier. Aim the rail, grab and pull in tight, go for that sunlit space between the pylons, and pray you'll make it. When the surf drum beats, the crowds are yelling, and the pier is swaying as the waves crash past. Wake up! You know you're at Huntington Beach, the central hub of competition surfing and home of one of the fastest straight-line barrels in California.

Situated 80 miles north of San Diego and 40 miles south of Los Angeles in Orange County, Southern California, this famous surf spot is home to many a classic wave and is world class on the right day. With 8 miles of beach around Huntington, waves and swell focus best at Huntington Beach Pier, giving it a well-deserved reputation for the best surf in the area. Here also is one of California's original surf clubs, and home to many of the surfers who pioneered the sport. Even some of the pioneering surf contests were held here, as far back as the 1920s. And since the late 1950s, the National Surfing Championships have been held here on a regular basis.

The waves can get big and gnarly, on both sides of the pier, and the best side depends on the swell direction, winds, and currents. The north side, with its big outer take-off peak, has a short right to the pier or a long left across the beach. "Shooting the pier" happens from the southern side. This is a hair-raising experience, especially the first time you do it. It's a left from the south side, which starts off well away from the pier on a good day and peels off to-ward the concrete pylons. The angles and variations while surfing are dependent on cornering, either tight to the wave's face, or holding a soft angle as if you were turning and cutting back. The trick is to time the pylons, which are 20 feet apart and parallel, to slip though the open gate and out the other side. On poor days, it tends to close out if the banks are not shaped well.

Often best in a southwest or southern swell, the waves angle across the face of the sandbanks, giving a nice peeling-off left. Head straight for, first, a tube ride, and then a walled-up wave to shoot the pier. Fortunately the currents and deeper water around the pier make it a hotdog performance wave as well, with rarely a tube actually ever going through the pier. That would make "shooting the pier" a lot more dangerous than it already is.

This is a great beach for surfing fun waves on good days and heavy, fast waves on the bigger days. You'll need experience when the surf is over 6 to 8 feet. If you're waiting out the sets or just hanging loose the California way, Huntington Beach is ideal for watching surfers up close from the pier. For beginners, wait until the conditions are no more than 2 feet and clean. The intermediates and experts come in when it gets bigger.

On summer evenings expect dozens of barbecues to light up on the beach beneath the spectacular sunsets. And if you're ready to mix it up with the crowds at night, Huntington Beach comes alive with its many bars, restaurants, and late-night surf shopping.

Photo R. Sumpter

Huntington Pier is a great wave. It's a beach break with right and left A-frame waves to shoot the pier.... You have to have the confidence and the understanding to do something like that; you have to have the right wave and be in the right spot. It's not easy, but you kind of just go for it.

Stephen Maitland,
Val Surf

Photo R. Sumpter

| Peak | Beachbreak | W Swell | |

Break: Beach break

Skill Level: Beginner to expert

Commitment: 6–10

Best Boards: Longboards, shortboards

Lifeguard: In season

Hazards: Strong waves over head high, rip currents, shallow sand bottom; pier pylons to haunt you if you shoot the pier. Rip can provide easy trip back out to the takeoff area.

Currency: U.S. dollar.

Going There: Visa required except by U.S. citizens. Vaccinations required except by U.S. citizens—tetanus, typhoid. Check with your doctor, health clinic, and embassy for up-to-date info.

Where to Stay: Waterfront Hilton, (714) 373–4999 or (714) 960–7873. Guesthouse International Huntington Beach, (866) 667–9330. Hotel Huntington Beach, (866) 667–9330. Best Western Regency (800) 359–2522. Beach Inn, (714) 841–6606. Book a Bed, +353 21 451 8993. Comfort Suites Huntington Beach, (800) 359–2522. Huntington Surf Inn, (714) 536–2444. Colonial Inn Surf Huntington Beach, admin@travellerspoint.com, (714) 536–3315, or fax (714) 536–9485. Huntington Beach Inn, (714) 536–7500, or fax (714) 536–6846

Finding the Break: From Los Angeles International Airport, exit toward Century Boulevard and take South Sepulveda Boulevard to the I–105 east ramp toward Norwalk. Merge east onto I–105 toward I–405 south toward Long Beach. Take I–405 south to Beach Boulevard toward Huntington Beach. Continue for 6 miles; you will see Huntington Pier. Park at a beach lot or meter.

Keep in Mind: Crowds in summer and fall.

Months	JF	MA	MJ	JA	SO	ND
Average Swell (feet)	5-6	4-5	3-4	3	3-4	6
Air Temp (C/F)	19/66	19/66	22/72	26/79	24/75	22/72
Water Temp (C/F)	14/57	14/57	16/61	17/62	17/62	14/57
Wetsuit	full	full	short	short	short	full
Average Sunshine p/d (hours)	7	9	9	12	9	7
Average Rain p/m (inches)	3	1	0-1	0	0-1	2
Average Surfable Days p/m	23	20	17	15	14	26

23. MALIBU
Southern California

Just imagine powering across the glassiest wave you've ever seen, at a place that helped shape the world of surfing, then pulling off the best aerial, floater, and turn you've ever practiced. These things happen at Malibu, one of Southern California's greatest breaks, if not the world's—a wave that has all the unique features you'd expect of the best.

Malibu is situated in the Golden State 10 miles east of Malibu Canyon in north Los Angeles County and 30 miles south of Rincon (Spot 24). Malibu is the original great sand point break, where Tom Blake first surfed in 1952 and shaped a surfing generation. Later, in the 1960s, Mickey Dora "Da King" rushed to fame at Malibu using his surfboard as a nose riding, arching, stalling, and trimming statement. Here he cast his own surf-style spell.

Whenever the surf starts breaking and swell lines stack up to the horizon, surfers gather to watch awesome-quality waves, still the criterion for performance surfing. This long right-hand point wave is best in a 4-to-6-foot swell. It's down-the-line surf all the way from the point. There's more wave face with sections, and enough wave face to hotdog the shoulders, ride the tube, and get—on a good day—a ride length of 500 to 600 yards or more, with nose rides of 20 to 30 yards.

On the bigger days, the full power of Malibu comes to light at the point. Waves line up as smooth swells protected by kelp beds at takeoff, and fire all the way across to the pier, with sections for cover-ups, head tips, tubes, and performance surfing. There was a time, back in the beginning, when there were few cars, no crowds, and *one man, one wave* was the rule. Surfers could have this amazing wave all to themselves. But no more. Still, this surf spot is ideal for beginners when it's small, and for experts when it's pumping.

Malibu's official name is Malibu Lagoon State Beach, originally called Surfrider Beach until the late 1950s. It is watched over by the 700-foot Malibu Pier, a prime vantage point from which to watch the waves. By 1929 the Pacific Coast Highway was built, opening access to the waves. Tom Blake began surfing here. So did Mickey Dora in 1952. And so began the style era. Mickey was joined by the most outstanding surfer of all time, Johnny Fain, whose arching right hand over the shoulder became the Malibu Turn, a move practiced to this day but rarely as well. Then came the shortboard revolution, threatening to render nose riding and hanging ten moves of the past. But with its glassy, consistent waves, Malibu has held on to its long-standing tradition, continuing to be one of the best longboard waves ever surfed.

Photo R. Sumpter

My favorite longboarding wave would be Malibu; that's the best longboard wave I've ever been on. . . . It's the perfect lined-up quintessential point wave, it's perfect for everything, nose riding, trimming, turning, locking in, everything.

Bryon DeBoer,
manager, Stewart Surf Boards

Photo Don Montgomery/mavsurfer.com

 Rights R.Point NW Swell

Break: Right-hand point break
Skill Level: Beginner to expert
Commitment: 7–10
Best Boards: Longboards, shortboards
Lifeguard: In season
Hazards: Seaweed and kelp can tangle your leash while waiting for sets. This is generally not a problem. Slow take-offs can cause late-takeoffs and wipe-outs as the barrel carries on down the line; some rips and currents.
Currency: U.S. dollar.

Going There: Visa required except by U.S. citizens. Vaccinations required except by U.S. citizens—tetanus, typhoid. Check with your doctor, health clinic, and embassy for up-to-date info.
Where to Stay: Malibu Beach Inn, (800) 462–5428. Malibu Shores (B&B), (310) 456–6000. The Santa Monica Hostel is located in Santa Monica in Los Angeles's west side, on the coast between Venice Beach and Malibu. Reservations (800) 909–4776, direct

(310) 393–9913, or fax (310) 393–1769.
Finding the Break: *From I–10:* Take I–10 west toward the beach. After the 4th Street/5th Street exit in Santa Monica, I–10 turns into the Pacific Coast Highway (PCH). Follow the PCH north into Malibu. *From I–405:* Take I–405 to I–10 (Santa Monica Freeway) and follow directions above. Or take I–405 north to I–101 (Ventura Freeway). Take I–101 north toward Ventura. Continue into the Calabasas area and exit onto Malibu Canyon Road. Follow Malibu Canyon Road west through the mountains. You will eventually come out to the ocean; continue past Pepperdine University. At a signal, turn left onto the Pacific Coast Highway (PCH) and continue south. Proceed south past the Malibu Fire Station. Keep your eyes open for Malibu beach.
Keep in Mind: Always crowded.

Months	JF	MA	MJ	JA	SO	ND
Average Swell (feet)	5–6	4–5	3–4	3	3–4	6
Air Temp (C/F)	19/66	19/66	22/72	26/79	24/75	22/72
Water Temp (C/F)	14/57	14/57	16/61	17/62	17/62	14/57
Wetsuit	full	full	shorty	shorty	shorty	full
Average Sunshine p/d (hours)	7	9	9	12	9	7
Average Rain p/m (inches)	3	1	0–1	0	0–1	2
Average Surfable Days p/m	23	20	17	15	14	26

24. RINCON

Southern California

Ever dreamed about what a perfect surf spot might look like? Ever wondered what makes the perfect point surf break? And have you thought about waking up every morning at a dream break to perfect surf? If your answer is yes, then look no farther, Rincon fits your dreams perfectly. Rincon Beach State Park offers classic views and a winding path through trees to the heart of mouthwatering waves pouring in around the point.

The paddle out is a feast for the eyes as you launch into pearly white and green tubes. The takeoff is stunning, a perfect blend of solid swell underfoot and driving power behind your ankles. You pump your legs and fly high into the lofty crest, then snap and hang, holding the line in the air. Toe forward to go straight, heel pressed back to stall. Like an elastic slingshot the wave shoots you forward a long way out on the shoulder.

Situated 10 miles north of Ventura Beach and 2 miles south of Aguadilla, straddling the county lines of Santa Barbara and Ventura in Central California, is the famous surf break of Rincon. Historically, waves were ridden here almost from the beginning, when Don Freeth surfed and lifeguarded at Redondo Beach in 1907. It includes the following sections: Domes, Dead Man's, Indicator, The Point, Maria's, Pistons, Dogman's, Tres Palmas, and Little Mal-

ibu. Rincon is the queen of the coast, and the quintessential perfect right-hand point break. To connect the entire area, you would ride for more than a mile, and from several high vantage points, it's possible to see this bay fill with curving swells and surf lines as they fan out on the shoreward side.

The Rincon Beach County Park is an unspoiled beauty spot, and this popular surf break is hard to beat for all-around surfing pleasure, with impressive waves that work in sizes from 2 to 12 feet. There are several amazing surf breaks to choose from in the lineup, but the best is the famous Rincon Point. From here you can see how far you can go; if you reach Route 101, you have surfed more than a mile and surfed one of the hottest waves in the world. The Rincon coast highway has many surf spots to explore, and the Santa Barbara coastline is 100 miles long with a surf break to suit all grades. For the beginner Mondos is an easy wave, and a really long ride. Rincon is for the intermediate to expert surfer, especially if it's over 6 feet, and ideal for the experienced on bigger days.

Rincon is one of the original great finds and today still rates as one of the best point breaks in the world. When a storm heads straight at California, this will be the spot highest on most people's list.

Photo R. Sumpter

Rincon has everything a surfer needs. It's got a big drop; you can hit the lip; you can pull into a barrel on certain sections; you can cut back and the wave will come through for you. You can ride all the way from the Point to the highway.

Seth Matson, event director,
Huntington Beach Pro/Junior Series

Photo R. Sumpter

Rights   R.Point   NW Swell

Break: Right point break
Skill Level: Intermediate to expert
Commitment: 3–10; 6–10 on a big swell
Best Boards: Longboards, shortboards
Lifeguard: None
Hazards: Undertow, boulder covered shoreline, rocky outcrops. Rip currents and pumping swells make the paddle out past incoming waves a judgment call. Get it wrong and you have to angle left toward the highway until the lull lets you through to the outer channel. Then the paddle is easier to the point.

Months	JF	MA	MJ	JA	SO	ND
Average Swell (feet)	5-6	4-5	3-4	3	3-4	6
Air Temp (C/F)	19/66	19/66	22/72	26/79	24/75	22/72
Water Temp (C/F)	14/57	14/57	16/61	17/62	17/62	14/57
Wetsuit	full	full	shorty	shorty	shorty	full
Average Sunshine p/d (hours)	7	9	9	12	9	7
Average Rain p/m (inches)	4	2	1	0	0	2
Average Surfable Days p/m	20	15	10	5	14	21

Currency: U.S. dollar.
Going There: Visa required except by U.S. citizens. Vaccinations required except by U.S. citizens—tetanus, typhoid. Check with your doctor, health clinic, and embassy for up-to-date info.
Where to Stay: Comfort Suites, (805) 566–9499. Prufrocks Garden (805) 566–9696. Coastal Getaways, (805) 969–1258 or (805) 969–1258. Santa Barbara Hostel (805) 963–3586.
Finding the Break: Easy to find. Take the Pacific Coast Highway (Route 101) north of Santa Barbara. You'll pass right by it.
Keep in Mind: If you're the first on a new swell, it won't be crowded for a while.

25. SAN CLEMENTE PIER
Southern California

You watch a dark blue swell emerge from the ocean. Check the watermark on the pylons and position yourself for the wave of the day. You take off and you must be fast. To shoot the pier through the narrow wooden pylons is a thrill. Few things in surfing compare. You start away from the pier on a right peak then head straight at it, charging up your bottle, cranking a few turns, testing the angles, aim, and zoom your way through.

Situated between Los Angeles and San Diego, the big icon at San Clemente is its famous 1,200-foot-long pier, the focal point for surfing fast, zippy waves. The waves here break fast and heavy. And while they're not that big, they can be gnarly, quick, and tricky. This is where the famous surfers of the past cut their teeth, and where today's surfers carve finely tuned patterns across glassy waves.

Considered one of the best contest waves on the West Coast (it always seems to have a good swell during a competition), San Clemente Pier works its magic in 2-to-3-foot lefts and rights when groomed by light offshore winds. The north side of the pier picks up a southwest swell, swinging in down the pylons. Some heavy left barrels peel off sandbars and short, fast, solid rights head to a shorebreak into the pier.

San Clemente is a unique Spanish-style beach and surf town, built on the hillsides overlooking the Pacific Ocean. The 2-mile strip of beach includes T Street, with its superb beach, reef, sandbars, and rocky outcrops that produce a variety of different classic breaks in winter and summer. Known for its consistency, T Street is a haven for bodyboarders and shortboarders alike. It has three separate breaks. Cropley's is a peaking right-hander that allows aerial maneuvers on good days, with a well-lined-up inside section. On a good day, it can be a long ride of up to 150 yards. There's also the Reef, which is mostly a right-hand reef break. During a south swell it has the occasional left barrel. Finally, there is the Beach House, a beach break with good lefts and rights.

San Clemente tries to be a relaxed, get-away-from-it-all place, and largely succeeds. It's ideal for the intermediate to expert surfer on the right day.

Photo R. Sumpter

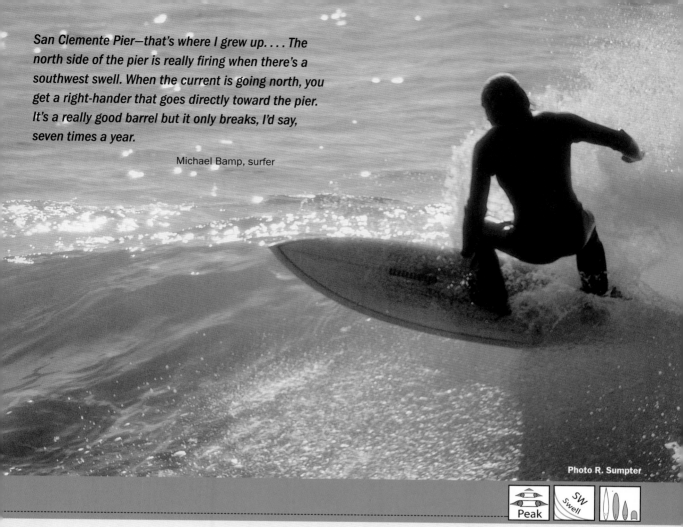

San Clemente Pier—that's where I grew up. . . . The north side of the pier is really firing when there's a southwest swell. When the current is going north, you get a right-hander that goes directly toward the pier. It's a really good barrel but it only breaks, I'd say, seven times a year.

Michael Bamp, surfer

Photo R. Sumpter

Peak

SW Swell

Break: Beach break
Skill Level: Intermediate to expert
Commitment: 3–10
Best Boards: Longboards, shortboards, bodyboards
Lifeguard: In season

Hazards: Rip currents, shallow sand bottom, close-outs; grinding shore break beside the pier
Currency: U.S. dollar.
Going There: Visa required except by U.S. citizens. Vaccinations required except by U.S. citizens—tetanus, typhoid. Check with your doctor, health clinic, and embassy for up-to-date info.
Where to Stay: San Clemente Inn, (949) 492–6103, or fax (949) 498–3014.
Finding the Break: Follow signs to the center of town and look for beachside parking and the pier. Walk past surf shops on the coastal path heading south to T Street for 400 yards.
Keep in Mind: Sometimes crowded at the pier, always crowded at T Street.
For More Information: San Clemente Beach Park, (949) 492–3156. Beach closure, (949) 667–3752.

Months	JF	MA	MJ	JA	SO	ND
Average Swell (feet)	5-6	4–5	3–4	3	3–4	6
Air Temp (C/F)	19/66	19/66	22/72	26/79	24/75	22/72
Water Temp (C/F)	14/57	14/57	16/61	17/62	17/62	14/57
Wetsuit	full	full	shorty	shorty	shorty	full
Average Sunshine p/d (hours)	7	9	9	12	9	7
Average Rain p/m (inches)	3	1	0-1	0	0-1	2
Average Surfable Days p/m	23	20	12	10	16	19

26. SAN ONOFRE
Southern California

A blistering 4-to-6-foot swell hits the California coast. It's a nice day and the question soon arises: *Where to go?* There are many spots from which to choose, but one that sticks in the mind and always produces a barrel load of fun is San Onofre.

This is a performance wave of great quality with its long sweeping walls and swell lines stacking up to the horizon. Situated between Los Angeles and San Diego, 3 miles south of San Clemente (Spot 25) and 2 miles north of Trestles (Spot 28), is the 3.5 miles of sandy beach known as San Onofre State Beach.

Set in a beautiful bay below the sandstone bluffs and cliffs of San Onofre, this surf spot is home to the now famous Hobie Alter San Onofre Classic. The rules of this competition require all contestants to ride a board manufactured prior to 1970. The equipment isn't all that's vintage: Contestants must also surf in the style performed back in the 1960s. And an original 1912 redwood surfboard owned by the great Duke Kahanamoku was one of the prizes of the vintage surfboard festival event. Hobie Alter (head judge) and Allen Seymour, two pioneers of the sport, run this contest to perfection.

It was Hobie Alter who invented the famous Hobie Surf-cat, a two-hull catamaran ideal for sail surfing. The catamaran went through its tests and trials here at San Onofre before finding its way to market. San Onofre was also home to Hobie's range of surfboard designs, like the Phil Edwards Triple Stringer model, that led the market for many years. San Onofre holds many modern events as well, and includes such prestigious happenings as the Surfrider Foundation Earth Day Celebration, the Rip Curl Grom Search contest, and the YMCA Surfing Series.

There are many peaks at San Onofre from which to choose. On the farthest takeoff area, there's a sand bottom with flat rocks and kelp, producing long, undulating lefts and rights. These waves, which rise from a long way out, feather and allow time to get into the best position for cruising left and right off perfectly formed 4-to-6-foot waves. This is a friendly place to meet people and share stories, and is favored as a nostalgic location for many longboarders who rate style as the only true way to surf. San Onofre is ideal for the longboarder, with almost flawless surf lines and fun peaks. But it can also be an ace spot for all surfers on the right day. One of the great discoveries of the 1960s, this spot was the sought-after wave, and still is today among top longboarders.

Photo J. Sumpter

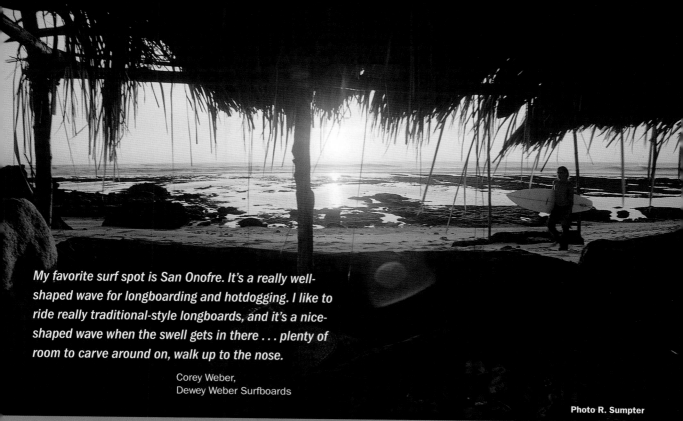

My favorite surf spot is San Onofre. It's a really well-shaped wave for longboarding and hotdogging. I like to ride really traditional-style longboards, and it's a nice-shaped wave when the swell gets in there . . . plenty of room to carve around on, walk up to the nose.

Corey Weber,
Dewey Weber Surfboards

Photo R. Sumpter

Break: Beach break

Skill Level: Beginner to expert

Commitment: 7–10

Best Boards: Longboards, shortboards

Lifeguard: May to September

Hazards: Some rip currents, shallow sand bottom, rocky outcrops, strong onshore wind conditions. Offshore winds produce a long paddle against tidal flows to a huge choice of breaks.

Currency: U.S. dollar.

Going There: Visa required except by U.S. citizens. Vaccinations required except by U.S. citizens—tetanus, typhoid. Check with your doctor, health clinic, and embassy for up-to-date info.

Where to Stay: There is no overnight camping at San Onofre Surf Beach; the near-est spot is the Bluffs Campground. Travel I–5 and turn onto Basilone Road (south of San Clemente). Drive 3 miles south on Basilone Road, which runs di-rectly into Bluffs Campground. San Clemente Inn, (949) 492–6103, or fax (949) 498–3014.

Finding the Break: The beach site is located off I–5, south of San Clemente. Exit Basilone Road and travel 1.5 miles south. Make a right turn at Surf Beach and follow signs.

Keep in Mind: Always crowded.

For More Information: San Mateo State Park, (949) 361 2531. San Onofre State Beach, (949) 492–4872. Beach clo-sure, (949) 667–3752.

Months	JF	MA	MJ	JA	SO	ND
Average Swell (feet)	5–6	4–5	3–4	3	3–4	6
Air Temp (C/F)	19/66	19/66	22/72	26/79	24/75	22/72
Water Temp (C/F)	14/57	14/57	16/61	17/62	17/62	14/57
Wetsuit	full	full	shorty	shorty	shorty	full
Average Sunshine p/d (hours)	7	9	9	12	9	7
Average Rain p/m (inches)	3	1	0–1	0	0–1	2
Average Surfable Days p/m	23	20	17	15	14	26

27. SUNSET CLIFFS
San Diego, Southern California

If you ever want to surf a magical place, a bit out of the way, with a lot of juice—a place so good it may seem like an optical illusion—then Sunset Cliffs is the place for you. It's a heavy, well-lined-up series of seaweed-covered rock reef peaks flowing into sandy lagoons. A few distant points will haunt you. The wave-riding choices put on the pressure by delivering hot, glassy, A-frame peaks, solid walls, and sneaker sets breaking off outer reefs.

A world-famous icon in today's global surfing scene, California is blessed with some of the best surfing coastline in the world. Near the Mexican border is the city of San Diego, with a coastline of pumping waves and glassy barrels that wrap into sun-bleached coves and bays. The stretch of coastline nearest to the border, from Point Lomar to Crystal Pier San Diego, is called Sunset Cliffs—a section of bluffs and panoramic views overlooking the Pacific Ocean that lasts for nearly 2 miles. Sunset Boulevard Road runs the length of the cliffs. Three main beaches lie below.

The break of Newbreak Beach, which has ace lefts and rights when there's a good swell, is peaky at high tide when it nears the cliffs. At low tide it becomes a barrel when the kelp beds and sandy bottom help form its classic waves. Sunset Cliffs will pick up south swells when La Jolla and San Diego are flat. Getting to the beach is no easy feat, requiring a little ingenuity and a lot of determination. But then again, who ever said that good things come easy? Best walked at low tide, the paths to the beach can be dangerous. Garbage Beach at Ladara Street gains its moniker from the large amounts of odoriferous kelp found there. Steps lead down to this beach, making the going a little easier. When the surf at Sunset Cliffs is 4 to 6 feet plus, you'll find a classic left and right break producing superb waves.

The next break is called No Surf Beach. And finally, farther south past a number of unnamed breaks, you'll find the Surf Country, so named for its variety of surf spots. Going north there are other good breaks, such as Swami's, Blacks, and Windansea. Sunset Cliffs is an adventurous surf spot, and with the right conditions it's in a class of its own. This is the ideal, off-the-beaten-path site for the expert surfer.

Surf hard, tread softly, and let the rhythm of the sea rule: That's the method best suited for surfing Sunset Cliffs. In California, good surf is just a matter of patience, and the best surf in the world sometimes needs a little more than others. At Sunset Cliffs the first signs of a new swell will have longboarders riding weightless on the nose, standing on the tip hanging five or ten toes, and head-dipping the wave's pitching curls. By the time it's over and you have chased the seven seas and surfed all 840 miles of California's coastline, Sunset Cliffs is still one of the greats—if you can handle the walk.

Photo R. Sumpter

*Sunset Cliffs, you know, I just like that wave. It's a great wave;
not very crowded; a good longboard wave; a good winter wave,
best at 3 to 4 feet. . . . You get locked into a good lined up wave.*

Bryon DeBoer,
manager, Stewart Surf Boards

Photo R. Sumpter

Peak

Beachbreak

W
Swell

Break: Beach break
Skill Level: Expert
Commitment: 7–10
Best Boards: Longboards, shortboards
Lifeguard: None
Hazards: Rip currents, shallow rock ledges, sand bottom. Several steep cliff paths require careful inspection in variable conditions. Paths are dangerously narrow in places and have vertical drops to the beach. New steps have improved access.
Currency: U.S. dollar.
Going There: Visa required except by U.S. citizens. Vaccinations required except by U.S. citizens—tetanus, typhoid. Check with your doctor, health clinic, and embassy for up-to-date info.
Where to Stay: Inn at Sunset Cliffs, (619) 222–7901 or (806) 786–2543; fax (619) 222–4201. Ocean Villa Inn, (619) 224–3481; fax (619) 224–9612. La Jolla Shores vacation rental, (916) 652–9353. Seacoast Inn, (858) 459–8271. Chula Vista Campsite, (800) 562–9877.
Finding the Break: Sunset Cliffs sits between Point Loma Nazarene College to the south and Adair Street to the north along Sunset Cliffs Boulevard. Take I–8 west, which turns into Sunset Cliffs Boulevard. Street parking is also plentiful on Sunset Cliffs Boulevard.
Keep in Mind: Not usually crowded, even in a good swell because elsewhere has easier access.
Surf School: San Diego Surfing Academy, (760) 230–1474.

Months	JF	MA	MJ	JA	SO	ND
Average Swell (feet)	5–6	4–5	3–4	3	3–4	6
Air Temp (C/F)	19/66	19/66	22/72	26/79	24/75	22/72
Water Temp (C/F)	14/57	14/57	16/61	17/62	17/62	14/57
Wetsuit	full	full	shorty	shorty	shorty	full
Average Sunshine p/d (hours)	6	7	10	12	11	7
Average Rain p/m (inches)	3	1	0–1	0	0–1	2
Average Surfable Days p/m	23	20	17	15	14	26

28. TRESTLES
Southern California

Once you're out and in position, you beam with delight as you stroke into a soft arching swell. The level of wave height pitches and drops on a glassy groundswell, there's a faint cross-wave, a wedge that's shifting over the brow of the swell, and the resulting V catches your fins, giving real power to a fast takeoff. Your spirit soars as you sail down, wind back up to a slashing turn, and then rail-slide a hard cutback into the curl. On the next forehand turn you get air 4 feet high and slide down the face again. This is jamming. This is Trestles.

One of the best surf spots in California, this is where A-frame waves bounce off submarine channels, creating dreamlike performance. Despite all the barriers being broken these days, there's still no greater test than to push yourself over the edge at Trestles, a complex wave that will test your skills to the limit.

Four great breaks provide a working playground where any maneuver you've kept in your dreams can be executed: Cottons for big-wave power turns, Uppers for peaks and pockets, Lowers for carving lefts and rights, and Church for all your dreams. When Mother Nature hits California with an onslaught of Pacific storm systems, the result is one of the world's greatest high-performance waves. Situated 3 miles south of San Clemente and a one-hour drive south of Los Angeles, Upper Trestles, San Mateo Creek Mouth, and Lower Trestles spread south off San Onofre State Beach Park. Trestles is famous for consistently producing superb right-hand point surf, with an occasional left, off a triangle shaped lineup. It's ideal for the intermediate to expert surfer.

This narrow, sandy beach, with a high tide line of pebbles, winds and curves out around the bays and points, spreading out into a reef takeoff that is the wonderland of waves. In the 1960s surfing at Trestles was second only to Malibu as a wave. In those days it meant difficult and dangerous access, by parking off a small pull-out near the edge of the freeway. Then, after crossing the Santa Fe Railway tracks, you had to dodge the U.S. Marines, who guarded and patrolled the beach, where their military base was located. The thought of marine gunsights focused on you while surfing always added an extra zing and dimension to a day of good waves! Today Trestles is part of the San Onofre State Beach Park, a public state park with several parking lots, one offering a sea view and easy beach access to the surf. Some things have changed here. But the waves have always delivered.

Photo R. Sumpter

When the surf is good, Trestles is really the place that everybody loves to go down to. Trestles would definitely rate in the top five surf spots of California.

Meg Bernardo, administrative director,
ASP North America and for Surfing America

Photo © ASP Tostee

Peak	R.Point	NW Swell	

Break: Reef break
Skill Level: Intermediate to expert
Commitment: 5–10
Best Boards: Shortboard
Lifeguard: In season
Hazards: Shallow rock and sand bottom, rip currents. This doesn't usually cause a problem but the rip currents can. On a good day the pebble beach stretches out to the lines of swells. Watch out for the mixed seabed. Holding position on big days causes you to surf toward Church.
Currency: U.S. dollar.
Going There: Visa required except by U.S. citizens. Vaccinations required except by U.S. citizens—tetanus, typhoid. Check with your doctor, health clinic, and embassy for up-to-date info.

Where to Stay: San Mateo Campground features family camping at its best and is near the famed surfing spot at Trestles Beach. The campground is located 1 mile east of I–5 on Cristianitos Road, just south of the city of South San Clemente.
Finding the Break: A 125-car parking lot is located on the northeast corner of the intersection of Cristianitos Road and El Camino Real in South San Clemente. A paved 0.5-mile trail runs west to Trestles Beach.
Contest: Boost Mobile Pro (WCT), September
Keep in Mind: Always crowded.
For More Information: San Mateo State Park, (949) 361–2531. San Onofre State Park, (949) 492–4872.

Months	JF	MA	MJ	JA	SO	ND
Average Swell (feet)	5-6	4-5	3-4	3	3-4	6
Air Temp (C/F)	19/66	19/66	22/72	26/79	24/75	22/72
Water Temp (C/F)	14/57	14/57	16/61	17/62	17/62	14/57
Wetsuit	full	full	shorty	shorty	shorty	full
Average Sunshine p/d (hours)	7	9	9	12	9	7
Average Rain p/m (inches)	3	1	0-1	0	0-1	2
Average Surfable Days p/m	21	20	17	12	14	20

29. MAVERICKS
Half Moon Bay, Northern California

As a mountain climber at the summit, you're at the top of the world. There's just time to look down, feel the wind, and see the distant bays, bluffs, and coves. Then you lean forward and drop down into the belly of the monster, driving a fin deep into the veins of the wave's torso. Like a serpent, the fin's wake snakes and twists over awesome boils that disappear, never to be seen again. The rushing, pent-up fury of the wall passes. You have ridden a mountain and survived.

Mighty Mavericks is a deep-water reef, situated 0.5 mile out from Pillar Point at Half Moon Bay, 20 miles south of San Francisco. It got its name from Mavericks the dog, who used to accompany one of the early surfers here. The story of Mavericks is one of the epic chapters in surfing's colorful history. It all started with Jeff Hawks driving past Half Moon Bay fifteen years ago and noticing the Pillar Point waves, breaking perfectly but huge, out beyond the rocky shore. No one wanted to surf it with him, so the next chance he got, he surfed it alone. It took years for Jeff to find some buddies to come with him, but at last in January 1990 Dave Schmidt and Tom Powers joined and started a leak to the world about Mavericks. The years passed, and in 1994 Peter Mel and friends had a big day; a photo appeared on the front cover of *Surfing Magazine.* Still more years passed, and in January 1998 Perry Miller was towed in to giant Mavericks, ten times his height. The frenzy for big waves swept the world.

In the quest for exciting new breaks to surf, surfers are like a nut looking for a bolt. The search, the discovery, the first paddle out, and the perfect wave ridden lock the psyche together. New breaks are often found on uncharted

Judging wave height is done with a surfer (of a known height) riding a wave's face. The surfer's height is used to estimate the distance from the highest point of the wave's peak to its trough. The prime wave-hunting season is December through April.

California's immensely varied landscape lies on one on the world's most geologically active zones, part of the "Ring of Fire" that girdles the Pacific Ocean. The San Andreas Fault runs for 600 miles and marks the meeting point of the Pacific and North American plates.

coasts in remote countries, but what makes the Mavericks story so much bigger is that we're talking *big* surf—the biggest waves in the world, and just 20 miles south of San Francisco, where surfing has been popular since 1964.

Until only a few years ago, only Steve Hawks had surfed Mavericks on a regular winter basis. He was the first. Since the media covered Jeff and a group of friends out in 60-foot-plus surf, the world has gone mad about Mavericks. The photographic evidence has fascinated both surfers and the general public. Today groups of surfers wait for bigger and taller swells to produce waves larger than the year before. Riding them raises the bar on the biggest ridden wave in the world.

Photo Paul Ferraris

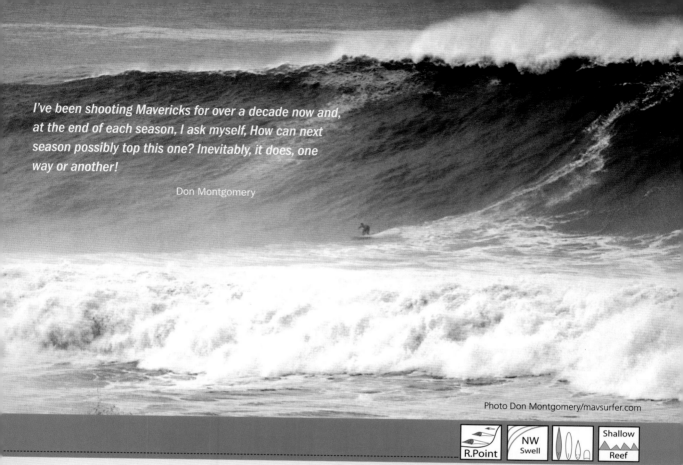

I've been shooting Mavericks for over a decade now and, at the end of each season, I ask myself, How can next season possibly top this one? Inevitably, it does, one way or another!

Don Montgomery

R.Point | NW Swell | Shallow Reef

Break: Right-hand reef break
Skill Level: Expert
Commitment: 10–10
Best Boards: 8-to-12-foot rhino gun
Lifeguard: None
Hazards: Giant waves, dangerous rip currents, rocks and gullies to shore break. The takeoff area sweeps into a bowl-shaped ledge platform and either holds enough water to surf or goes dry. The wave face then gets tiers of breaking waves forming on the middle section. A clean faced bottom near the rocks or close to the impending breaking lip are the only places to go to escape being impaled on rocks.
Currency: U.S. dollar.
Going There: Visa required except by U.S. citizens. Vaccinations required except by U.S. citizens—tetanus, typhoid.

Check with your doctor, health clinic, and embassy for up-to-date info.
Where to Stay: Beach House, Pillar Point, (800) 359–2522. The Mill Rose Inn, (650) 726–8750. Half Moon Bay Lodge, (650) 726–9000. Half Moon Bay State Park and Camping (800) 444–7275 or (650) 726–8819.
Finding the Break: From San Francisco and points north, exit the city on I–280 south, take Route 1 south to Half Moon Bay, and park at Pillar Point, a small parking area.
Keep in Mind: The few car spaces will fill up quickly at Pillar Point when the surf's big. Park where you can (allow extra time) and expect a long walk. It's well worth it.

Months	JF	MA	MJ	JA	SO	ND
Average Swell (feet)	6–8	4–5	3–4	3	4	6
Air Temp (C/F)	13/56	16/61	19/67	22/72	23/74	15/60
Water Temp (C/F)	7/45	10/50	12/55	14/58	15/59	9/49
Wetsuit	full	full	full	full	full	full
Average Sunshine p/d (hours)	6	9	8–9	10	9	5–6
Average Rain p/m (inches)	4	1	0	0	1	3
Average Surfable Days p/m	8	2	1	0	0	1

30. SANTA CRUZ
Northern California

Santa Cruz is one of the world's greatest and most consistent surf breaks. This small-to-big-wave spot boasts water the color of blue ice that hits rock sediments entering Santa Cruz and fires up a hotdog wave from Natural Bridges to Cowells Beach. It's sheltered from most prevailing winds, yet exposed to virtually all the best swells.

Steamer Lane is only one of fifteen great breaks at Santa Cruz and is a piping-hot point surf barrel that got its name from the steamships that cruised past here at the turn of the twentieth century to arrive at Santa Cruz Harbor. The point break is a savage crash out into rocks if you get it wrong and have to bail. But if you crack the right ride, you'll need precision on takeoff and first turn. Then drive a rail-to-tail spurt into the green face pocket and execute power trim, a javelin-throw speed run to the first of four takeoff areas. This is where you can cut back, slow up, and reset your geography for the breaking section. Fortunately, the rocks are a little farther away via natural curvature of the bay as they go down the line, but it helps to keep your concentration. From here on a perfect day, you can fly across fast—and possibly closed-out—sections, making this one of the most exciting rides in the world.

Situated 75 miles south of Mavericks (Spot 29) near San Francisco and 100 miles north of Santa Barbara, Steamer Lane and Pleasure Point are the famous breaks at Santa Cruz to which you must go. Steamer Lane is famous for its big surf and has been considered prime training ground for decades. One of the first locals to surf at Santa Cruz was Harry Mayo; in 1936, at the age of thirteen, he built paddle boards at Mission Hill Junior High with his friends and started the first formal surf club in 1938. Still, it wasn't until Jack O'Neill made wetsuits available in the late 1950s that surfing in Santa Cruz flourished year-round.

Since then, Santa Cruz has been considered the capital of Northern California surfing. How does a little coastal town grow to become one of the biggest surfing venues in the world? Why does surfing heap so much attention on this little place with big waves? It's because Santa Cruz has fifteen reef and points, all of which break like crystals on the right day, accommodating a huge surfing fraternity. Breaks like Cowells Beach and West Cliff Drive, plus countless lesser-known spots, ensure a vibrant and thriving surf scene. This miracle of geography makes Santa Cruz a mecca for long- and shortboard surfers of all levels.

Walk along West Cliff Drive, a paved path that winds for miles along the ocean, and see some of the best waves and views in Santa Cruz. The promenade offers gorgeous ocean views as well as glimpses of surfers, dolphins, sea lions, and the occasional passing whale. Along the way, stop at two surf monuments: the bronze surfer statue at the Pelton steps, and the remodeled brick lighthouse that is now the Surfing Museum. Displays at the museum offer visitors a glimpse of more than one hundred years of surfing history in Santa Cruz, starting with the arrival of two Hawaiian princes in 1885. Just off Lighthouse Point, see Seal Rock, a tiny island strewn with sea lions and seals.

Santa Cruz is also located on the Monterey Bay Marine Sanctuary, one of the largest protected marine areas in the world. The bay is home to 26 species of marine mammals, 96 species of seabirds, 345 species of fish, and 4 species of turtles. Watch otters, harbor seals, and other sea life play in the waves as you surf the shoreline. Santa Cruz Wharf is lined with seafood restaurants and shops, stretching 0.5 mile into the Santa Cruz Harbor. Built in 1914, the wharf is a pretty place to take a stroll and check out Steamer Lane waves up close.

Photo John McGinty, overthefalls.com

Big days at Steamer prepared me for Hawaii, and its epic waves are my favorite performance surf spot in Northern California.

Rod Sumpter

Rights	Lefts	S Swell	

Break: Right-hand reef break

Skill Level: Intermediate to expert

Commitment: 6–10, 9–10 if big

Best Boards: Shortboards up to 8-foot, 10-inch guns

Lifeguard: None

Hazards: Rip currents, rock entry, jagged crevices. Lots of rocks to avoid during the walk. There are many jump off points to get to the Santa Cruz and Streamer Lane breaks, all of which require good timing and judgment of swells. This can be dangerous if handled wrong.

Currency: U.S. dollar.

Going There: Visa required except by U.S. citizens. Vaccinations required except by U.S. citizens—tetanus, typhoid. Check with your doctor, health clinic, and embassy for up-to-date info.

Where to Stay: The Adobe B & B, (831) 469–9866. Santa Cruz Hostel, (831) 423–8304. Best Western, (831) 477–0607. Santa Cruz Kamping, (831) 722–0551 or (800) 562–7701.

Finding the Break: From San Francisco take Route 1 south into Santa Cruz, where it becomes Mission Street. Go down Mission Street, through three lights to Bay Street. Turn left and follow Bay Street to the end. Turn right onto West Cliff Drive and head past the surf breaks. Steamer Lane is on the left side of the lighthouse.

Surfing Schools: Club Ed Surf School, (831) 464–0177 or (800) 287–SURF. Richard Schmidt Surf School, (831) 423–0928.

Keep in Mind: Crowded on every good swell and on weekends.

Months	JF	MA	MJ	JA	SO	ND
Average Swell (feet)	5–6	4–5	3–4	2–3	3–4	6
Air Temp (C/F)	13/56	16/61	19/67	22/72	23/74	15/60
Water Temp (C/F)	7/45	10/50	12/55	14/58	15/59	9/49
Wetsuit	full	full	full	full	full	full
Average Sunshine p/d (hours)	6	9	8–9	10	9	5–6
Average Rain p/m (inches)	4	1	0	0	1	3
Average Surfable Days p/m	25	23	20	11	18	24

31. CAPE HATTERAS
North Carolina

A finger of tiny islands sticks out into the Atlantic ready to catch any available swell and turn raw wave juice into a pumping top-quality surf concoction. Cape Hatteras has all the right topography to make this place great, and it pulls in big Atlantic swells to make it the focus of East Coast surfing. When it does fire on all cylinders, these door-stopping sandpit barrels are strewn over 70 miles of dunes, and a four-by-four pickup truck gets the pick of the surf crop. This is where the Wright brothers first flew an aircraft. This is where gob-smacked surfers in the 1960s first found a local wave paradise. This is where wave hunting is so much fun.

Situated 120 miles south of Norfolk, Virginia, and 160 miles north of Wilmington, North Carolina, this line of small islands called the Outer Banks curves out into the Atlantic where the Gulf Stream meets the Labrador Current. This dynamic chain of sandy islands provides some of the best waves and surf spots along the East Coast.

There are many breaks from which to choose, but one of the best is called the Lighthouse. Although the Cape Hatteras Lighthouse was actually moved inland in 1999 (the Atlantic was about to suck it in) surfers still call the break Cape Hatteras Lighthouse. This is a beach break with a sand point giving a right-hander on the rim of the sandy bay. The right point is part of a sandbar spit that juts out into the bay, 200 yards offshore. It is this break that has, in part, made Hatteras world famous. This is the sought-after wave in the area in any swell direction, although there are dozens of ace breaks and potential breaks that all work in the same swell. Other breaks include surf spots to the north, at Rodanthe and Oregon Inlets, both of which have a lot of sandbars and consistent waves. To the south, there's Frisco, Cape Lookout National Seashore, and Wrightsville Beach.

For thousands of years this island chain has survived the barrage of wind and sea. Today the long beaches and dunes produce the ideal environment for wave riding, and all are still beauty spots. Fishing is also very popular here on the Outer Banks, and surfing is prohibited within 300 yards of the fishing pier. Wrightsville Beach requires surfers to stay 500 feet away from its commercial fishing piers.

The Italian explorer Amerigo Vespucci first set foot on the beaches here in the sixteenth century and, thankfully, the coastline has remained largely untouched since then; you can still see waves that, on the right day, are world class. This is an ideal surf spot for the beginner and intermediate surfer, with a few days a year reserved exclusively for the expert.

Cape Hatteras Lighthouse is the tallest in North America and, at 280 feet, the light can be seen 20 miles out to sea. It has warned sailors for more than a century of the treacherous Diamond Shoals, the shallow sandbars that extend 14 miles into the ocean off Cape Hatteras. Dubbed the Graveyard of the Atlantic for its treacherous currents, shoals, and storms, the Outer Banks lives up to its name countless times a year and provides East Coast surfers with everything they need to rip it up in the pounding surf.

Photo R. Sumpter

If you want big surf, you go to Cape Hatteras on the Outer Banks. The continental shelf at the cape is very steep and narrow, allowing the full brunt of the Atlantic Ocean's waves to reach the shoreline.

Stan Riggs,
professor of marine geology,
East Carolina University

Photo R. Sumpter

| Peak | R.Point | Beachbreak | NE Swell |

Break: Beach break
Skill Level: Beginner to expert
Commitment: 1–10 on most days; 10–10 during hurricane swells
Best Boards: Shortboards, longboards, bodyboards
Lifeguard: None
Hazards: Dangerous rip currents, shallow sand bottom. Watch out for bumping into things in the water, it might be a shark but it's more likely to be a turtle coming onto the beach.

Currency: U.S. dollar.
Going There: Visa required except by U.S. citizens. Vaccinations required except by U.S. citizens—tetanus, typhoid. Check with your doctor, health clinic, and embassy for up-to-date info.
Where to Stay: Holiday Inn Express in Hatteras Village, (800) 359–2522. Comfort Inn Hatteras Island, Buxton, (866) 236–9330. Outer Banks Hostel, Kitty Hawk, (252) 261–2294 or (877) 453–2545. There are also plenty of

choice motels, hotels, and camping areas in the park. Call the seashore headquarters at (252) 473–2111.
Finding the Break: Not as easy to find since the lighthouse was moved inland about 1,000 yards. Follow Route 12 to the village of Buxton. Look for the lighthouse and turn toward the Atlantic coast; the Cape Hatteras Lighthouse surf spot is the tiny bay at the L-shaped corner of the coastline with a sand point. You'll see where the lighthouse used to be.
Surf School: Corolla Surf School, (252) 453–9283.
Keep in Mind: Rarely crowded except during good surf days on summer weekends.
For More Information: Cape Hatteras National Seashore, Manteo, North Carolina, (252) 473–2111.

Months	JF	MA	MJ	JA	SO	ND
Average Swell (feet)	2-3	2	1-2	0-1	1-2	2-3
Air Temp (C/F)	5/42	8/48	23/75	29/85	20/69	5/42
Water Temp (C/F)	5/42	7/47	16/61	19/67	17/62	12/54
Wetsuit	full	full	full	spring	full	full
Average Sunshine p/d (hours)	5-6	7	8	9	7	5-6
Average Rain p/m (inches)	3	3	4	4	3	3
Average Surfable Days p/m	10	8	5	3	7	9

32. OCEAN CITY
Maryland

Small Atlantic swells arrive, then flop and fizzle away, lapping at the shoreline. But the expectations rise and East Coast surfers are coiled and ready to strike. From across town you can smell the waves in the air—it's the surf report saying the swells are up. At last, it's time to paddle out into the salty waters of the Atlantic and bury yourself into the best barrels of the day.

Ocean City, Maryland, picks up the occasional sought-after classic swell. Yes, the swell here is fickle, and these good waves are rare. But the topography as the Atlantic Ocean meets the land does allow the right conditions for great surf. With its miles of beach, Ocean City can be a fabulous surf spot on the right day. Other nearby breaks includes Dewey Beach, Bethany, Rehoboth, Fenwick Island, and local Delaware surf spots. In the late summer and fall, at the height of the hurricane season, the eastern seaboard is often brushed (or even slammed) by one of these massive storms. But when one of these storms turns north well offshore and heads back out to sea, the phrase *Right time, right place* is very apt. During these few times each year the Atlantic rises up, casting the perfect swells westward to comb the beach breaks, groins, jetties, and piers of the eastern seaboard, forming seriously heady waves.

When the surf's up, places like 8th Street, with its shifting sandbanks, could be the spot. Or it might be half a dozen other spots that surfers flock to. There are twenty-seven popular breaks on the South Beaches of Ocean City alone, running from 64th Street to 2nd Street. On the North Beaches there are spots from 140th to 67th Streets, with ace breaks hosting lefts and rights of true quality. Ocean City with its many breaks is the ideal spot for the beginner—there are a lot of small, mushy days on which to learn. But it's also great for the expert when those storms are brewing offshore and the surf is big.

It always seems to be summer in Ocean City, and its growth has increased dramatically since starting out as a small fishing village in 1875. Besides being a surfing and sunbathing magnet, the city draws anglers from all over the world when it hosts the White Marlin Open, the world's largest marlin-fishing tournament, held in the late summer.

Ocean City now boasts more hotels than the eyes can count, seventeen championship golf courses, 160 restaurants, nature tours, 3 miles of the world-famous boardwalk, and 10 miles of white-sand beaches. There are free summer concerts on the beach every Wednesday and Sunday that include pop, country, rock, Caribbean, and jazz music. On the boardwalk at the inlet, the Life-Saving Station Museum displays artifacts recovered from many shipwrecks, including guns, ship bells, a large collection of shipwreck china, and a very extensive shark exhibit. More than 5,700 people have been saved from 300 disasters on the coast of Ocean City. There is also the Roland E. Powell Convention Centre, which is host to many surf product shows.

Photo R. Sumpter

What we get compared to say, California, is that we can get the quality, just not the consistency. When it's good here it's very good, but we get a lot of flat days, and a lot of uncooperative winds. When it's up and good, it's as challenging as anywhere.

Lee Gerachis,
Malibu's Surf Shop, Ocean City

Photo R. Sumpter

Beachbreak | NE Swell

Break: Beach break

Skill Level: Beginner to expert

Commitment: 1–10; during a hurricane swell, 10–10

Best Boards: Shortboards, longboards, bodyboards

Lifeguard: In season

Hazards: Dangerous rip currents, shallow sand bottom. The shore dump is gnarly and the undertow strong in onshore conditions with waves over 6 feet. Watch out for hurricane swells.

Currency: U.S. dollar.

Going There: Visa required except by U.S. citizens. Vaccinations required except by U.S. citizens—tetanus, typhoid. Check with your doctor, health clinic, and embassy for up-to-date info.

Where to Stay: The Harrison Group of Hotels has top-name hotels; call (800) 638–2106. Ocean City Campground, (410) 524–7601 or fax (410) 524–4329.

Finding the Break: A good place to start is in front of Malibu Surf Shop (410–289–3000). Go north to find many breaks toward 64th Street.

Keep in Mind: Rarely crowded except during good surf days on summer weekends.

Months	JF	MA	MJ	JA	SO	ND
Average Swell (feet)	2	2	1	0–1	1	2
Air Temp (C/F)	5/42	8/48	23/75	29/85	20/69	5/42
Water Temp (C/F)	5/42	7/47	16/61	19/67	17/62	12/54
Wetsuit	full	full	full	spring	full	full
Average Sunshine p/d (hours)	5–6	7	8	9	7	5–6
Average Rain p/m (inches)	3	2	1	0	1	3
Average Surfable Days p/m	15	12	5	3	2	9

33. SEBASTIAN INLET
Florida

A postcard-perfect spot, Sebastian Inlet is a place to pop some aerials at First Peak, do a rail slide or maybe a 360-degree lip launch, throw some curves and arches, then disappear into the barrel and come out smiling.

One of the best breaks on the East Coast, Sebastian Inlet is situated 15 miles south of Melbourne Beach (a good shortboard beach break) and 15 miles north of Vero Beach (a good bodyboard break). It's located right next to the Indian River County line. This is the most famous surf spot in Florida, and certainly its most consistent. At First Peak, a right-hander that lines up along the north jetty and is protected from southerly winds, the peak wedges up from 4 feet to overhead on takeoff. Breaking off a shallow sandbar and throwing a lip-launch curtain, it makes a mean barrel. On a good day, when conditions are right, the wave continues as a walling tube with peaky sections. At the end of the section called Second Peak is a high-performance right and occasional left, and down the line is a section called Third Peak.

There are 3 miles of Atlantic seaboard beach here, with numerous waves to surf. One of these is Monster Hole, one of the best breaks when there's a big swell. Just south of Sebastian Inlet in the river mouth, this long left and occasional right-hander is a gnarly big-wave spot. It can be double overhead and has a fast takeoff and drop to a big barrel. Waves farther north tend to need just the right swell and banks to crank. One such break that picks up any swell if it's around is Shark Pit, with its A-frame peak.

In 1886 the first inlet here was dug by hand. In 1971 Sebastian Inlet was made into a state park, at which time the south jetty was built. Today sand dredging at the mouth of the inlet helps Monster Hole maintain a consistent wave, and the new bridge and extended north jetty are capturing more swell than ever for First Peak.

Sebastian Inlet is a quality surf break with areas to suit the beginner on small days, going north up the beach a bit. First Peak and Second Peak are ideal for the expert.

Photo R. Sumpter

Sebastian Inlet is a hotdog, a really rippable wedge wave off the jetty.

Colin McPhillips,
2000–2002 World Longboard Surfing Champion

Photo R. Sumpter

R.Point | Beachbreak | SE Swell

Break: Beach break
Skill Level: Beginner to expert
Commitment: 2–10
Best Boards: Longboard, shortboard
Lifeguard: In season
Hazards: Rip currents, shallow sand bottom, sharks. Paddle out can be slow during big days. Overhead waves wedge up and hit low tide bars to produce heavy, fast, thick sections impossible to avoid.

Currency: U.S. dollar.
Going There: Visa required except by U.S. citizens. Vaccinations required except by U.S. citizens—tetanus, typhoid. Check with your doctor, health clinic, and embassy for up-to-date info.
Where to Stay: Ferndale Lodge Sebastian, (561) 589–5247; fax (561) 388–6035. Captains Quarters Sebastian, (561) 589–4345; fax (561) 589–4346. Palm Court Resort, (561) 231–2800. Sea Horses Cottages, (561) 231–6402. Surf & Sand Oceanfront, (561) 231–5700. Islander Inn, (561) 231 4431; fax (561) 589–5100.

Finding the Break: The waves are at Sebastian Inlet State Park located off Highway A1A, between Melbourne and Vero Beach, on the Brevard–Indian River county line. Park entrance fee $3.50.
Keep in Mind: It's always crowded at First Peak, with plenty of waves going north.
For More Information: Sebastian Inlet State Recreation Area, (321) 984–4852.

Months	JF	MA	MJ	JA	SO	ND
Average Swell (feet)	3	2–3	1–2	1–2	2–3	3–4
Air Temp (C/F)	25/77	28/82	31/88	32/90	30/86	25/77
Water Temp (C/F)	17/63	19/66	24/75	26/79	25/77	21/70
Wetsuit	shorty	shorty	vest	none	none	shorty
Average Sunshine p/d (hours)	7	8	12	14	13	7
Average Rain p/m (inches)	3	4	7	6	3	5
Average Surfable Days p/m	20	17	15	9	14	22

Photo R. Sumpter

LATIN AMERICA
AND THE CARIBBEAN

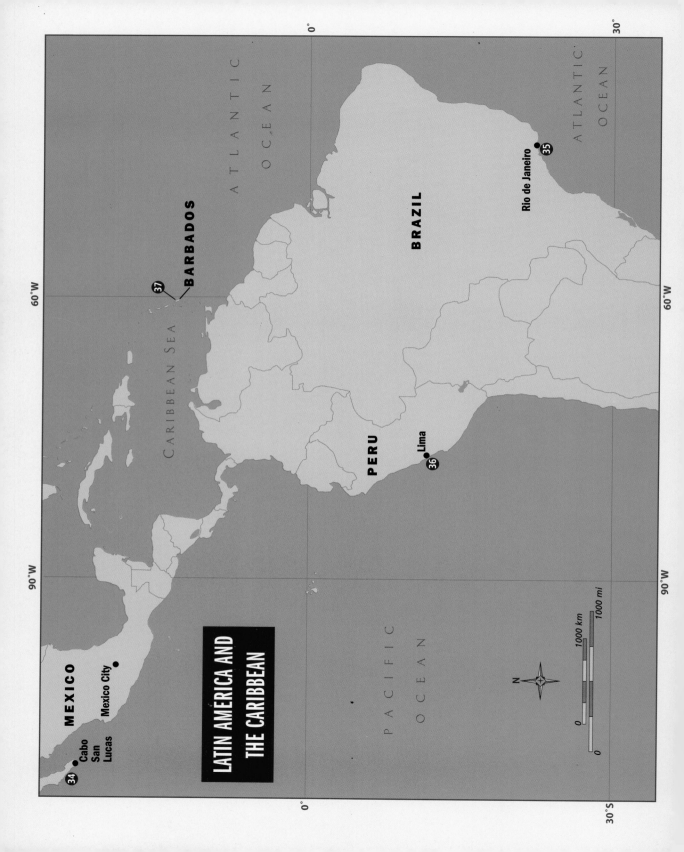

LATIN AMERICA AND THE CARIBBEAN

MEXICO

Cabo San Lucas

Mexico City

BARBADOS

BRAZIL

Rio de Janeiro

PERU

Lima

ATLANTIC OCEAN

ATLANTIC OCEAN

PACIFIC OCEAN

CARIBBEAN SEA

N

1000 km

1000 mi

0° · 30° · 60°W · 90°W · 60°W · 0° · 30°S

34 · 35 · 36 · 37

Mexico, Brazil, and Peru are Latin America's main surf countries in a region rich in waves, where the surf spots are full ranging—from big to small, from clean to mushy.

The vastness of South America's coasts thwarts all who surf here, but individual surf spots shine like golden jewels, ready and waiting to be ridden. You just need willpower and an adventurous spirit to try out these magic countries.

Starting in the north, Baja California and Mexico's western coast both offer classic groundswell surf on the Pacific Ocean side in May to October from the frequent tropical storms that pass close by. The three outstanding surf destinations are Cabo San Lucas at Baja's southern tip, with breaks like La Rocca and Todos Santos; Manzanonelo-Colima farther south in Mexico; and the big-wave beach break of Puerto Escondido, 190 miles south of Acapulco. These are the best surf areas in Mexico.

Brazil's surf is some of the most demanding in the world, where tightly packed zipping, pounding, short, fast beach breaks crunch bones and test surfers to the limit in consistent 3-to-6-foot waves. These beach destinations are sandwiched between reef and point surf locations that have all the hallmarks of lonely, wild, deep-water peaks. Brazil's huge coastline receives swells from the South Atlantic trade winds in the winter and from the North Atlantic in summer.

Some of Brazil's best surf starts in the north on the island of Fernando de Noronha 250 miles northeast of Natal on the northeast elbow of Brazil. The island has a variety of quality reef breaks. Farther south, Rio de Janeiro's great city is a hive of cafes, restaurants, nightclubs, and surf shops. Surfboard manufacturers, fruit markets, and beach culture add to the allure. When the waves pump in the right swell and the right winds are blowing, the surfing in Rio is epic. São Paulo, farther south of Rio, features skyscrapers as well as a long string of beaches, reefs, and points that create the best surf you could ever wish for.

Peru is the third largest country in South America, with regular offshore winds and a consistently good swell from the Humboldt Current created by the Andes Mountains. The Pacific Ocean receives big surf from May to October, and places like Cabo Blanco in the department of Piura at the very north of Peru are best at Christmastime, when they pick up swell from the Cocos Ridge and North Pacific. Heading south 250 miles is Chicama, a truly great wave with its fast, long left point peeling off lots of sections. Punta Rocas is the big-wave spot, 60 miles to the south of Lima, having the biggest and most spectacular surf in Peru with waves up to 30 feet. It's a long paddle out to the break, but well worth it if you're into huge waves.

The Caribbean Sea and the Atlantic Ocean provide Barbados with medium to big surf consistently. The island's location far out in the Atlantic allows waves to travel thousands of miles on the bottom of the sea before reaching a coral reef that mingles with stretches of beaches all around Barbados's coastline. Whether a swell approaches the island from the north, west, or east, Barbados is guaranteed to have surf somewhere along its shores at almost any time of year. The best surf spot is on its west coast at Soup Bowls, where the heavy, barreling surf is a highly demanding wave for the experienced surfer. On the east coast—often the glassy side of the island—beach and reef breaks from Brandons near Bridgetown to Accra Beach, and places like Freids, Cottons Bay's beach, and Rockley Beach have softer and easier waves, than the wild, rough, and serious hard-core west.

Latin America has everything a surfer hungry for adventure could want: the prospects of perfect waves, an enormously diverse coastline, and a colorful and lively culture.

34. LA ROCCA

Cabo San Lucas, Mexico

Mexico is lucky enough to receive the two best extremes of surfing: small quality waves and big quality waves. They come from the Pacific Ocean swells that swing onto Baja's Cabo San Lucas peninsula. At La Rocca the waves are generally small—the kind that you're not afraid of, but that still provide the ultimate fun of hanging ten, arching turns, and trimming. Longboarders revel in these small waves, since their boards perform best and don't drag as they would on 20 footers. Soft, clean, and perfect for holding a rail and carving big turns—why surf scary big waves, when you can have total fun on head-high perfection?

At the other end of the scale is the big surf of Cabo San Lucas at Todos Santos, where the waves can turn into huge gun barrels, glinting steel in the noonday sun and striking awe into the township that overlooks the bay. When a mighty swell hits, the big-wave riders get out their guns and face the pounding shorebreak eye to eye. It's a shoot-out with some of the most powerful waves in the world.

La Rocca is situated on Mexico's Baja California peninsula, part of the surf coastline that runs from San Jose del Cabo in the south to Todos Santos in the north. This is a 15-mile stretch of classic breaks country that winds along Route 19. La Rocca is a right-hand break off a rocky outcrop, producing a quality right-hand wave for nose riding and roundhouse cutbacks. The length is from 50 to 100 yards; it's a good longboarding wave at 3 to 4

feet. It can also hold 6-8 feet in the right swell.

Along Route 1 on the southeast coast, about 2 miles before the town of San Jose del Cabo, is the most popular break—Costa Azul. This is a reef point break that holds good shape up to overhead, and can be lots of fun even on smaller waves. The point, reefs, and beaches pick up ace conditions when there is a *chubasco* (a wind that blows from the coast of California off the Mexican mainland), or when the Southern Hemisphere brings in a swell from below the equator.

When the waves are flat in Cabo San Lucas, it can be a whole different scene up the west coast past Todos Santos. From the tip this 60-mile stretch of coastline offers some of Baja's best beaches and surf breaks, only without the crowds. Once you're on Route 19 northbound, just look for the side roads heading west toward the ocean. When you set foot on some of these deserted breaks, odds are you're the only person for miles. Todos Santos is one of the best big-wave spots in the world, with several breaks to the south of the town at Playa San Pedrito and Playa Los Cerritos; to the north is La Pastara.

Baja first became popular in 1964 when it was discovered that easy-access breaks like K49 were just a day trip from San Diego. Many were pioneered by Windansea Surf Club and Long Beach Surf Club members. Poor roads were the primary reason that Cabo San Lucas took so long to become popular.

Twenty million years ago seismic upheavals along the San Andreas Fault caused a narrow finger of land (Baja) to separate from the mainland of Mexico. At its widest point Baja is only 120 miles across. The waters of the Pacific filled the gap, creating the Gulf of California. The central region is dominated by the Vizcaino Desert with a landscape of giant cacti, cirios, and wind-polished boulders. The southern Cabo San Lucas area is mainly desert, with some mountainous regions and lush vegetation. Fine sandy beaches and rugged rock formations are splendid against the emerald sea.

If you're here in the autumn and the surf is flat, check out the thousands of California gray whales that migrate south from Alaska's Bering Strait to central Baja's Pacific coast. Weighing twenty to forty tons apiece, these mammoths of the deep can be viewed from points at Cerritos, or by boat on one of the many tours offered.

La Rocca I rate as fun and playful. The best wave was probably in the final, a 9.4 wave. I hung ten, hit the lip, cut back, and just kind of did a whole package of maneuvers.

Colin McPhillips,
2000–2002 World Longboard Surfing Champion

Photo © ASP Tostee

R.Point | Beachbreak | SW Swell

Break: Beach break and right-hand reef break
Skill Level: Beginner to expert
Commitment: 3–10
Best Boards: Longboard; shortboard or gun if it's big
Lifeguard: None
Hazards: Rocky headland, outcrops, and heavy beach break
Currency: Mexican peso.

Going There: Visas are required by all except by Irish or British subjects. Vaccinations required—hepatitis A, typhoid, tetanus, polio, malaria, and tuberculosis (if you're coming from infected areas). Check with your doctor, health clinic, and embassy for up-to-date info.
Where to Stay: Casa Del Mar, +52 (624) 144–0030. Cabo Surf Hotel Beachside, +52 (624) 142–2666. Hotels 4 Travellers, (800) 742–6081. Cabo Surf Hotel, (866) 608–9330. Coyote Cal's Mexico Hostel, +52 (646) 154 4080. Gran Baja Hotel Surf View, ewr2@apc.net.
Finding the Break: From Los Cabos Airport, take the four-lane Route 1 going south (first exit to the right when leaving the airport). Continue past San Jose del Cabo for about 10 miles. After passing La Jolla de Los Cabos and the Rosta Azul beach, follow the coast road to La Rocca, and then head southwest and around up the west coast to Todos Santos, turning off the highway onto sand and dirt tracks to find many spots.
Keep in Mind: There's surf year-round, but the south coast is best April to May; the west coast, November to December.

Months	JF	MA	MJ	JA	SO	ND
Average Swell (feet)	3	2–3	4	3–4	3–4	3
Air Temp (C/F)	26/79	27/81	32/90	36/96	34/92	27/81
Water Temp (C/F)	24/75	24/75	25/77	27/81	28/82	26/79
Wetsuit	vest	vest	none	none	none	none
Average Sunshine p/d (hours)	6	6	7	8	7	5
Average Rain p/m (inches)	1	1	2	5	6	1
Average Surfable Days p/m	19	16	12	14	17	20

35. RIO DE JANEIRO
Brazil

Rio has one of the best beach breaks in Latin America and some of the finest tubes in the world. And like its annual Carnival, Rio's unlocked Atlantic waves hit the beaches and light up the many beach breaks. When the waves are this big, the hordes of tourists evacuate the water, allowing surf-starved surfers to flock to the emerging action as if marching in the Samba Parade. And in classic Carnival atmosphere, the days down here never end—at sunset the beach spotlights come on to shine on nighttime surf. The rich sounds of jazz combined with the sweet songs of the sea leave surfers riding barrels until the fat lady sings.

Situated along 45 miles of white, sandy beaches, the city of Rio de Janeiro is dramatically set between rain-forest-clad cliffs and the deep blue sea. This is South America's first true surf city, with surf spots running from northeast to southwest along its many beach breaks. Here you'll find a variety of waves between April and September, the very best of which arrive in July and August.

Brazil's tropical coastline stretches for 11,919 miles. While just a small piece of this vast run, Rio's 45 miles offers number of famous beaches and surf spots. Starting in the north, the fast tubing waves of Ipanema (meaning "dangerous waters") create a left-hand beach break with epic peaks. Then there's Copacabana, below the famous landmark of Sugar Loaf Mountain, with its heavy shorebreak and right-hand waves. As a bonus, Copacabana is right in front of the seething main beach scene and glare of city skyscrapers. Barry Manilow would love the surf here. Continuing south, you then have the right reef break called P5 and a left break called P6, both breaking shallow bays 400 yards from shore on sand-covered reefs. The next break is Leme, a sand-bottomed peak that's very short, with both right- and left-handers often closing out. Express Escoriao is next in line, delivering a ripping right-hand beach break. A reef break called Shore Break and a beach break named Ria da Urca with a fine right-hander follow. The coast at Harpooner becomes one of the best river point breaks around, with choice of point break and beach break to surf with fine-quality waves on the right day. The next break is called Prainha and is one of the more famous beaches in Brazil, having left and right breaks depending on swell and tide. Triangle Peaks give plenty of piping barrels at this ace break.

Rio de Janeiro rightly claims more than twenty quality surf spots, and most are beach breaks. This is an ideal place for the beginner on small days, and for experts when it's pumping perfection.

Overlooking Rio's beach life is the famous *Cristo Redentor,* standing with his arms outstretched atop Corcovado Mountain. Rio is an exciting contrast of forested mountains and sun-drenched beaches.

From its sandy beaches to the Amazon jungle, Brazil is the largest country on the South America continent (four times the size of Mexico), with a population of nearly 159 million people. In 1494 Portugal first claimed Brazil, and independence came in 1922. And while Portuguese is the national language, English is easily considered a second language, spoken in just about all areas of the country, especially those travelers and tourists are likely to frequent such as Rio. Expect to find pleasantly comfortable temperatures year-round, since most of the country lies immediately south of the equator and seasonal changes are very nominal.

Surfing the Amazon

The Amazon River runs through Brazil as it travels across the heart of South America, a distance of 4,000 miles. The river has a wave called *pororoca*, which breaks as a wave between São Domingos do Capim in Para state, and Arguari in Amapa state, Amapa's capital. This river tidal wave is caused by an incoming tide and a full moon, usually after the dry season. It is surfable, but very tricky, because the river is flowing at 5 miles per hour and the wave comes at 20 miles per hour in the opposite direction. This causes much debris, not to mention confusion among the deadly creatures in the river. It's rated dangerous.

Photo © ASP Tostee

Rio's got some good sandbars. It's a pretty tough beach break—there's a lot of closeouts—but on the right swell it has moments where you can get a good barrel and high performance. . . . Down the beach, Ipanema is actually a really good left; it's up there in the top twenty in the world.

Andy Irons,
2002–2003 World Surfing Champion

Photo © ASP Tostee

Rights | Lefts | Peak | Beachbreak | S Swell

Break: Beach breaks and reef breaks
Skill Level: Beginner to expert
Commitment: 3–10
Best Boards: Shortboard
Lifeguard: In season
Hazards: Rips and currents can be mega; heavy shorebreaks. Rocky patches along the beach and underwater, rock shelves and jagged reefs.
Currency: Brazillian real.
Going There: Visa required. Vaccinations required—hepatitis A, typhoid, tetanus, polio, malaria, and tuberculosis. Check with your doctor, health clinic, and embassy for up-to-date info.
Where to Stay: Aroador Inn, +55 021 523 0060, or fax +55 021 511 5094. Caesar Park, +55 021 525 2525, or fax +55 021 521 6000. Copacabana Palace, +55 021 548 7070, or fax +55 021 235 7330. Ipanema Inn, +55 021 523 6092, or fax +55 021 511 5092. Pria Ipanema, +55 021 540 4949. Club Med Village Rio das Pedras, +55 021 688 9191, or fax +55 021 688 3333.

Finding the Break: Ipanema Beach is 12 miles from Santos Dumont airport and 20 miles from Rio de Janeiro International Airport.
Surf Schools: Prainha Surf School, +55 047 449 1617. Barra/Floripa, +55 048 232 3149.
Keep in Mind: Crowds.

Months	JF	MA	MJ	JA	SO	ND
Average Swell (feet)	2	2	2–3	4	3	2
Air Temp (C/F)	28/84	27/82	25/77	25/77	24/76	26/80
Water Temp (C/F)	26/78	25/77	23/74	21/70	20/68	22/72
Wetsuit	none	none	vest	vest	shorty	shorty
Average Sunshine p/d (hours)	7	6–7	6	6	7	5–6
Average Rain p/m (inches)	5	4	3	2	2	4
Average Surfable Days p/m	4	6	5	3	2	5

36. PUNTA ROCAS
Peru

Like a cascading avalanche high in the Andes, a wave sprayed with Inca gold comes flying down the face of Peru's best surf spot, Punta Rocas. This is an A-frame wave, looking like a hollow pyramid made from warm crystals, cracking and bending under pressure. The curl line is as smooth and poetic as the condor that glides the thermals out to the blue Pacific. The great Aztec god folds its wings, and the wind turns offshore. You're taking off and making the drop into the wave's melting pot, and as it throws out an almighty sheet of water, you slingshot out the back-door section. The angle of attack has to be pulled up or the collapsing curl will J-knife you into oblivion.

Punta Rocas is ideal for the expert surfer year-round, but it's also a place where beginners can find a few small-swell days and calm beach breaks—generally in the summer—to call their own. This excellent surf spot lies amid arid desert with rocky scrubland and barren hills, with the odd palm tree dotted about. Standing atop 75-foot cliffs and looking down to the ocean, this break puts on a display. Access to the beach is along winding, rocky paths.

The paddle out on a 10-to-15-foot day starts at the shorebreak, where the pounding waves rattle the nerves and timing a lull is vital to passing the grinding waves washing up the sloping beach. The big blue smooth-face waves on the horizon some 700 yards out draw you on through the shore dump by way of an outgoing rip current. Still, it's tricky not to become mince-pied. Beyond the beach break and before Punta Rocas's A-frames, you see the awesome waves close up.

The best option is to paddle to the farthest possible takeoff area and wait for the right swell. A late takeoff is best, one that will jettison you into a vertically curved turn along the clean jaws of a smooth wall for 100 yards. It's a gnarly midsection threatening to shut down and close out, blowing your pixels off. But hang in there. The wave holds up and you're through the tight part. You reach the flatter performance wave, great for turns, and are off the lip before the wave finally backs off into the channel.

Peru's first surf spots are situated just a twenty-minute drive from Lima, the capital city, and thirty minutes from Jorge Chavez International Airport. There are breaks such as Waikiki, El Camotal, Tres Picos, the left point of Herradura, and Miraflores, with its fun, soft waves. Two hours farther south are the heavy breaks of Punta Rocas, breaking over a granite ledge where the Peruvian National Championships are held each year. Kon Tiki is a big-wave *bombora*-style break, and Pico Alto is a good big-wave spot from 8 to 25 feet, with a left and right peak comparable to Sunset Beach on Oahu. To the north is one of the world's longest lefts at Chicama, a fast left breaking off a rock and sand bottom with possible rides of up to 2 miles. In general the entire coastline, particularly along the first two-hour drive south of Lima, is a gold mine of surf spots, beaches, points, and sand and reef breaks.

One hour south of Lima is Punta Hermosa, where there are fifteen breaks within a mile stretch of coastline. Big winter swells (April to October) are usually in the 10-to-15-foot range and are chilled by the Humboldt Current, which rises up from Chile, bringing cool water from southwest South America. You'll definitely need a full wetsuit here. In summer use a spring suit when there's an average swell running; the surf is generally a nice 3 to 6 feet.

The good spots on the northwest coastline are at and near El Alto. These breaks are at Punta Restin, Cabo Blanquillo, and Cabo Blanco, all of which are lefts. Over the border in Ecuador, the best surf spots are between Salinas and Manta. The second-ever World Surfing Championships were held in 1965 at Waikiki, Punta Rocas, and at Kon Tiki's *bombora* waves, in 15 feet of surf. Felip Pomar from Lima won the championships and was the first Peruvian to surf many of the big wave's breaks.

Photo J. Sumpter

Archaeologists have unearthed textiles and pottery that depict surfing in Peru, dating back to 50 B.C., a time when the tortora reed was woven into a type of canoe used by fishermen who sat at the back to paddle. This could possibly be the oldest surfing craft. The 12-foot-long canoe is still used today at Huanchaco in Santa Rosa, and at Pimental in La Libertad.

I had some of my best, biggest waves at Kon Tiki—18 feet plus. I rate it in my top three big-wave spots of the world.

Rod Sumpter

Photo J. Sumpter

Rights	Peak	Beachbreak	W Swell

Break: Right-hand reef break

Skill Level: Expert

Commitment: 7–10

Best Boards: Shortboards to big-wave guns

Lifeguard: None

Hazards: Big triple-overhead waves crash in a *Bombora*-style avalanche. Dangerously heavy; expect to be held down a minute. A strong 12-foot leg leash required.

Currency: New sol.

Going There: Visa required by U.S., Canadian, Australian, Japanese, and EU citizens; others should check with their embassies. Vaccinations required—hepatitis A, typhoid, tetanus, polio, malaria, tuberculosis (children only). Check with your doctor, health clinic, and embassy for up-to-date info.

Where to Stay: Punta Rocas, Kahunas Surf Host & Spa, +51 (0) 1 430 7407 or fax +51 (0) 1 430 7407. Peru Adventures Lodge Punta Hermosa, +51 (0) 1 230–8316. Surfcamp San Bartolo, +51 (0) 1 430 7407. In northern Peru Hostal Las Olas +51 (0) 74 858 109; also overlooks the sea, and is great value with prices including breakfast. Mancora Hostels string out along the southern end of the Panamerican Highway: the Hospedaje Crillon, +51 (0) 74 858 000; Hostal Sausalito, +51 (0) 74 858 058. Mancora Vacation rentals, Lima, +51 (0) 1 221 4259. Beach Bungalow rentals, Mokala, Vichayito, Mancora, +51 (0) 74 968 4889. Crillon Hotel, Avenue Nicolas de Pierola, Lima, +51 (0) 14 283 290.

Finding the Break: From Lima International Airport head for Lima and take the Panamerican Highway south. Travel for 20 miles and you will pass Punta Hermosa. In 1 mile turn right for Punta Rocas. Drive down the winding hill to the beach parking area.

Surf School: Kahunas Surf Host & Spa, +51 (0) 1 430 7407.

Keep in Mind: Rarely crowded.

Months	JF	MA	MJ	JA	SO	ND
Average Swell (feet)	3	4	4–5	4	3–4	2–3
Air Temp (C/F)	26/80	25/78	20/68	21/70	21/70	24/76
Water Temp (C/F)	18/64	19/66	17/63	15/59	16/61	17/62
Wetsuit	spring	spring	full	full	full	spring
Average Sunshine p/d (hours)	6–7	7	4	1	2	4–5
Average Rain p/m (inches)	0	0	1	1	2	0
Average Surfable Days p/m	19	17	8	6	18	20

37. SOUP BOWLS
Bathsheba, Barbados

Shot like a bullet from the barrel of a painter's tube, these 6-foot-high blue-eyed waves look picture-perfect Barbados, swaying palm trees and all. Their clean, glassy, see-through walls are transparent, and the surfability possibilities seem endless. A wave to smack, tuck, kick, and vanish into on these hot dreamy waters.

Barbados is part of the West Indies, situated 1,600 miles southeast of Miami and 175 miles northeast of Trinidad and Tobago. Soup Bowls, at Bathsheba, is by far the island's most famous and best break, with international and local championships being held here since the 1960s. It's a fast right-hand reef break with a short barrel and cut-back section and an inside-out shorebreak over ledgey coral pocket holes.

After a difficult paddle out over coral studded with urchins, the takeoff is mighty—from 6 to 8 feet. This is a very powerful, heavy wave when the winds are northeast. The best season for waves is from November to March, with a length of ride 50 to 100 yards on a good day. The next break is High Rock, a peak that walls up and surges to the south 100 yards, giving quality steep drops and fast walls around some striking eerie rock formations. Then comes Tent Bay, a left and right with awesome power, a shallow coral reef, caves, a channeled seafloor, and more strange rocks strung along the landscape.

Bathsheba Bay is the first vista you see when arriving down Horse Hill around the winding tropical road—a strik-

> Legend has it that Bathsheba, wife of King David, bathed in milk to keep her skin soft and white—like the foaming waters of Bathsheba Bay.

ing panorama of white surf, blue sea, and palm trees. Beginners can find beach breaks on the west coast at spots like Rockley Beach. Other breaks around the island are Batt's Rock, Sandy Lane, Tropicana, Gibbs, Maycocks Beach, and Duppies. Soup Bowls, at Bathsheba, is an ideal surf spot for the expert.

In 1536 the first known mention of Barbados is found in an official document issued by King Ferdinand of Spain. Recently shell tools unearthed at Heywood Beach, a surf spot north of Speightown, have revealed a date of 1630 B.C. It is thought that people arrived here from Venezuela on seafaring canoes up to 90 feet long.

Barbados is one of the islands missed by Christopher Columbus on his voyages of discovery. It was discovered, instead, by a Portuguese explorer named Pedro a Campos in 1536, while on his way to Brazil. He named the island Los Barbados for the bearded fig tree he found growing in abundance here.

The sand of the beautiful beaches of Barbados ranges in color from pink to white, 80 miles of which are open to the public. The island is 21 miles long by 14 miles wide.

Photo R. Sumpter

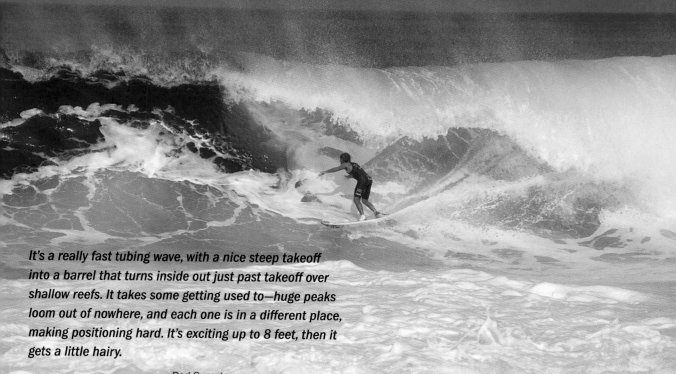

It's a really fast tubing wave, with a nice steep takeoff into a barrel that turns inside out just past takeoff over shallow reefs. It takes some getting used to—huge peaks loom out of nowhere, and each one is in a different place, making positioning hard. It's exciting up to 8 feet, then it gets a little hairy.

Rod Sumpter

Photo R. Sumpter

Rights | NE Swell

Break: Reef break
Skill Level: Intermediate to expert
Commitment: 5–10
Best Boards: Shortboard
Lifeguard: None
Hazards: Tiptoe over coral seashore to a pounding shorebreak. Huge closeout waves that get more difficult from knee to waist high and dangerous in over-head waves.

Currency: Barbados dollar.
Going There: Visa required by all except British and Irish passport holders. Vaccinations required—yellow fever, typhoid, tetanus, polio. Check with your doctor, health clinic, and embassy for up-to-date info.
Where to Stay: Bajan Surf Bungalow, Bathsheba, (246) 433–9920, or fax (246) 433–9278. Sea-u Guest House, Bathsheba, (246) 433–9450, or fax (246) 433–9210. Edgewater Inn, Bathsheba, (246) 433–9900, or fax (246) 433–9902. Crane Beach Hotel, (246) 423–6220, or fax (246) 423–5343. Atlantis Hotel Tent Bay, Bathsheba, (246) 433–9445, or fax (246) 433–7180.

Finding the Break: From the airport take the coast road to Bridgetown and follow signs for Bathsheba. While the distance from the airport is 19 miles, the total driving time is fifty minutes due to winding, narrow, steep roads.
Keep in Mind: Some crowds December to February.

Months	JF	MA	MJ	JA	SO	ND
Average Swell (feet)	3-4	3	2-3	3	3-4	4
Air Temp (C/F)	28/84	30/87	30/87	30/87	29/86	29/85
Water Temp (C/F)	24/75	24/75	25/77	26/79	27/81	25/77
Wetsuit	none	none	none	none	none	none
Average Sunshine p/d (hours)	9	9	8	9	8	8
Average Rain p/m (inches)	2	1	3	6	6	7
Average Surfable Days p/m	17	15	10	8	14	19

Photo R. Sumpter

NORTHERN
EUROPE

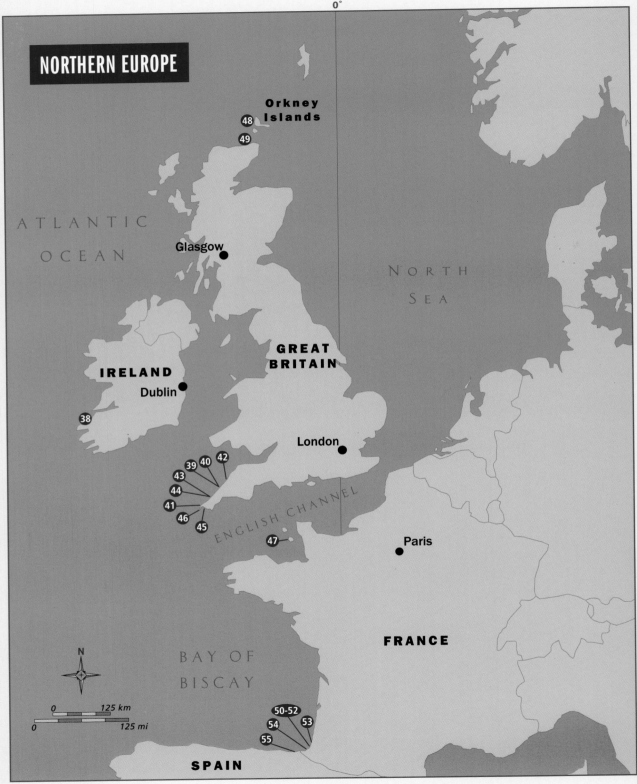

NORTHERN EUROPE

Orkney Islands

48
49

ATLANTIC
OCEAN

Glasgow •

NORTH
SEA

IRELAND

Dublin •

GREAT
BRITAIN

38

London •

39 40 42
43
44
41
46   45

ENGLISH CHANNEL

47

Paris •

N

BAY OF
BISCAY

0   125 km
0   125 mi

FRANCE

50-52
53
54
55

SPAIN

0°

The North Atlantic is the big swell machine in Europe, created by low-pressure systems crossing the great ocean from Newfoundland, Greenland, and Iceland in winter, and often sending swell as far as North Africa. Big surf in winter, smaller in summer, swell is sent to every nook and cranny along Europe's coast and to hundreds of surf locations. The best waves are in four areas: Ireland's west coast, Great Britain's southwest coast of Cornwall, Scotland's north shore, and southern France, where the Bay of Biscay collects the swell and rolls out waves consistently.

It is Ireland's west coast that first receives these mighty long-distance groundswells, the same swell that hits the west coast of the Dingle peninsula. Blessed with the best bays, points, reefs, and beaches, the peninsula is a haven for good waves, making it one of the best areas to surf in Europe.

Britain's southwest county of Cornwall is the UK's first and most consistent year-round North Atlantic surf area. It picks up the brunt of Atlantic storms and long-distance swells. This is Britain's most surfed coastline, with summer waves on thirty beaches. Although crowded in summer, Cornwall's beaches are deserted in winter, so fall is a good time to surf.

Six hundred miles to the north, Scotland's north shore is at its best in the fall as well. At Thurso East the perfect right reef break is famed for being the best wave in the entire country. The north shore of Scotland's Caithness County has much to offer the traveling surfer, with perfect waves, big surf, and epic scenery.

The North Atlantic swells reach southern France's beaches in the Bay of Biscay, a horseshoe-shaped bay that also touches on northern Spain. Here the Atlantic swells arrive and hit a deep-water canyon. The area just off the beaches is called Golfe de Gascogne, and is a deep-water swell builder for all the breaks between Bordeaux and Biarritz. Places like Hossegor in the north offer quick breaking waves and amazing rides. To the south in the center of Biarritz city is a beach break of mini tubes at Cote de Basque. With its sheltered profile from big storm waves, it is ideally protected beside the promenade and castle for good surf. South from Biarritz are the great breaks of Guethary, a legendary big-wave reef break of sheer beauty and the best in France. Lafitenia is an awesome point wave on the right day.

Just to the southeast the Biscay Plain and the European continental shelf hug the north coast of Spain, and the water above remains deep, even up close to the coast. Big waves enter this corner of the ocean, and when they hit the Continent, at places like Mundaka in northern Spain, they can be huge, perfect, and scary.

The northern area of Europe is a rich contrast of surfing styles, with both remote and wild locations and accessible and busy surfing centers.

38. DINGLE PENINSULA

County Clare, Ireland

The great outdoors doesn't get any bigger than Ireland's southwest coast. And with the wild Atlantic Ocean, it is rarely flat. The Dingle peninsula has just about everything a surfer could want: abounding surf beaches and epic-quality reef waves by the boatload—a stunning green patchwork of surf, mountains, and valleys. Surfers who like clean glassy waves and a barrel of Guinness won't have to wait very long for either here at Dingle.

The Dingle peninsula sports a geographic feature not found elsewhere—three coasts facing north, west, and south on which to surf, each coast protected from strong winds by mountains. When there's a pumping swell coming in from the Atlantic, the coasts at Dingle offer a lot of unimpeded surf from which to choose. Even on relatively flat days, there are usually some waves on offer.

"The Dingle," as it is called, measures just 10 by 20 miles. Surfers first discovered it in the 1960s when longboarders trekked up the west coast, discovering and plotting many of today's most fabulous breaks. Indeed, this is one of the world's ultimate surf locations, with remote points and bays yet to be surfed for the first time.

On the north coast to the east of the peninsula at Tralee Bay, there are numerous surf spots from which to choose. Here you'll find Sandy Bay, a beach break for beginners that's lifeguarded in summer. Right around the headland of Magharee is Garry Williams Point, a right-hand wave picking up any swell around. This break is often best when elsewhere is flat. There is Mossie's, a right-hand point reef wave that provides a classic ride off rock platforms and is best in southern winds. Farther around Brandon Bay is Dumps, a gnarly closeout dumping beach break.

Brandon Bay, a majestic horseshoe, has numerous other beach breaks, including Fermoyle Strand and Golane Strand. The soft sand here can be a graveyard for overenthusiastic vehicles, which can be seen coming from the town of Dingle from on top of Ireland's highest mountain pass, Conner Pass.

At the west-facing corner of the peninsula is Bally David, a big right-hand wave. The beach break at Smerwick Harbor offers excellent low-tide waves, even if a big swell is running. On the peninsula's west coast is Coumeenole, a good left. This break is very tidal, with rip currents and hollow waves, and quite gnarly. On the south coast you'll find Inch Beach, a longboarder's dream wave, and Inch Reef, a long right-hand reef break that peels alongside the cliff road. Parking and access are difficult, but the waves are worth it.

Few surf locations can boast so many fantastic waves for the beginner, intermediate, and expert surfer alike. On the right day, the Dingle is ideal.

When the surf or the weather isn't cooperating for some good wave riding, the wild splendor of Kerry's scenery can keep you very busy indeed. The Ring of Fire, Ireland's most famous tour, is just south of Dingle. This is the honey pot, a scenic route circling the Iveragh peninsula, providing a dramatic mix of rugged moorland and mountains, lakes, rivers, cliffs, and beaches. The Dingle peninsula is also a unique floral delight, with water lilies and subtropical gardens. The area is steeped in history, having a wealth of ring forts, high crosses, and other ancient monuments. Dingle Oceanworld, an aquarium near Dingle Harbor, is also worth a visit, as the aquarium features creatures of the deep and houses relics of the Spanish Armada.

Photo R. Sumpter

Dingle peninsula—a wide variety of surf, from points to beach breaks. It's a narrow spit of land so it can be offshore on one side and onshore on the other, big on one side and small on the other side. Very uncrowded, not many surfers, pretty much an in-the-middle-of-nowhere feeling, but has excellent waves, some of the best waves in Europe.

John Sumpter,
1997 Ligger Bay Surfing Champion

Photo R. Sumpter

Rights	Lefts	R.Point	Beachbreak	N Swell	SW Swell	

Break: Point, reef, and beach breaks
Skill Level: Beginner to expert
Commitment: 5–10
Best Boards: Shortboard, longboard
Lifeguard: None
Hazards: Dangerous rip currents, shallow sand bottom. Rocky beaches, bays, and points create a variety of dangers when entering the lineup and wiping out. Numerous seals can cause some quick heartbeats in the water.

Currency: Euro.
Going There: No visa is required by U.S., British, Australian, Canadian, Japanese, and other EU citizens. All others require a visa. Vaccinations required—check with your doctor, health clinic, and embassy for up-to-date info.
Where to Stay: Doyles Townhouse Dingle, +353 (0) 66 51174. Aisling House, Castle Gregory, +353 (0) 66 39134. Guest House Dingle, +353 (0) 66 59882.

Skellig Hotel Sea View, +353 (0) 66 51144, or fax +353 (0) 66 51501. Alpine Guest House, +353 (0) 66 51250, or fax +353 (0) 66 51966. Anchor Caravan Park, +353 (0) 66 39157.
Finding the Break: Easy to find. From Dublin airport head for the southwest coast and the county of Kerry. The slender Dingle peninsula, the northernmost arm of Kerry, stretches into the sea. From the Ring of Kerry, the Dingle is reached by continuing on the N70 to Castlemaine, and then heading to Annascaul on the R561 that passes Inch Beach. From here all the surf spots are found with ease.
Surf School: Jamie Knox Surfing School, +353 (0) 66 39411.
Keep in Mind: No crowds and great scenery.

Months	JF	MA	MJ	JA	SO	ND
Average Swell (feet)	7	5	2	1	2	6
Air Temp (C/F)	6/44	10/50	16/61	21/71	18/66	10/50
Water Temp (C/F)	8/46	9/48	11/52	17/63	13/56	9/48
Wetsuit	full	full	full	spring	full	full
Average Sunshine p/d (hours)	2	4–5	4–5	7	4–5	2
Average Rain p/m (inches)	3	2	2	1	2	3
Average Surfable Days p/m	20	17	16	12	18	22

39. CRANTOCK
Cornwall, Southwest England

Simply one of the best and fastest waves in Cornwall, this outrageous left at low tide packs a barrel, and long walls of water comb in beside the river mouth. The right is a gun-ho, smack-down-the-line fast, haul-ass affair, westward as far as you can go.

Situated on the north Cornwall coast 1 mile south of Fistral Beach, Newquay (Spot 40) and 2 miles north of Perranporth (Spot 44) are the many great beach breaks of Crantock and the Gannel River, flanked west and east by the Pentire headland. Crantock becomes a bay at low tide and is sheltered from most of the prevailing wind directions. It's a fickle break, but the beauty of Crantock is choice. The first and most famous wave is the left-hand river-mouth beach break, which draws in a swell up the Gannel River, providing the perfect topography to make waves as if from a machine. The breaking waves run along the edge of the beach and peel off fast to rip on. This is the ultimate surf break in the area, almost as if it was built to fit everyone's idea of the classic setup. Here, it's best in September to November.

At high tide in all swell directions—west, northwest, north—the headland peak in front of the river-mouth right-hander is a classic full-faced performance wave. When there's a big swell running, a right-hander forms against the river flow. Almost like a "stopper" wave, this right trough peak races across the bay, peeling off at speed with a soft open face and plenty of green water under the curl line. It's a hotdog wave for longboards. This connects the beach break in the middle of the beach with a central peak, outer bank peak, and Kiddies Corner, making Crantock a superior mix of fun to challenging surf when the swell's up.

The paddle out is easy in the fast-flowing river, and the takeoff is reached in a few strokes. Crantock is lifeguarded in the summer months and has waves to suit all surfing grades, depending on the conditions—ideal for the expert when it's over 6 feet.

Crantock's beach and sand dunes cover a 1-square-mile area and are of special natural beauty. They are surrounded by green rolling hills and bounded on the east by the Gannel River, where a small passenger ferry joins to Pentire at Newquay.

The parish of Crantock is in the deanery of Pydar; St. Carantacus founded it in the fifth century. The son of a Welsh chieftain, he went to Ireland where he met St. Patrick, and they studied together. They went their separate ways and St. Carantacus came to Cornwall, to rest in the Gannel. The village is mentioned in the Domesday Book of 1086.

Photo R. Sumpter

Crantock has a very good selection of waves. . . . The farther you go down the beach, the bigger the surf gets. There's a very good right-hander at the end, only really surfable at low to midtide—except in dry periods, when high tide can be perfect.

John Sumpter,
1997 Ligger Bay Surfing Champion

Photo R. Sumpter

| Rights | Lefts | R.Point | Peak | N Swell | |

Break: Beach break, left and right river-mouth break

Skill Level: Beginner to expert

Commitment: 2–10

Best Boards: Longboard, shortboard

Lifeguard: In season

Hazards: River rips and currents at high tide make the takeoff tricky and, on big days, dangerous. Most low tide waves under chest high peel sweetly, but for waves larger than this, unexpected sections close-out heavily.

Currency: Pound sterling.

Going There: No visa is required by U.S., Australian, Canadian, Japanese, and EU citizens. No vaccinations required, except yellow fever if you're coming from an infected area. Check with your doctor, health clinic, and embassy for up-to-date information.

Where to Stay: Crantock Beach Holiday Park, +44 (0) 1 637 831 005. Pennaville House, +44 (0) 1 637 830 302.

Finding the Break: From Newquay go west on the A3075 for 2 miles, turn right at the sign for Crantock. Park at the beach car park (fee June to October) and walk up the dunes to the waves.

Keep in Mind: Crowded in July and August.

Months	JF	MA	MJ	JA	SO	ND
Average Swell (feet)	4	4	3	2	3	4–5
Air Temp (C/F)	6/44	10/50	16/61	21/71	18/66	10/50
Water Temp (C/F)	8/46	9/48	11/52	17/63	13/56	9/48
Wetsuit	full	full	full	shorty	spring	full
Average Sunshine p/d (hours)	2	4–5	4–5	7	4–5	2
Average Rain p/m (inches)	2	2	1	1	2	2
Average Surfable Days p/m	10	11	8	7	12	14

40. FISTRAL BEACH

Newquay, Cornwall, Southwest England

Crisp clean lines, blue sky, and head-high waves grind in on a new swell that increases with a light offshore wind. The swell stacks up five to a set behind the first break, where a right-hander runs off fresh low-tide sandbars that are the special shortboard feature of Fistral. It's a typical pumping swell after a long flat spell, and it's now a hooting sight. The peak loops and buries its hook in dry sand, forming perfect lefts and rights of 50 yards on this low tide, and other peaks along the beach all start to happen. By half tide it's become a longboard wave; by high tide, a fun soft wave.

Fistral Beach, Britain's most famous surf spot, is situated 60 miles southwest of the city of Plymouth and 12 miles north of Truro, Cornwall's capital and cathedral city. It regularly hosts the Association of Surfing Professionals leg of the European circuit—along with Hossegor (Spot 53) in France—and the UK National Championships have been held here since 1966. Fistral's surf is as dependable as any in Cornwall, and the town of Newquay has good facilities.

Because its white sand beaches face northwest, it picks up any summer Atlantic swells available, making it much less likely to be flat in summer, and very consistent in winter. In fact, there are many winter days that can be too big to surf—days when the waves are blown out or are rough stormy whiteouts driven by gales.

Newquay has five beaches: Fistral on the western side of Newquay Bay, and Towan, Great Western, Tolcarne, and Lusty Glaze on the eastern side. These are sheltered from the prevailing southwest winter gales and, although near totally flat in summer, provide good beach waves through the Newquay Bay area from autumn through spring.

There are four key breaks at Fistral. Starting from east to west, the Cribber is a big-wave spot that I first surfed in 1965; it's the UK's number one big-wave spot, breaking at 20 to 25 feet. This is the only wave in the UK that starts to compare with the big waves of Hawaii's Waimea Bay (Spots 14 and 15) or Mavericks in California (Spot 29). Next is Little Fistral, a small cove within Fistral Bay that only becomes visible at low tide. Beside the headland, this is a classic left opposite the old lifeboat house. Little Fistral is the sought-after wave in the winter months, when it needs a 6-to-8-foot west swell. The wave peels off a hollow takeoff area and winds down to the corner of the beach cove. The main break at north Fistral is split into two breaks, a consistent right from a channel rip, and a left bank with lefts and rights on both sides, peeling to the middle of the beach. This is a fun wave in most conditions, ideal for longboarders, shortboarders, and bodyboarders on various days. South Fistral has a pumping left off the corner cliff, which has a long wall and powering hook. There are excellent middle sandbanks, sheltered in the corner from the prevailing southwest winds. Fistral is offshore in south to southeast wind, and is ideal for everyone from beginners to experts.

Newquay's seafaring life dates back to the nineteenth century, when fishermen braved the mountainous seas. The town's coat of arms includes four pilchards, with the Cornish-language motto *Ro-an-mor,* meaning "gift from the sea." Groups of men called "huers" would keep watch from the top of the cliffs and alert the fishermen when they saw the vast shoals of pilchards entering the bay. Surfers do the same spotting today—not in search of pilchards, however, but rather of the bay's best surf.

The town of Fistral is quite friendly with the local surf crowd, as displayed in 1997 when the mayor led a parade of surfers though the center of town to celebrate the beginning of the National Marine celebrations.

Photo R. Sumpter

Fistral . . . [it's] the type of wave you could possibly surf from giant storm surf to 1 foot on the beach and everything in the middle. I've got really good barrels and I've seen some really good surfing.

Andy Irons,
2002–2003 World Surfing Champion

Photo J. Sumpter

Peak	Beachbreak	N Swell	

Break: Beach break

Skill Level: Beginner to expert

Commitment: 2–10

Best Boards: Longboard, shortboard

Lifeguard: In season

Hazards: Heavy low-tide waves and danger near the rocks.

Currency: Pound sterling.

Going There: No visa is required by U.S., Australia, Canadian, Japanese, and EU citizens. No vaccinations required, except yellow fever if you're coming from an infected area. Check with your doctor, health clinic, and embassy for up-to-date information.

Where to Stay: Fistral Beach Hotel Sea View, +44 (0) 1637 874 277. Westward Ho Hotel, +44 (0) 1637 873 069. Surf Beach Hotel, +44 (0) 1637 874 340. Tremont Hotel Pentire, +44 (0) 1637 872 984. Fistral Backpackers, +44 (0) 1637 852 100. Harvey Court Backpackers, +44 (0) 1637 875 775. Newquay Surf Reef Lodge, +44 (0) 1637 878 088. Newquay Surf Lodge Backpackers, +44 (0) 1637 859 700. Newquay Holiday Park, +44 (0) 1637 871 111. Hendra Paul Farm, +44 (0) 1637 874 695. Croftlea Holiday Park, +44 (0) 1637 852 505. Hendra Holidays, Newquay, +44 (0) 1637 875 778, or fax +44 (0) 1637 879 017.

Finding the Break: From the Newquay airport turn right, travel 2 miles, and turn right onto A3059. Continue for 5 miles and follow signs to Fistral Beach from Newquay center. Park at the beach.

Keep in Mind: Crowded June to September.

For More Information: Newquay Tourism Office, +44 (0) 1726 223 300 or +44 (0) 1637 854 020.

Months	JF	MA	MJ	JA	SO	ND
Average Swell (feet)	6	5	4	2–3	3	4–5
Air Temp (C/F)	6/44	10/50	16/61	21/71	18/66	10/50
Water Temp (C/F)	8/46	9/48	11/52	17/63	13/56	9/48
Wetsuit	full	full	full	shorty	spring	full
Average Sunshine p/d (hours)	2	4–5	4–5	7	4–5	2
Average Rain p/m (inches)	2	2	1	1	2	2
Average Surfable Days p/m	15	12	11	8	16	18

41. GWITHIAN
Cornwall, Southwest England

This is a wave that breaks farther and farther out on an outgoing tide, each set getting bigger and bigger the farther you go. By the time you've caught three waves, you're half a mile out and getting locked in deeper. The green wall starts thin, then thickens toward the inside section before either blowing out or peeling off forever, peeling down smaller and smaller toward shore. On a high tide the waves are a shore dump. But by half tide the bay takes shape and is filled with line after line of perfect corduroy, a stoking sight.

Situated 8 miles south of Fistral Beach, Newquay (Spot 40), and 3 miles north of Porthmere, St. Ives (Spot 46), is the classic surf break of Gwithian, a left-hand peak much prized in the center of a small bay called St. Ives Bay. There are several breaks close to the rim of the coast, the best of which is Gwithian. Also considered a beauty spot and designated a wildlife protection area, its left-hand big takeoff peak and hooking curl lines are amazing.

This sweeping, bowling left-hander is a muscleman challenge when the swell's up over 8 feet. From 6 feet plus to double overhead, it's quite a unique site. The left-hander starts working as swell lines nearly 0.5 mile out in the bay hit the main sandbanks, forming a beautiful triangular-shaped wave. The open face of the wave allows the left-hander to break evenly and peel with plenty of scope to maneuver on a shortboard. There are gullies under the water leading from the river mouth out to sea, which have carved a groove—or rather a snaking S-shaped channel—into the sandbars, forming the perfect takeoff area with in-teresting sections all the way to the beach. Gwithian is good for longboarders on smaller days of 2 to 4 feet, although it's fickle by nature, requiring a solid southwest groundswell of 4 feet or bigger and a light southerly wind to make it great. If you're lucky enough to arrive on a new swell that's increasing from a local low-pressure system, coupled with a long-distance Mid-Atlantic swell, then the conditions will simply be magic.

From the dunes parking area, the marram grass rolls across to a steep 30-foot drop. Paths track down to the beach. From here the world is your oyster. There are good waves on the right side of the beach as well, toward the Godrevy lighthouse. These waves show up at low tide, breaking off sandbanks with short hollow peaks. Some rocky platform areas, opposite the lighthouse, can pack a punch, especially the rocky outcrops producing short tricky waves like a shallow reef break. Gwithian is ideal for the beginner when it's small, and excellent for the intermediate to expert when it's pumping at 6 feet plus.

Gwithian is a small village lying almost at sea level between Hayle and Portreath. Hayle river mouth is a substantial inlet and port where huge sand dunes back onto the shore of St. Ives Bay, about 3 miles long and 1.5 miles wide. They make up the second largest sand dune system in Cornwall, and are one of the largest to be found in the United Kingdom. A right-hander peels off the right side of Hayle river mouth at the sandbar entrance, where high tide on a big swell can offer a perfect wave.

Photo R. Sumpter

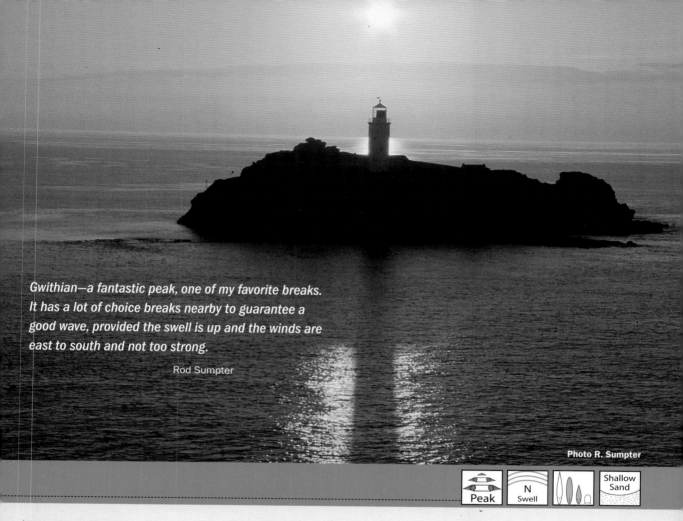

Gwithian—a fantastic peak, one of my favorite breaks. It has a lot of choice breaks nearby to guarantee a good wave, provided the swell is up and the winds are east to south and not too strong.

Rod Sumpter

Photo R. Sumpter

	Peak	N Swell		Shallow Sand

Break: Beach break
Skill Level: Beginner to expert
Commitment: 2–10
Best Boards: Longboard, shortboard
Lifeguard: In season
Hazards: Rip currents from the river after heavy rain; murky water

Currency: Pound sterling.
Going There: No visa is required by U.S., Australia, Canadian, Japanese and EU citizens. No vaccinations required, except yellow fever if coming from an infected area. Check with your doctor, health clinic, and embassy for up-to-date info.

Where to Stay: Beachside Holiday Park, +44 (0) 1736 753 080. Riviere Sands Holiday Park, +44 (0) 1736 752 132. Sandbank Holidays, +44 (0) 1736 752 594. Tom's Self-Catering Holidays, +44 (0) 1736 753 010. St. Ives Bay Holiday Park, +44 (0) 1736 752 274.

Finding the Break: From the Newquay airport, turn right leaving the airport, and travel 2 miles. Turn left onto the A3059 and continue 3 miles to the A30. Head south, following signs for Redruth-Penzance, and turn off at Hayle. Take the Gwithian B3301 road to the beach parking area.

Keep in Mind: Crowds in July and August.

Months	JF	MA	MJ	JA	SO	ND
Average Swell (feet)	6	5	3	1	2–3	4–5
Air Temp (C/F)	6/44	10/50	16/61	21/71	18/66	10/50
Water Temp (C/F)	8/46	9/48	11/52	17/63	13/56	9/48
Wetsuit	full	full	full	spring	spring	full
Average Sunshine p/d (hours)	2	4–5	4–5	7	4–5	2
Average Rain p/m (inches)	2	2	1	1	2	2
Average Surfable Days p/m	15	12	11	8	16	18

42. MILLOCK
Cornwall, Southwest England

Famous for its challenging and demanding takeoffs and walls, which are thick and powerful, Millock is a fast, down-the-line type of wave. There are sections that wall fast and tubey, having a high degree of fast performance barrels for the shortboard only. The groundswell separates into a mighty, rough-towering, fast-forming A-frame peak at take-off, or as an inside takeoff area that thunders a wave wall close to the rock point. The closer to shore, the better, because the sculpted left-hand tubes seem to be picture perfect. They become more lethal closer to the bone-breaking granite rocks.

Situated 7 miles south of Bude and 40 miles north of the city of Plymouth is the small hamlet of Millock, which has one of the best left-hand reef breaks in Cornwall. Millock can hold waves up to 12 feet, and it feels like a big wave with all the haunting, rugged appearance of storm-blown surf. It never seems to be friendly and nice. Instead it's aggressive and hard as boots when you wipe out. And it's as treacherous as any when it comes to navigating a way from the parking lot out through a pebble beach with 5-foot-tall granite clumps of rock barring your entrance. Then caves and gullies surged by the heavy shorebreak stand ready to trap or snap a leg. The best height here at Millock

is at 6 to 8 feet on a new swell with lulls. This is the ultimate left when conditions are right.

The tiny hamlet of Millock is opposite the surf with just a dozen houses, one post office, and very little parking. The nearest comfortable parking is from the top of the towering cliff above Millock. From here you can see the waves peeling off beautifully—a dream wave from 200 feet up, looking like an easy surf. But beware, it's not easy.

Although it's somewhat fickle, Millock does break quite often. It needs a big southwesterly swell and wind to turn southerly or southeast, helping to line up ace waves. From the outer reef that holds up and feathers to the takeoff, the steep walling drop all the way through several middle sections to a grinding shorebreak are very fast. The wave keeps up the pressure to stay in front of the curl in order to make it, or to kick out. This is a classic ride of 500 yards or more on a good day. Millock is best in spring and autumn and is a classic break ideal for the expert to advanced surfer.

Because Millock can be fickle, other beaches in the area worth mentioning are Widemouth, Crookletts, and Summerleaze. If Millock is blown out, you might get a wave at one of these three nearby beaches. None has the thrill of surfing Millock, but are all certainly worth a look.

Photo R. Sumpter

It could be the best left-hander in Cornwall. It's quite a heavy wave that only breaks when it gets quite big so it starts to work when most other beaches are beginning to get closed out, too big.

John Sumpter,
1997 Ligger Bay Surfing Champion

Photo R. Sumpter

| L.Point | NW Swell | | Shallow Reef |

Break: Left-hand reef break

Skill Level: Expert

Commitment: 7–10

Best Boards: Shortboard

Lifeguard: None

Hazards: Below the 100-foot cliffs, the pebble beach of gray stones is hard to walk on. Blocks of rocky slabs guard the sea, ledges of boulders 4 feet high with narrow gaps, and a savage shore dumping waves make the get-out very hard. Rips pull you left into the breaking wave and sneaker sets almost close out in the channel. The bigger the swell the harder it gets.

Currency: Pound sterling.

Going There: No visa is required by U.S., British, Australian, Canadian, Japanese, and other EU citizens. No vaccinations required, except yellow fever if you're coming from an infected area. Check with your doctor, health clinic, and embassy for up-to-date info.

Where to Stay: Bay View Inn, Widemouth, +44 (0) 1288 361 273. Waverly Bungalows, +44 (0) 1288 361 673. West Wooley Barns, +44 (0) 1288 331 202. Old Lifeboat House, +44 (0) 1288 354 542. Whins Chalet, +44 20 8994 8754. Bude Meadows Campsite, wendy@budemeadows.com.

Finding the Break: From the Exeter airport take the M5 to Exeter, then the A30 to the Okehampton bypass. Turn off for Bude on the A3079 and follow signs to Widemouth. Take the coast road at Widemouth Beach and go west for 2 miles to Millock. (Note the narrow one-way roads and difficult parking in summer.)

Keep in Mind: Some crowds when the surf's up.

Months	JF	MA	MJ	JA	SO	ND
Average Swell (feet)	6	3–4	2	1	2	5–6
Air Temp (C/F)	6/44	10/50	16/61	21/71	18/66	10/50
Water Temp (C/F)	8/46	9/48	11/52	17/63	13/56	9/48
Wetsuit	full	full	full	shorty	spring	full
Average Sunshine p/d (hours)	2	2	1	1	2	2
Average Rain p/m (inches)	2	2	1	1	2	2
Average Surfable Days p/m	10	5	4	1	1	8

43. PENHALE CORNER
Cornwall, Southwest England

This is a wave that pitches out a tube right from the takeoff and hollows all the way in through to the inside. It's one of the most famous breaks in the southwest of England.

The fabulous beach break of Penhale Corner is situated 3 miles south of Fistral Beach, Newquay (Spot 40), and 10 miles north of Truro, the cathedral city and capital of Cornwall. At low tide this beach is 500 yards wide and 2 miles long. The corner wave beside the cliff is the sought-after wave in the area. It's a right peak to a long fast wall and plenty of sections, some barrels, and some open-face performance sections to a shorebreak. At high tide the beach is 50 yards wide to the foot of huge sand dunes, rising as high as 100 feet and rolling inland for 0.5 mile. The beach, with its many left and right peaks, is a magnificent sight, set next to Perranporth Beach, a total of 3 miles of white sand and some of the largest dunes in Europe.

There are several named breaks from which to choose, starting from the west with Snaps, a nice left at half tide on a 6-foot-plus swell. Then there's the Pit, a left and right straight out front from the gun range signpost. The Pit picks up most swells, and, consistent in all conditions, it's the most popular spot here. Army Camp, a series of lagoon-shaped sandbars in the beach, forms excellent surf setups and a whole host of ace surf conditions, including Penhale, where the army has jurisdiction over the land above the high-tide mark (but not the sea). This is also where one of

The Cornish legend tells how some local pagan Irish captured St. Piran. Jealous of his miraculous healing powers, they tied a millstone around his neck and threw him off a cliff and into the sea during a storm. As Piran hit the water, the millstone bobbed to the surface like a cork, the storm abated, and he was saved. Such magical things happen only in legends! Piran landed at Perran Beach, to which he gave his name, and built a small chapel on Penhale sands. He lived there for many years as a hermit working miracles for the local people. He is the patron saint of Cornwall.

Cornwall's best right-hand sand points can be found. Here also, millions of freshwater shells were recently found, providing evidence that freshwater lakes existed here for thousands of years before the emergence of the present coastline. A must-surf spot for any surfer, Penhale Corner is ideal for beginners in small surf conditions, and great for intermediate to expert surfers if it's 3 to 5 feet or bigger. The surf becomes dangerous at over 10 feet.

Photo R. Sumpter

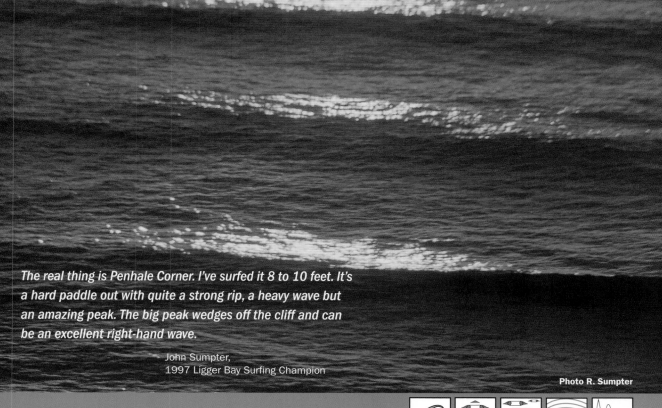

The real thing is Penhale Corner. I've surfed it 8 to 10 feet. It's a hard paddle out with quite a strong rip, a heavy wave but an amazing peak. The big peak wedges off the cliff and can be an excellent right-hand wave.

John Sumpter,
1997 Ligger Bay Surfing Champion

Photo R. Sumpter

 Rights Peak Beachbreak N Swell

Break: Beach break
Skill Level: Intermediate to expert
Commitment: 4–10
Best Boards: Shortboard
Lifeguard: None
Hazards: Wedge waves peak and the bounce off the cliff makes a triangle wave hammer the inside. Paddling out in anything over head-high is heavy going. Steep shorebreak at high tide.
Currency: Pound sterling.

Going There: No visa is required by U.S., British, Australian, Canadian, Japanese, and other EU citizens. No vaccinations required, except yellow fever if you're coming from an infected area. Check with your doctor, health clinic, and embassy for up-to-date info.
Where to Stay: Perran Sands Holiday Campsite, +44 (0) 1872 573 241. Atlantic House Sea View, +44 (0) 1872 572 259. Ponsmere Hotel, +44 (0) 1872 572 225. Haven Holiday, +44 (0) 1872 573 551. Holywell Bay Holiday Park, Newquay, +44 (0) 1870 220 4646. Peranporth Youth Hostel, Droskyn Point, +44 (0) 1872 573 812. The Meadow Caravan Park, Holywell, +44 (0) 1872 572 752.

Finding the Break: From the Newquay airport turn right, leaving the airport, and travel 2 miles. Turn left onto the A3059 and continue 3 miles to the A30. Head south, following signs for Redruth-Penzance. Turn off at the Perranporth signs; when you see Perran Sands Holiday Center, 1 mile before Perranporth, turn right into the center, drive past the main office, and park at the top of the hill overlooking the beach dunes. Walk from here to the sea, heading right (north) to the end of the beach for Penhale.
Keep in Mind: Rarely crowded.

Months	JF	MA	MJ	JA	SO	ND
Average Swell (feet)	6	5	3	1–2	3	4–5
Air Temp (C/F)	6/44	10/50	16/61	21/71	18/66	10/50
Water Temp (C/F)	8/46	9/48	11/52	17/63	13/56	9/48
Wetsuit	full	full	full	shorty	spring	full
Average Sunshine p/d (hours)	2	4–5	4–5	7	4–5	2
Average Rain p/m (inches)	2	2	1	1	2	2
Average Surfable Days p/m	15	12	11	8	16	18

44. PERRANPORTH
Cornwall, Southwest England

Escaping from the first set wave, a left-wedging peak, there's time to get the third wave in the set. It's come in from "enticers" under the shadow of the cliff wall, and meets a bounce swell off Droskyn rocks. You turn, dig in the tail, and free-fall down the wedgy wave until gravity stops pulling. You then must turn left before the powerful washing-machine curl pulls you in and cleans you up.

Situated 5 miles west of Fistral Beach, Newquay (Spot 40), and 10 miles north of Truro, the capital of Cornwall, is the superb white beach of Perranporth, 3 miles long with many named breaks. Within Perranporth there are three breaks of quality. Droskyn Corner is the first, with a left-hand barrel wedge beach break beside the cliff, working best at low to half tide, and having a short right into the rip. Then there's Chapel Rock, a left and right peak off sandbars in front of a 60-foot freestanding rock in the middle of the beach. This is the favorite left on a west swell, with a steep, barreling, hooking takeoff that can run for 300 to 500 yards on a good day. It can be the perfect left, with a long wall,

ideal for roundhouse cutbacks and long nose rides. This is often the best wave on the beach. And finally there's Flat Rocks, a right-hand wave from the edge of the hill in the middle of the beach, which separates Perran Sands from Perranporth. This wave is very hollow at low tide and builds on the incoming high tide into a performance wave for longboards and shortboards when it's over 4 feet. Perranporth is a must-surf spot for beginner to expert shortboarders and longboarders alike, depending on conditions.

This seasonal seaside resort has surf almost year-round, with excellent surfing facilities in summer and a population that has seen a long history of wave riding. Bob Head and I rode the first Malibu longboards here in 1964 and 1965. Before the Malibu longboards arrived, surfing was performed by lying down on three-ply boards, 4 to 5 feet long, with a curved front. These bodyboards have been used since 1908. But stand-up surfing really began about 1937 with swimmers like Pip Staffieri riding hollow ply boards with a keel.

Photo R. Sumpter

Perranporth's possibly my favorite break—it's my home break. There are so many peaks you can go to. The Chapel Rock is very good. It catches most of the swell and is very different from low to high tide. Low to mid-tide is best for barrels, and high tide for performance surfing.

John Sumpter,
1997 Ligger Bay Surfing Champion

Photo R. Sumpter

Peak	Beachbreak	N Swell		Shallow Sand

Break: Beach break
Skill Level: Beginner to expert
Commitment: 2–10
Best Boards: Longboard, shortboard
Lifeguard: In season
Hazards: Sneaker-set waves close out the best waves at three-quarter high tide. Big, grinding, low-tide barrels. Going right into the Droskyn Bay and around the cliffs at high tide can and does trap novice surfers who then need to be rescued by helicopter.

Currency: Pound sterling.
Going There: No visa is required by U.S., Australian, Canadian, Japanese, and EU citizens. No vaccinations required, except yellow fever if you're coming from an infected area. Check with your doctor, health clinic, and embassy for up-to-date info.

Where to Stay: Atlantic House Sea View, +44 (0) 1872 572 259. Ponsmere Hotel, +44 (0) 1872 572 225. Haven Holiday, +44 (0) 1872 573 551. Tregundy Farm House, +44 (0) 1872 570 1863. Perranporth Youth Hostel, Droskyn Point, +44 (0) 1872 573 812.

Finding the Break: From the Newquay airport turn right, leaving the airport, and travel 2 miles. Turn left onto the A3059 and continue 3 miles to the A30. Head south, following signs for Redruth-Penzance. Turn off at the Perranporth signs and park at the beach.

Keep in Mind: Crowded in July and August.

Months	JF	MA	MJ	JA	SO	ND
Average Swell (feet)	6	5	4	2–3	3	4–5
Air Temp (C/F)	6/44	10/50	16/61	21/71	18/66	10/50
Water Temp (C/F)	8/46	9/48	11/52	17/63	13/56	9/48
Wetsuit	full	full	full	shorty	spring	full
Average Sunshine p/d (hours)	2	4–5	4–5	7	4–5	2
Average Rain p/m (inches)	2	2	1	1	2	2
Average Surfable Days p/m	15	12	11	8	16	18

45. PORTHLEVEN
Cornwall, Southwest England

Porthleven is not for the fainthearted. It's a demanding wave—steep, heavy, and hollow—that breaks shallow over flat rock ledges. This steep peak is at the entrance to Porthleven Harbor near rocks that make for hairy positioning. How deep can you go and still make the drop, then carve around the barrel or through it?

Situated on the south coast of Cornwall in the curve of Mounts Bay, 3 miles west of Helston and 4 miles east of Praa Sands, is Britain's southernmost fishing village of Porthleven, and one of Cornwall's best surfing locations. This right-hand reef of sloping rocks is the perfect steep drop and barrel for surfers looking to drop in and carve. There is also a harbor wall peak named the Pier, with a quality left and right break off outcrops of rock, forming barrels here on most swells.

In the winter the predominant swell and most storm systems come up from the Bay of Biscay, giving a south swell just right for Porthleven. But if the waves are too big, they can get blown out hard. In summer the swell is more northwest from the central Mid-Atlantic, and this favors the north coast of Cornwall, wrapping only a little swell around to the south coast, and to Porthleven only on occasion. Possibly the best time for good swells along the south coast and Porthleven is during either springtime, around April and May, or in the autumn in September and October.

Porthleven is best at three-quarter to high tide, and holds waves from 2 to 12 feet. At low tide it's a suck-out barrel on dry rocks, but if the waves are over 6 feet, it peaks on a second reef farther out. In all, it's a handful of pumping waves at 6 to 8 feet for the expert surfer.

In the deanery of Kerrier, the name *Porthleven* is a compound of the words *porth* and *elvan*. *Porth* is Cornish for "port." Elvan is the name of the Celtic saint who came to these shores in the fifth century. Elvan's port is a picturesque beauty spot sitting tightly against the cliffs along the south coast of Cornwall.

The beach of Porthleven is a shingle shorebreak and connects to Loe Pool, a beach break with a large freshwater lake separated from the sea by a sandbar. Legend says that King Arthur's sword Excalibur lies at the bottom of the lake. The next break going east is Gunwallow, where a stream cuts a path across the beach and into the shorebreak, forming a little left sand point where fast hollow waves peel off with power. This is a fairly consistent beach break when there's a south swell.

West of Porthleven is Praa Sands, a 3-mile-long beach facing southwest, with good waves the entire length. The western end is more sheltered, out of the predominant west winds.

Photo R. Sumpter

Porthleven is a very sucky right-hand reef break, which, when it's working, is Britain's best wave.

John Sumpter,
1998 Ligger Bay Surfing Champion

Photo R. Sumpter

R.Point	Peak	S Swell		Shallow Reef

Break: Right-hand reef break
Skill Level: Expert
Commitment: 6–10
Best Boards: Shortboard
Lifeguard: None
Hazards: The high cliff path to the harbor entrance with rocky outcrops, shallow rocks and ledges make this a rock-hopping trip to the surf. It does not get any easier in the water. Steep takeoffs and walling waves close to rocks.

Currency: Pound sterling.
Going There: No visa is required by U.S., Australian, Canadian, Japanese, and EU citizens. No vaccinations required, except yellow fever if you're coming from an infected area. Check with your doctor, health clinic, and embassy for up-to-date info.
Where to Stay: Willavean, +44 (0) 1326 573 732. The Gables, +44 (0) 1326 561 049. Poldown Caravanning and

Camping, +44 (0) 1326 5745. Praa Sands camping, +44 (0) 1736 763 222. Lower Pentreath Farm, Praa Sands, +44 (0) 1736 763 221. Praa Sands Holiday Village, Praa Sands, +44 (0) 1736 762 201. Prussia Cove Caravan & Camping, +44 (0) 1736 762 488. Boscreage Caravan Park, Ashton, +44 (0) 1736 762 231 or +44 (0) 1736 763 398.

Finding the Break: From the Newquay airport turn right and travel 2 miles. Turn left onto the A3059 and continue 3 miles to the A30. Head south, following signs for Redruth-Penzance, and turn off at Camborne. Follow signs for Helston, then Porthleven, and park at the harbor or in the west side of town past the Ship Inn, where there is some parking.

Keep in Mind: Crowded when the surf's up.

Months	JF	MA	MJ	JA	SO	ND
Average Swell (feet)	6	5	3	1	2	3-4
Air Temp (C/F)	6/44	10/50	16/61	21/71	18/66	10/50
Water Temp (C/F)	8/46	9/48	11/52	17/63	13/56	9/48
Wetsuit	full	full	full	shorty	spring	full
Average Sunshine p/d (hours)	2	4-5	4-5	7	4-5	2
Average Rain p/m (inches)	2	2	1	1	2	2
Average Surfable Days p/m	10	8	5	3	6	7

46. PORTHMERE BEACH

St. Ives, Cornwall, Southwest England

The barrel looms. You send out an arm and pull into the tube. The wave cascades all around and you punch out of the pocket, smothered in foam. St. Ives is where the clear waters of the Gulf Stream touch the white sandy beaches of southwest England, making the coast look as tropical as the beaches in Tahiti. Add a low tide and the surf here is top-to-bottom hollow, pitching out some heavy tubes. Early-summer swells make this an ace spot.

Situated 10 miles north of Penzance and 12 miles east of Lands End, Porthmere Beach, St. Ives, is one of Cornwall's best surf spots and finest beaches. There are three key breaks here. Starting from the east end, you'll find a right-hand beach break in front of a rock hill known as St. Ives Headland, or the Island. This shallow sand-bottomed right-hander is the ultimate Cornish beach break, pumping in barrels as soon as the swell is 4 feet. This can be the best right-hander in all Cornwall.

The next break in line is between the Clodgy Point channel and the outcrop of rocks dominating the left side of the bay called Gowna Rock. Even in onshore conditions, the mushy peak here can be ace, and the wave holds an open face ideal for longboarders and bodyboarders who surf this stretch of the beach. If it's a more northerly swell, the break is a right; if it's a southwest swell, it's mostly a left.

Clodgy Point, to the far west of the beach, is the third break along Porthmere Beach. On big spring low tides, this break is a fantastic left on a day with a north swell and light southerly winds. Beginners do best at the west end of the beach where the waves are softer. The St. Ives Harbor breakwater has good lefts when Porthmere Beach is closed out or has a big swell running. Porthmere is ideal for all grades of surfers when the conditions are right, and classic for the expert when it's perfect.

For those who need a break from the surf, Porthmere Beach has much more going for it than just waves. Art galleries abound, including the famous Tate Gallery at Porthmere Beach, which overlooks a peaking left and right in the middle of the beach. The quaint Cornish fishing village of St. Ives has a lot of waves and even more charm for those lucky enough to spend time here. It's long been home of artists, who flock to the area because of its clear, soft light and picture-postcard conditions.

Photo R. Sumpter

When there's a huge west swell and Porthmere is completely closed out, St. Ives breakwater will be great. That big swell wraps around from Porthmere and it just peels and peels.... I rate Porthmere as the number one surf spot in Britain.

Rob Tanner, local surfer

Photo R. Sumpter

Peak	Beachbreak	N Swell	

Break: Beach break and left-hand breakwater

Skill Level: Beginner to expert

Commitment: 1–10

Best Boards: Longboard, shortboard

Lifeguard: In season

Hazards: Shallow sand bottom, rip currents. Waves hit hard at low tide and they backwash and shore dump at high tide.

Currency: Pound sterling.

Going There: No visa is required by U.S., Australian, Canadian, Japanese, and EU citizens. No vaccinations required, except yellow fever if you're coming from an infected area. Check with your doctor, health clinic, and embassy for up-to-date info.

Where to Stay: Atlantic Hotel, +44 (0) 1736 796 177. Belays Croft Hotel, +44 (0) 1736 796 304. Channings Hotel, +44 (0) 1736 799 500. Chy An Creet, +44 (0) 1736 796 559 or +44 (0) 1736 796 304. St. Ives Backpackers, +44 (0) 1736 799 444. Harleguins, +44 (0) 1736 798 511. Premier Apartments, +44 (0) 1736 798 798. Tregenna Farmhouse, +44 (0) 1736 795 588.

Finding the Break: From the Newquay airport turn right, leaving the airport, and travel 2 miles. Turn left onto the A3059 and continue 4 miles. Turn right onto the A39, go 2 miles, and join the A30 going west toward Penzance. Travel 12 miles, turn off at St. Ives, and follow signs to Porthmere Beach. (Note the narrow streets.) Park at the beach.

Keep in Mind: Summer crowds when the surf's up.

Months	JF	MA	MJ	JA	SO	ND
Average Swell (feet)	5	4	3	1–2	3	4
Air Temp (C/F)	6/44	10/50	16/61	21/71	18/66	10/50
Water Temp (C/F)	8/46	9/48	11/52	17/63	13/56	9/48
Wetsuit	full	full	full	shorty	spring	full
Average Sunshine p/d (hours)	2	4–5	4–5	7	4–5	2
Average Rain p/m (inches)	2	2	1	1	2	2
Average Surfable Days p/m	12	10	9	6	16	18

47. SECRETS

St. Ouens Beach, Jersey, Channel Islands

It's high tide and the waves peel off. The conditions are just right as a hotdog performance wave for longboards. At low tide the waves become supertubes that vary between fast hairy closeouts and makable barrels ideal for shortboards.

Situated 20 miles west of northern France and 100 miles south of England are five islands: Sark, Alderney, Guernsey, Herm, and Jersey. These are the Channel Islands.

Facing west on the biggest island is the classic beach break of St. Ouens (pronounced wons), a 5-mile-long beach along the island of Jersey. The Channel Islands have many surf spots, primarily on Jersey and Guernsey, with some on Alderney. But the best and most consistent spot is St. Ouens Beach, Jersey, comprising four main breaks.

Starting in the southwest of Jersey Island, you'll find Corbiere, a remote seascape that overlooks a rocky bay with reef waves boiling over numerous rocks and a channel out to the famed big-wave spot. This break is not for the faint-hearted. This is a big peak at 12 to 15 feet, and the area has spectacular wave splash-ups and many wave possibilities, most of which are too dangerous to surf.

The next beach break is called Les Brayes, a break with some heavy waves off a mixture of rock and sandbars. There are strong rips and gnarly waves here at Les Brayes, making this break ideal only for the expert.

Then there are the beach break peaks that run for 2 miles up to an area known as the Water Splash. It's here that the neck of the horseshoe bay has built shelves and patches of flat rocks and sandbanks, in an ideal beach break setup. The tidal range here is 40 feet, making low tide and high tide completely different. At high tide the little contours and gullies in the sandbanks offer perfect bars to produce good clean swell lines. This helps it to become the most consistent wave on Jersey. It's a 500-yard walk to the water at low tide.

North from here lies a 2-mile stretch of fine beach breaks; at the end of this is Secrets, probably the finest wave in Jersey. When there's a light easterly wind and a big west swell to push up to this part of the bay, lefts and rights form off sand- and rock bars, making the clean, glassy barrels near perfect. These waves are ideal for the intermediate to expert surfer when conditions are right.

Photo R. Sumpter

My favorite wave on Jersey. I will always remember winning my first British title at Water Splash and surfing the classic waves of Secrets.

Rod Sumpter

 Peak Beachbreak NW Swell

Break: Beach break
Skill Level: Beginner to expert
Commitment: 3-10
Best Boards: Shortboard, longboard
Lifeguard: In season
Hazards: Rip currents, shallow sand bottom.
Currency: Pound sterling.

Going There: No visa is required by U.S., Australian, Canadian, Japanese, and EU citizens. No vaccinations required, except yellow fever if you're coming from an infected area. Check with your doctor, health clinic, and embassy for up-to-date info.
Where to Stay: Channel Islands Travel

Reservations, +44 (0) 1534 746 181. Watersplash Night Club, jayne@jaynes jersey.com. The Jersey Hospitality Association, St. Helier, +44 (0) 1534 721 421, or fax +44 (0) 1534 722 496.
Finding the Break: From Jersey Airport take a right turn at the traffic circle toward St. Brelade. Follow the B36 for 1.5 miles. At the traffic lights turn right and head toward St. Ouens Bay. Drive along the coast, heading north past the Watersplash Night Club for 2 more miles to the last beach parking area. This is Secrets.
Keep in Mind: Rarely crowded.

Months	JF	MA	MJ	JA	SO	ND
Average Swell (feet)	6	5	3	2	2-3	3-4
Air Temp (C/F)	6/44	10/50	16/61	21/71	18/66	10/50
Water Temp (C/F)	8/46	9/48	11/52	17/63	13/56	9/48
Wetsuit	full	full	full	shorty	spring	full
Average Sunshine p/d (hours)	3	4-5	6	9	5	3
Average Rain, inches p/m	4	3	2	2	3	4
Average Surfable Days p/m	14	12	10	7	11	18

48. SKAILL BAY
Orkney Islands, Scotland

You might expect a perfect wave like this only in a lost world—a swell breaking like softened gold, sliding down the face of a liquid barrel. What makes this break shine above the rest is its power and beauty, two rippable points in this lost world.

Skaill Bay lies 100 miles northeast of Great Britain on the west coast of Kirkwall, Orkney Islands, Scotland. These islands have much surf potential—and much yet to be discovered, because there are many unexplored reefs and bays. There are seven main islands, Kirkwall, Weststray, Rousay, Sanday, Shapinsay, Stronsay, and Hoy, surrounded by some of the fiercest Atlantic Ocean conditions that the winter season can deliver. The summer can be quite calm thanks to the Gulf Stream, which passes by at Thurso. It is here that the ferry crosses daily from the mainland to the Orkneys.

Kirkwall is blessed with one of the best sandy beaches in Europe, and has a tidal range of 25 feet. One of the best and most consistent breaks is Skaill Bay, a superb horseshoe bay with two point surfs and a long beach break that handles almost all wind conditions, from northeast to southwest. The best time of year to come for surf is spring or autumn in April or May and September or October. Ideal for the adventurous surfer.

From the moment you arrive, Orkney seduces you with its seascapes, its wildlife, and its unhurried pace of life. There are about seventy islands within the Orkney archipelago, only seventeen of which are inhabited. Exploration never ceases, as you see far-off sandy beaches, points, and peaks, and more waves are found, more breaks discovered. There's always another island worth checking out.

The area is very rural, and there is the possibility of bed-and-breakfast accommodations, but most surfers camp above the beach.

Photo S. Sumpter

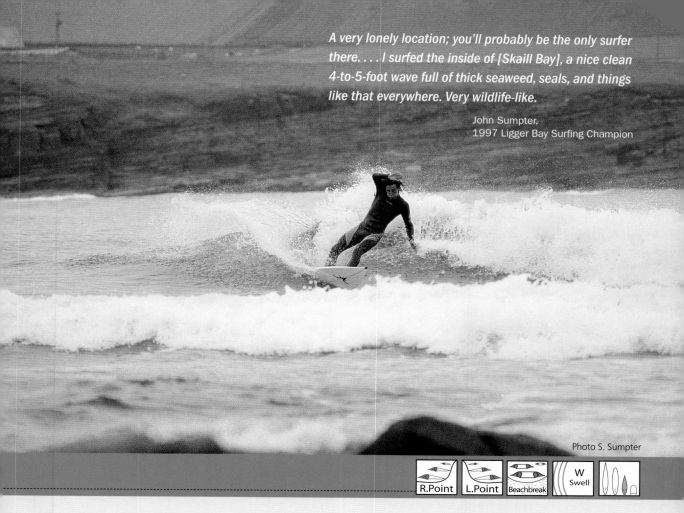

A very lonely location; you'll probably be the only surfer there. . . . I surfed the inside of [Skaill Bay], a nice clean 4-to-5-foot wave full of thick seaweed, seals, and things like that everywhere. Very wildlife-like.

John Sumpter,
1997 Ligger Bay Surfing Champion

Photo S. Sumpter

| R.Point | L.Point | Beachbreak | W Swell | |

Break: Beach break and right and left point break

Skill Level: Intermediate to expert

Commitment: 6–10

Best Boards: Shortboard

Lifeguard: None

Hazards: Rip currents, shallow sand and rock bottom. Seasonal seaweed in September can cause leg rope problems.

Currency: Pound sterling.

Going There: No visa is required by U.S., Australian, Canadian, Japanese, and EU citizens. No vaccinations required, except yellow fever if you're coming from an infected area. Check with your doctor, health clinic, and embassy for up-to-date info.

Where to Stay: The Tourist Office, +44 (0) 1856 850 716. Standing Stones Hotel, +44 (0) 1856 850 449. Stromness Hotel, +44 (0) 1856 850 610. Youth Hostel, +44 (0) 1856 850 589. Point of Ness Campsite, +44 (0) 1856 873 535.

Finding the Break: From Scabster Harbor (next to Thurso), take the car ferry to Stromness and head north on the A967 to Aith. Then take the coast road to Skaill Bay.

Keep in Mind: Rarely crowded.

Months	JF	MA	MJ	JA	SO	ND
Average Swell (feet)	4–5	5	3	1	3	4–5
Air Temp (C/F)	6/43	10/50	16/61	15/59	14/47	9/48
Water Temp (C/F)	5/41	7/45	10/50	14/58	12/54	8/46
Wetsuit	full	full	full	full	full	full
Average Sunshine p/d (hours)	1–2	3	4	7	4–5	1–2
Average Rain, p/m (inches)	4	3	2	1	3	4
Average Surfable Days p/m	12	10	5	3	9	14

49. THURSO EAST
Caithness, Scotland

You drive the nose of the board hard into the cracking lip. The narrowness of the arching tunnel is serpentine as it spits and blows like the Loch Ness Monster, slingshotting your ride into a winding maze of heady updrafts like a dram of golden scotch whiskey.

Also known as the Castle Reef at Thurso because of the seventeenth-century castle opposite the break, this classic surf spot is made famous by its barreling tubes, peat-brown Atlantic salt water, and uncrowded space. Situated at the northeast tip of Scotland, on the Caithness peninsula, the coastline is also known by local surfers as the North Shore for its many surfing breaks. These breaks lie between the beach breaks of Sandwood Bay, 55 miles to the west of Thurso town, and Gills Bay, with its good lefts and rights, 30 miles to the east. Thurso East is a world-class right-hand reef break with a straight-down-the-line tube for 150 to 300 yards, breaking heavily over slabs of Caithness sandstone and kelp-covered flat rocks. The en-tire coastline of the North Shore picks up swell easily and is pounded by winter storms and mountainous seas. In spring and fall the breaks seem to line up all at once—this is the best time of year to surf. It's an ideal surf spot for the intermediate to expert.

Other must-see North Shore places include Brimmes Ness to the west, 4 miles from Thurso—a big-wave spot with three challenging reef breaks, the Bowl, the Cove, and the Left. Durness, a few miles to the east, has soft beginners' waves and excellent longboarders' peaks. The whole lineup and choice across the bay is quite amazing. Another key spot on the North Shore is Melvich, a beach break set below 100-foot hills and rolling countryside, a beauty spot with a river mouth left, a sand point right, and beach breaks. But all along the coast, you'll find remote beaches, points, and reefs. The North Shore has the ideal surf spots for the beginner, intermediate, and expert. It's just a matter of looking and finding the right conditions.

Photo Denny Peat

For me the most memorable barrel wave in the world. It's here that speed barrels make you hold your breath and emerge tranformed, enlightened forever.

Rod Sumpter

Photo Denny Peat

R.Point | NE Swell | Shallow Reef

Type of Break: Right-hand reef break
Skill Level: Intermediate to expert
Commitment: 6–10
Best Boards: Longboard, shortboard
Lifeguard: None
Hazards: Flat shallow rock bottom, rips and currents. Murky water due to peat bogs used for burning in open fires fil-tering into Thurso River. Dangerous paddle out and wipeouts when waves are double overhead.
Currency: Pound sterling.
Going There: No visa is required by U.S., Australian, Canadian, Japanese, and EU citizens. No vaccinations required, except yellow fever if you're coming from an infected area. Check with your doctor, health clinic, and embassy for up-to-date info.
Where to Stay: Royal Hotel, +44 (0) 1847 893 191. Murry B & B, +44 (0) 1847 895 759. Thurso Campsite, +44 (0) 1955 603 761. Scottish Tourist Office, +44 (0) 131 332 2433.
Finding the Break: From the Edinburgh airport take the M85 north to Perth, then head north on the A9 to Pitlockry and then Inverness. Follow the A9 to Wick, then the A882 to Thurso East. Park near the old castle.
Surf School: Harper's Hire, +44 (0) 1847 893 179.
Keep in Mind: Crowded in September and October when the surf's up.

Months	JF	MA	MJ	JA	SO	ND
Average Swell (feet)	6–8	6	4	2	3–4	5–6
Air Temp (C/F)	6/43	10/50	16/61	15/59	14/47	9/48
Water Temp (C/F)	5/41	7/45	10/50	14/58	12/54	8/46
Wetsuit	full	full	full	full	full	full
Average Sunshine p/d (hours)	1–2	3	4	7	4–5	1–2
Average Rain p/m (inches)	4	3	3	2	4	5
Average Surfable Days p/m	12	10	8	5	11	14

50. BIDART PLAGE

Biarritz, Southern France

From way out at sea you can see brilliant set waves balance on the horizon, then disappear and re-form like a mirage. It's one long, slow, feathering, breaking wave, and it's down this drop-in that longboarders love to play. It gives them plenty of time to do four or five deep carving turns before it's showtime.

Situated 4 miles south of Biarritz and 20 miles north of the Spanish border, Bidart Plage is the perfect fun beach

break wave when everywhere else is flat. When southwest France and the Bay of Biscay are calm, and there is little chance of surfing, Bidart seems to pick up some swell. There can be strong rips and currents flowing, making positioning demanding. But once you've got your position, the length of ride is 50 to 100 yards and can be magic on the right day. Bidart is ideal for the intermediate to expert surfer wanting to find some waves on small days. When it's over 6 feet, it's for experts.

A small hilltop town between Route 10 and the sea, Bidart has little of the hustle and bustle that you're likely to find in Biarritz. This is where the Pays Basque countryside and coast meet to create a world all its own, with neat white houses with red roofs and shutters and a unique language and folklore. The two main towns along the coast are Biarritz and St. Jean de Luz, and are less than 20 miles from the first peak of the Pyrenees Mountains. These spectacular mountains are great for hiking; the lower slopes are covered with vineyards that produce the local wine.

Surfers, however, will find most surf spots at the base of cliffs. Most spots are beach breaks, Bidart's having lovely white sand. Bidart became recognized as a surfing venue in 1965 when longboarders showed their skills and captured the imagination of the local swimming and bodysurfing population. In 1975 Film de Surf, the surfing film festival at the Pax Cinema, held the first international championships at Bidart.

There is a short stretch of coastline here, with several other breaks located south of Bidart. First is Milady Plage, a good left and right beach break. Then there's Plage Marbella, which is tucked under steep cliffs and has some rocky outcrops that produce classic right-handers and the occasional left. There's Cote de Basque (Spot 51), a longboard and shortboard wave at low tide with some bodyboarder inside peaks. And when there's a very big swell, the harbor at St. Jean de Luz starts to work, as does the big-wave spot farther out of Belharra Reef. The two other beaches close by are d'Ilbarritze, a good bodyboarding wave with fast hollow sections, and Plage de l'Uhabia, a beach break mainly for bodyboards that has a sand point right in the middle of the area where the swimming flags go in summer. Outside the summer season, this can be a good longboard or shortboard wave. These are long narrow beaches, and nowhere near are good as Bidart for waves.

Photo R. Sumpter

Bidart—a fun beach break wher...

Colin McPhilli...
2000–2002 Worla...

Photo V. Sumpter

Beachbreak

NW Swell

Break: Beach break
Skill Level: Beginner to expert
Commitment: 2–10
Best Boards: Longboard, shortboard
Lifeguard: In season
Hazards: A steep sand slope and sub-merged rock patches make a savage shorebreak from 4 to 6 feet at high tide. Entry and surfing to the shore is a hit-and-miss game.

Currency: Euro.
Going There: No visa is required by U.S., Australian, Canadian, Japanese, or other EU citizens. All others require visas. For vaccinations required, check with your doctor, health clinic, and embassy up-to-date info.
Where to Stay: Bidart Rentals, +33 (0) 5 59 54 67 60 or fax +33 (0) 5 59 54 67 61. Chemin Dorréa Bidart, +33 (0) 5

59 54 74 90, or agencepetit@ wanadoo.fr. Maisons du Sud Ouest, +33 (0) 5 59 47 59 60, or fax +33 (0) 5 59 47 59 69. Pays Basque, +33 (0) 5 59 26 56 62.
Finding the Break: The Biarritz airport is just 5 miles away (a ten-minute drive). Or use the Bordeaux airport to fly into the country for this spot. Biarritz is the closest city to Bidart Plage. South from Biarritz, follow the coastal route—it's signposted.
Surf School: Logoondy Surf Camp, +33 (0) 5 59 24 62 86.
Keep in Mind: Very crowded in July and August.

Months	JF	MA	MJ	JA	SO	ND
Average Swell (feet)	5–6	5–6	4–5	2–3	4	5
Air Temp (C/F)	12/54	14/57	20/68	24/75	22/72	15/57
Water Temp (C/F)	11/52	13/55	16/60	21/70	19/66	12/54
Wetsuit	full	full	shorty	shorty	spring	full
Average Sunshine p/d (hours)	3	4–5	6–7	8	6–7	3
Average Rain p/m (inches)	3	2	2	1	2	2
Average Surfable Days p/m	19	16	14	10	18	20

51. C... Biarritz, Southern France

...nall- ...eing the ...a hotdog- ...rds ride best ...ding is great at ...ges. High tide sees ...ose, and carving swan turns. ...en the heavens go black during a ...avy surf spills in around the castle point, makin... e really long rides.

Situated 10 miles south of Bayonne and 15 miles north of the Spanish–French border, Cote de Basque Plage and Grande Plage are the two beaches closest to the city center, with fine facilities and famous for their quality waves. Cote de Basque picks up a northwest swell with a point wave breaking off the promenade at the end of the horseshoe bay. Going north, next to the castle, a magic point wave forms on big days. On the 2-to-4-foot days, it's ideal for the longboarders. There are several beach breaks producing superb rights and lefts from rocky outcrops, all the way south to Bidart Plage (Spot 50). These beach breaks peak and loom up during tidal changes and last for only an hour or two while breaking over the right conditions. At low tide there can be entirely different waves, faster and hollower. The farther south you go, the bigger the waves are, in general, and it's these bigger waves that give Cote de Basque its reputation as a classic point break. It's ideal for beginner, to expert, depending on the conditions.

Biarritz is the center of French surfing in southern France, and this area is famous for having a number of world-class breaks. Grande Plage is a fast, heavy beach break with top-to-bottom barrels if the swell is over 5 feet.

The Empress Eugenie liked the beaches of Biarritz, and by her visits she made it a fashionable resort in the 1850s. Nobility followed, staying in the coastal establishments that have now become grand hotels and casinos overlooking Cote de Basque and Grande Plage.

When it's smaller, the waves are softer and more fun. Other places to surf, starting at the Spanish–French border, are the river-mouth breaks of Hendaye, with a good left and right and ideal for intermediate to expert surfers, and Hendaye Plage, good for beginners. There's also St. Jean de Luz, Guethary (Spot 52) for the expert only, and Lafitenia (Spot 54), for the intermediate and expert surfer. The next beach break north of Biarritz is La Chambre d'Amour beach and groin breakwater, a fast, hollow wave, good from low to midhigh tide. The coast changes, and several beach breaks going north produce nice waves at Les Sables d'Or, Les Corsaires, and 2 miles of surfable breaks to La Barre beach.

In 1957 Joel de Rosnay was the first French surfer to surf Biarritz beaches. He did it on a Californian Dewey Weber model imported board. He started the craze at Cote de Basque and soon formed the French Surfing Federation. By 1965 his style, and overseas surf traveler stars like Billy Hamilton and Mark Martinson, were seen in film making epics like *Waves of Change* at Cote de Basque. France began to boom to the surf rhythm.

Photo R. Sumpter

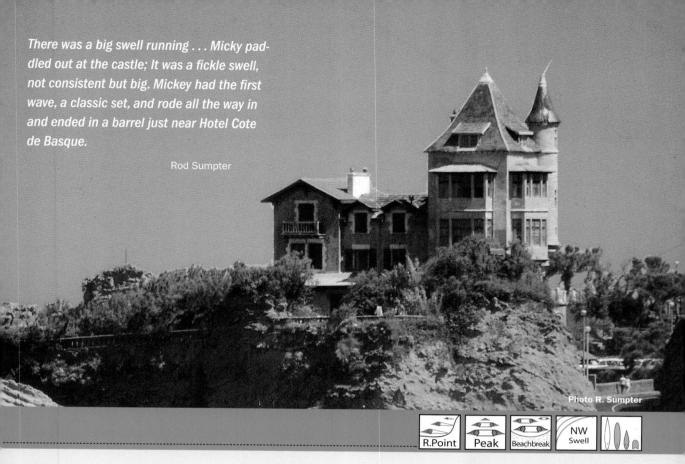

There was a big swell running . . . Micky paddled out at the castle; It was a fickle swell, not consistent but big. Mickey had the first wave, a classic set, and rode all the way in and ended in a barrel just near Hotel Cote de Basque.

Rod Sumpter

Photo R. Sumpter

| R.Point | Peak | Beachbreak | NW Swell | |

Break: Beach break and point break
Skill Level: Beginner to expert
Commitment: 2–10
Best Boards: Longboard, shortboard, bodyboard
Lifeguard: In season
Hazards: Shallow sand bottom and strong rips sweep south on any swell over head-high.
Currency: Euro.

Going There: No visa is required by U.S., Australian, Canadian, Japanese, and EU citizens. All others require visas. For vaccinations required, check with your doctor, health clinic, and embassy up-to-date info.

Where to Stay: Hotel du Palais, +33 (0) 5 59 41 64 00, or fax +33 (0) 5 59 41 67 99. Holiday Rentals Biarritz, +33 (0) 5 59 24 04 91. Les Maisons du Biar-ritz, +33 810 059 753. Victoria Surf Biarritz, +33 (0) 5 59 22 27 28. Paradisco, mncd@noos.fr. Hotel Louisiane, +33 (0) 5 59 24 95 77.

Finding the Break: From Biarritz Parme Airport exit toward Biarritz. Follow signs for the beach, a ten-minute drive. That will lead to Avenue de la Marne; turn right and follow Place du Poète Louis Guillaume–Avenue de la Reine Nathalie. Follow signs for Cote de Basque, and park at the beach promenade parking area. Or use Bordeaux airport to fly into the country for this spot; Cote de Basque is south of the city of Biarritz.

Surf School: Plums Surf School, +33 (0) 5 59 24 08 04.

Keep in Mind: Very crowded in July and August.

Months	JF	MA	MJ	JA	SO	ND
Average Swell (feet)	4–5	4	3	2	3	5
Air Temp (C/F)	12/54	14/57	20/68	24/75	22/72	15/57
Water Temp (C/F)	11/52	13/55	16/60	21/70	19/66	12/54
Wetsuit	full	full	shorty	shorty	spring	full
Average Sunshine p/d (hours)	3	4–5	6–7	8	6–7	3
Average Rain p/m (inches)	3	2	2	1	2	2
Average Surfable Days p/m	19	16	14	6	18	20

52. GUETHARY
Pays Basque, Southwest France

Big bold peaks and strong swell lines march in and rule Guethary's lineup. The awe-inspiring sets pile up to the horizon and weave toward you like a surfacing dolphin. You're in the right spot and ready to go when the wedge shifts and you fling yourself into a killer avalanche, beating it to the bottom. The downdraft and speed send you out from under the bowl and blow you across the face.

Situated 3 miles south of Cote de Basque (Spot 51) and 12 miles north of the Spanish border, beside Bidart Plage (Spot 50), is the all-time classic break of Guethary. Guethary is (90 percent of the time) a long, open-face right-hander. Ten percent of the time it turns into a classic left peak with a length of ride of 300 to 500 yards on a good day. The consistent right-hand peak and walling waves are what Guethary is famous for, and on big days it can hold a smooth wave from 5 to 20 feet. The cliffs protect it from offshore winds, and waves can be ridden in glassy conditions, usually best with a light southeast wind and a northwest swell direction.

The peak looms up way out the back, and you can see it weave its way through a gully to where the takeoff point is. It's a shifting peak, so positioning is important; you need to judge the size to move in or out accordingly. Once launched into the massive face, it pitches out like Sunset Beach (Spot 12) and shuts the first envelope smoothly. The wall bowls and barrels and the face swings in like Honolua Bay (Spot 20). It lines up perfectly to carve and trim, the wall pushing turbo barrels and then softening, making it good for longboarding. It's a magic wave rated by most as the best in France, and a world-class act to follow, without a doubt. This is the ideal surf spot for the intermediate on 3-to-5-foot days, and for the advanced to expert surfer when bigger.

There are two other unique reef breaks just west of Guethary, both of which have classic features. Cenitz has a mega takeoff and drop to a soft shoulder, which is good for bottom turns. Avalanches has a big peak and mushy shoulders.

And some of France's biggest waves are a few miles south of Guethary at a place called Belharra Perdun. It's a deep reef, about 0.5 mile offshore at St. Jean de Luz. Michel Larronde rode these waves at 35 to 40 feet in 2001 as a tow-in surfer aided by a personal watercraft.

Photo R. Sumpter

Guethary's a good wave—it's Sunset in a wetsuit. Big long drop, long face, big long right, big carving turns, roundhouse cutbacks.

Colin McPhillips,
2000–2002 World Longboard Surfing Champion

Break: Right- and left-hand reef break

Skill Level: Intermediate to expert

Commitment: 5–10

Best Boards: Shortboard, longboard

Lifeguard: In season

Hazards: Rocky outcrops; a tough shifting peak left and right; shallow inside section; harborwall trail to rock entry

Currency: Euro.

Going There: No visa is required by U.S., Australian, Canadian, Japanese, or other EU citizens. All others require visas. For vaccinations required, check with your doctor, health clinic, and embassy for up-to-date info.

Where to Stay: Homelidays Guethary, +33 (0) 1 40 47 00 09, or fax +33 (0) 1 40 47 00 61. Bidart Rentals, +33 (0) 5 59 54 67 60, or fax +33 (0) 5 59 54 67 61. Le Grande Hotel, +33 (0) 5 59 26 35 36, or fax +33 (0) 5 59 51 99 84.

Finding the Break: From Biarritz Parme Airport exit toward Biarritz. Follow signs toward the beach. That will lead to Avenue de la Marne. Turn right and follow Place du Poète Louis Guillaume–Avenue de la Reine Nathalie. Turn left and follow Avenue de la Reine Victoria 300 yards to Cote de Basque.

Surf School: Lagoondy Surf Camp, +33 (0) 5 59 24 62 86.

Keep in Mind: Very crowded in July and August.

Months	JF	MA	MJ	JA	SO	ND
Average Swell (feet)	8	6	4–5	2	4–5	6
Air Temp (C/F)	12/54	14/57	20/68	24/75	22/72	15/57
Water Temp (C/F)	11/52	13/55	16/60	21/70	19/66	12/54
Wetsuit	full	full	shorty	shorty	spring	full
Average Sunshine p/d (hours)	3	4–5	6–7	8	6–7	3
Average Rain p/m (inches)	3	2	2	1	2	2
Average Surfable Days p/m	21	12	14	5	14	20

53. HOSSEGOR
Landes, Southwest France

This beach break has a perfect right A-frame wave that turns into an emerald-green barrel. It's this hallmark that ranks Hossegor as one of the great beaches of France. Longboarders come to play and refine their performance skills, compare the wine, and take in the culture on the small, glassy, hot and hazy days. But it's the shortboarders who rule the kingdom of big waves, who fly and float the barrel. They draw swords and do battle at one of the world's major surf contest sites, the Association of Surfing Professionals world tour.

Found 60 miles north of Hendaye Plage on the Spanish border and 100 miles south of the city of Bordeaux, Hossegor is famous for its world-class beach break. Frequent, strong North Atlantic swells hit the Hossegor sandbars and produce waves that range from 3 to 20 feet. The town is backed by the Lac d'Hossegor, a famous sailboarding venue, and the waters stretch all the way to the beach. The beach area largely consists of sand dunes, marram grass, and a long wilderness beachfront into the sea. Hossegor nestles in between the two other surf towns of Seignosse and Capbreton, both of which are good spots, but neither has the surf flair or quality waves of Hossegor.

The ideal time to surf Hossegor is in September or October, when the crowded summer droves of tourists in the water and beach-ball maniacs from Paris have disappeared. In the fall and also during the early winter, Hossegor sees its fair share of surf travelers from all over the world.

One of the most amazing aspects of Hossegor is its ability to pick up a new swell and jump from 3 to 5 feet in the morning when you're surfing a 5-foot, 10-inch by 20-inch fishtail, to 20 feet in the afternoon—you'll need your 8-foot-10 by 19-inch rhino gun. When it's big the whole concept of beach break surfing goes a bit strange. Set waves that form as an A-frame break into the first 100 yards as predicted, then often shove out into a death-defying closing-out wall, best likened to a trip to nowhere or a speed run past the wedge and shorebreak. When it's breaking 6 to 8 feet, you can't beat Hossegor's shaped waves. It's like a folding piece of glass on a calm day, without a hint of chop; you can carve its every form for 300 yards.

The entire French coast seems to be made for surfing. Starting in the south is the river-mouth break of the Hendaye border, where surfing right lets you cross into Spain, while going left keeps you in France. This is a soft wave and can be lots of fun. Then there's St. Jean de Luz, a big-wave spot that breaks in the mouth of the harbor. Off the north jetty is a heavy right and several reef breaks working off different tides in the harbor itself; these are for the expert surfer only. Lafitenia (Spot 54) is a superb right-hand point break. Many people regard Guethary (Spot 52) as the best wave in France, a long right with excellent shape. There's also a rare, left reef peak of exceptional quality that heads toward the start of Bidart Plage (Spot 50), a beach break with soft to heavy barrels. The small cliff-terraced beach breaks at Cote de Basque (Spot 51) have a good longboarding wave. This is the place where, historically, most of French surfing began. Then there's Grande Plage in the center of the city, a beach that picks up swell and is usually short, heavy, and fast for the intermediate to expert surfer. Les Sables d'Or comprises the two nice beach breaks of Chambre d'Amour along with VVF camping, and if there's any swell at all it will be breaking here. Going north, there are other breaks with good waves in the right conditions, like Les Plages d'Anglet and Cavaliers—superfast, close-to-the-shore beach breaks. Other surf places of note still heading north are Boucau, Moliets Plage, St. Girons Plage, Mimizan Plage, and Lacanau Ocean. Finally, as the Bay of Biscay straightens, surfing spots and good surf locations thin out, but surf breaks can be found to the far north in Brittany.

Nestled against an emerald pine forest, caressed by the ocean, lined with endless beaches of fine sand is the town of Hossegor. The resort has integrated its various types of accommodations among the pine trees, and huge camping sites abound, but there is still a perfect balance with the original nature and beauty of the area. The ASP world tour of surfing, the European kite festival, the Motocross Enduro on the beach, and the Hossegor Pelote Basque Open all mingle in the full swing of the summer season. And when the sun goes down below the horizon, there are plenty of bars, surfers cafes, and restaurants from which to choose in this elegant French town.

Photo © ASP Tostee

I think Hossegor has the best sand bars in France. . . . It's just a quick right down the beach until it hits the dry sand. I rate Hossegor as France's number one surf spot at lower tide, but I like the high tide, when it's right on the beach, just a big barrel.

Andy Irons,
2002–2003 World Surfing Champion

Photo © ASP Tostee

Rights | Lefts | Beachbreak | NW Swell | | Shallow Sand

Break: Beach break
Skill Level: Beginner to expert
Commitment: 5–10
Best Boards: Shortboard
Lifeguard: In season
Hazards: Rip currents. Sandbars and shallow sand bottom make this an epic pad-dle-out in waves more than 15 feet high.

Currency: Euro.
Going There: No visa is required by U.S., Australian, Canadian, Japanese, or other EU citizens. All others require visas. For vaccinations required, check with your doctor, health clinic, and em-bassy for up-to-date info.
Where to Stay: Moser Immobilier, +33 (0) 5 58 43 51 05, or fax +33 (0) 5 58 43 81 57. Hossegor Rentals, +33 (0) 5 58 72 10 19. Agence Petit, +33 (0) 5 58 43 54 42. Agence Duran, Hossegor, +33 (0) 5 58 41 79 20, or fax +33 (0) 5 58 41 79 22.
Finding the Break: From the Bordeaux air-port head for Bayonne, which is the closest city to Hossegor. From Bayonne drive north to Seignosse, and on to Hossegor.
Surf School: Destination Surf, +33 (0) 5 07 19 82 59.
Keep in Mind: Very crowded in July and August.

Months	JF	MA	MJ	JA	SO	ND
Average Swell (feet)	6–8	5–6	4–5	2–3	4	6
Air Temp (C/F)	12/54	14/57	20/68	24/75	22/72	15/57
Water Temp (C/F)	11/52	13/55	16/60	21/70	19/66	12/54
Wetsuit	full	full	shorty	shorty	spring	full
Average Sunshine p/d (hours)	3	4–5	6–7	8	6–7	3
Average Rain p/m (inches)	3	2	2	1	2	2
Average Surfable Days p/m	26	22	16	12	18	25

54. LAFITENIA
Southwest France

Some of France's finest waves line up and break perfectly at the tiny bay of Lafitenia, where seamless sets wrap around a limestone point. The takeoff lets you hear the slicing sound of the fins carving off a jackknife rock-ledge section that wails as you pass. Then it's no-holds-barred across the straight-up wall that locks into the barrel.

Situated 400 miles southwest of Paris and 10 miles northeast of the Hendaye–Spanish border in the south of France is the area known as Basque country. This is where you'll find the classic surf spot of Lafitenia. Lafitenia is a magic right-hand point surf where perfect swell lines fill the beautiful bay. At the point, Surge Rock, a submerged rocky-cave formation on the seabed, produces a steep takeoff and wave face, then smoothes out into a classic walling ride. At 10 feet the wall lines up right across the bay for a superb classic ride at top speed—there are no cutbacks or holding back to make this wave. This fabulous spot is one of the few true point surfs in the entire Basque country region. It's a boulder-laid cove spreading out to a cliff face, then a solid rock plate and pebble seafloor to the shore. This unique feature allows slight changes to the stone banks, but the waves are mostly affected by swell direction and the winds. Ten miles south of Biarritz, where cliffs and quaint villages are the norm, Lafitenia is a sought-after break when the surf's up with a northeast swell and southeast wind. It's also sheltered from strong offshore winds; with its high cliffs, it stays glassy even during east to southerly gales. This is a magic surf spot ideal for the expert when it's pumping.

Lafitenia's first peak and second peak are unique. There are effectively two breaks at the same place, but the rider on the outer first peak has the right-of-way over the second. This is a very important etiquette rule in France (and the rest of the world, for that matter). The length of ride can be 250 to 500 yards on a really good day, when the northeast swell is wrapping and peeling off across the entire bay to the inner bay's boulders and pebbled beach.

Photo R. Sumpter

It was the time of the year when the Bay of Biscay gathers up raw swell from the Mid-Atlantic. . . . This was Glen [Short's] first time in France, and [he] was impressed by the quality, size, and speed of the French waves.

Rod Sumpter

Photo R. Sumpter

R.Point | NW Swell | | Shallow Reef

Break: Right-hand point break

Skill Level: Intermediate to expert

Commitment: 5–10

Best Boards: Shortboard, longboard

Lifeguard: None

Hazards: Shallow rock bottom. A steep trail to the pebble beach with 3-inch stones. Once out, a single underwater rock bluff makes the takeoff hairy and steep.

Currency: Euro.

Going There: No visa is required by U.S., Australian, Canadian, Japanese, or other EU citizens. All others require visas. For vaccinations required, check with your doctor, health clinic, and embassy for up-to-date info.

Where to Stay: Bidart Rentals, +33 (0) 5 59 54 67 60, or fax +33 (0) 5 59 54

67 61. Homelidays Guethary, +33 (0) 1 40 47 00 09, or fax +33 (0) 1 40 47 00 61. Bidart Rentals, +33 (0) 5 59 54 67 60, or fax +33 (0) 5 59 54 67 61. Le Grande Hotel, +33 (0) 5 59 26 35 36, or fax +33 (0) 5 59 51 99 84.

Finding the Break: From Biarritz Parme Airport exit toward Biarritz. Follow signs toward the town center; you will then find signs for the south coastal route to Bidart and Guethary. Still going south, continue for 1 mile. You will see Lafitenia on the right. Park at the top of the hill and walk down the path to the beach.

Keep in Mind: Very crowded in July and August.

Months	JF	MA	MJ	JA	SO	ND
Average Swell (feet)	7–8	5–6	4–5	2–3	4–5	6
Air Temp (C/F)	12/54	14/57	20/68	24/75	22/72	15/57
Water Temp (C/F)	11/52	13/55	16/60	21/70	19/66	12/54
Wetsuit	full	full	shorty	shorty	spring	full
Average Sunshine p/d (hours)	3	4–5	6–7	8	6–7	3
Average Rain p/m (inches)	3	2	2	1	2	2
Average Surfable Days p/m	10	11	7	4	7	12

55. MUNDAKA
Pays Basque, Northern Spain

When the Mundakain surf is big, you hear the waves crack and rumble. It's a stampede of rollers. You know taking off could be tricky, as set waves build up, clean up, and close out. So scary are these powerful peaks, they seem determined to shake you off. They fill the bay, splashing the banks as villagers watch you sail across the river channel, leaving your mark. A mighty seething section looms like a red cloak to the charging bull, and you move to go through the back door as it opens. Spain's mightiest wave peels off like the swirling skirts of the flamenco dancer. The matador in the center of the ring, the surfer draws his sword and carves his track, performing down the fading wave to the cobblestone shore.

Situated 20 miles east of Bilbao and 30 miles west of San Sebastian is Europe's longest left, the river-mouth wave of Mundaka. Nestled in the corner of the Bay of Biscay along the mouth of the River Guernika, Mundaka's classic waves draw surfers from all over the world. It's a small fishing village, and this beauty spot can boast one of the few rivers in Spain with truly clean water. Thanks to the nature reserve nearby, the water here is carefully monitored.

Mundaka can be infamous for having long flat spells with no surf, particularly in the summer. But in the winter months (October to March), the surf starts to roll in and the waves can be incredibly powerful, perhaps the best lefts in Europe, with a ride length of 300 yards or more.

The layout of the bay and river between Guernika and Bermeo shapes the terrain into a left sandbank, and the mix of river and inward swell is responsible for such fine waves. The beach also faces north and is protected from westerly winds. Getting in can be handled in several ways, the best of which is down the steep and very slippery steps to the harbor, past the fishermen and fishing lines, out the harbor entrance, and across the channel. Paddle out across the river rip and into the takeoff area. There can still be a rip current here, so you need to keep moving in order to hold a position. The takeoff to the wave is steep and the bottom trough is smooth with a lot of face to the wall. It's an easy barrel setup, the wall lines up ahead of you a long way; it's still a barrel and a race.

The wave has three sections, the first of which is tight to the tube, the curl thick and heavy, strong enough to blast you clean off your board. The wave softens for the second section, with more shoulder on which to maneuver. The third section fades a little in size as you surf down the river. It holds up nicely for a top turn or two to stay in the slot, then the wave barrels to the inside. Mundaka is a difficult, but classic world-class break ideal for expert surfers only.

There are many other surf breaks along the Basque coastline as well, one of the most popular being Sopelana, a beach break with good sectioning peaks facing northwest. Sopelana is a few miles north of the city of Bilbao. So if Mundaka is flat, head north and check out this break.

Beautiful Mundaka is high up on a picturesque windy road, where the view of the ocean is downright breathtaking. Green sloping hills cascade seaward as you drive north toward Bakio. The country here consists of a central plateau slanting to the southeast, parted by mountains and river valleys where Spain borders France. Surfing began in this beauty spot in the 1960s at Sopelana, when traveling French surfers from Biarritz brought in their surfboards in search of new waves. Today boards are locally produced at Pukas Surfboards, and a strong Spanish team makes an impressive show at the World Championships each year.

Photo © ASP Tostee

I rate Mundaka as the best left in Europe. It's hollow, powerful, and gnarly. I like the way it barrels on the inside as much as the takeoff hook. It's a classic wave when all the conditions come together.

John Sumpter,
1997 Ligger Bay Surfing Champion

Photo © ASP Tostee

 L.Point NW Swell

Break: Left-hand river-mouth break
Skill Level: Expert
Commitment: 6–10
Best Boards: Shortboard
Lifeguard: None
Hazards: River-mouth currents, shallow rocks, and sand bottom.

Currency: Euro.
Going There: No visa is required by U.S., Australian, Canadian, Japanese, or other EU citizens. All others require visas. For vaccinations required, check with your doctor, health clinic, and embassy for up-to-date info.

Where to Stay: Mundaka B & B, +44 (0) 1242 529 509, or fax +44 (0) 1242 228 401. Mundaka Campsite, almost on the beach (no phone). Hotel reservations, +34 9021 80743. Hotel Nervion Bilbao, room@netcomuk.co.uk, +44 (0) 020 7636 6888.

Finding the Break: From the Santander airport take the A8 east to Bilbao (or start from the Bilbao airport). Follow the C6313 to Bermeo, then follow signs around the winding coast to Mundaka. Parking is difficult.
Contest: Billabong (WCT), October.
Keep in mind: There are crowds both in and out of the water when the surf is up.

Months	JF	MA	MJ	JA	SO	ND
Average Swell (feet)	8	6	3-4	2	3-4	5
Air Temp (C/F)	12/54	14/57	20/68	24/75	22/72	15/57
Water Temp (C/F)	11/52	13/55	16/60	21/70	19/66	12/54
Wetsuit	full	full	full	shorty	spring	full
Average Sunshine p/d (hours)	3	5	7	8	7	3
Average Rain p/m (inches)	2	2	2	0	1	2
Average Surfable Days p/m	15	12	9	4	10	12

Photo R. Sumpter

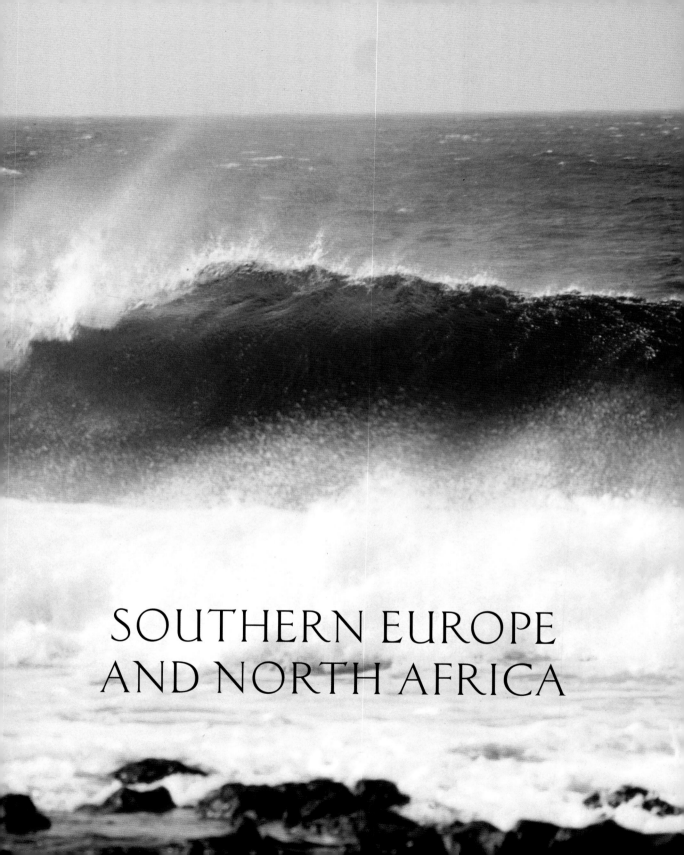

SOUTHERN EUROPE
AND NORTH AFRICA

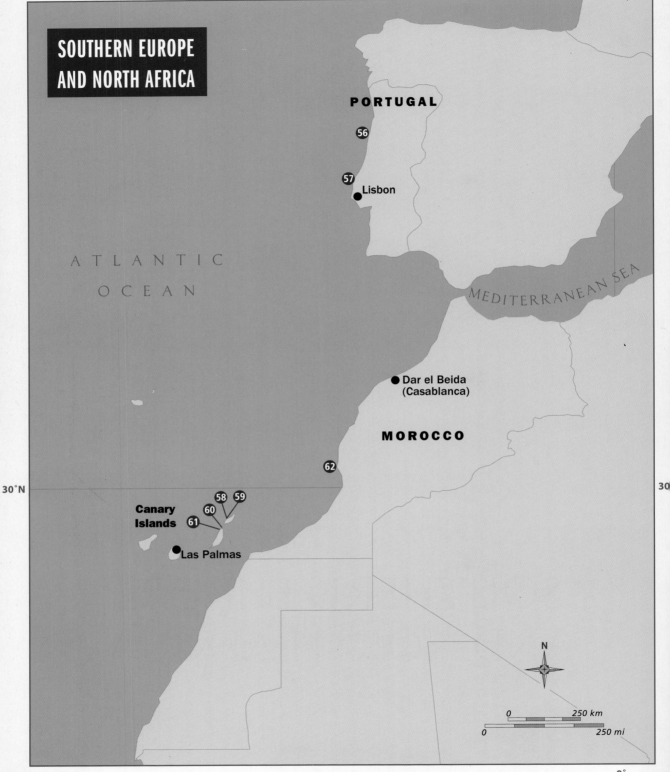

SOUTHERN EUROPE
AND NORTH AFRICA

PORTUGAL

56

57 ● Lisbon

ATLANTIC
OCEAN

MEDITERRANEAN SEA

● Dar el Beida
(Casablanca)

MOROCCO

62

30°N

58 59
60
Canary
Islands   61

● Las Palmas

N

0   250 km
0   250 mi

0°

0°

30°

Portugal, the Canary Islands, and Morocco are southern Europe's premier surfing locations, with brilliant surf, warm water, and colorful cultures. These countries of southern Europe and North Africa are a stronghold of quality waves and a boundless mix of remote locations that can be challenging to find even for the experienced traveler.

Portugal's west coast and the Atlantic Ocean create one of world's best surfing locations at places like Costa Nova, Averio, and Peniche. Costa Nova has beach breaks holding waves from 2 to 12 feet in an interesting area of lakes, salt mines, dunes, and waterways. And south from here, just north of Lisbon, is the ultimate beach break of Supertubos at Peniche. Cracking waves are set amid a centuries-old fishing village of tiny cottages and brightly painted boats.

Over the Straits of Gibraltar on Africa's northwest coast lies Morocco with its dry desert coastline and miles of rewarding surf for those with a four-wheel-drive vehicle. Places like Anchor Point are superb when the low-pressure depressions from the Azores push in a west swell. Only here will you find the king of Morocco also president of his local surf club.

Southwest of Morocco are the fabulous volcanic Canary Islands, which have great reef breaks to challenge the hard-core surfer to the limits. On Lanzarote, La Santa's right reef break is a perfect down-the-line hotdog wave. Across the bay, La Santa Lefts is a pounding top-to-bottom hard-core left. On Fuerteventura, the Bubble's break on the north shore of the island is a vertical thrill. At times the whole island can have surf. To the northwest of the chain is the tiny island of Lobos, accessible by ferry. The two surf points Lobos provides are unforgettable. A demanding right-hand reef break peels off around the north side of the island, and an equally good left can be found on the south side.

Southern Europe and North Africa hold some of the most adventurous surfing destinations around, with interesting and exciting cultures to enjoy along the way.

56. COSTA NOVA
Aveiro, Northern Portugal

When you arrive at Costa Nova, it doesn't take long to appreciate the fine waves. There's a peak in the middle that's got a kick like a mule's, and a suck on the face of the wave the size of three collapsing waterfalls. The end section is just right for zapping some snaps. This is a great big bold beach break, laid out to catch the North Atlantic swells. There are avalanching *bomboras* on big days, but on average it's just perfectly nice.

Situated 100 miles south of Oporto, Costa Nova is a classic beach break beside the jetty of Barra, an artificial canal that was built to provide access to the Atlantic for the local fishing industry. Inadvertently, this canal also formed one of the world's best surf spots. The waves here are of perfect proportions in the right swell and conditions, making this one of the best breaks, among many, along this stretch of coastline.

In 1965 I was traveling in Europe with a group of Australian surfers and found great waves in the Aveiro area. The locals watched with enthusiasm, and the sport has flourished ever since.

Barra Jetty at Costa Nova is best at 4 to 6 feet with a light east wind, but can hold waves of 15 feet plus. This is a big-wave spot during heavy seas, and in the lee of storms it can handle the biggest swells of all—over 25 feet and often well lined up and clean, sheltered by the 0.25-mile-long concrete wall stretching out to the horizon. The groin peak next to the beach and jetty has an easy paddle-out rip and an in-

The white sand beaches of Aveiro are huge, and the locals catch a lot of fish. The large nets are pulled up the beach by strong oxen, an age-old tradition. Brightly painted swan-neck fishing boats line the numerous canals, spanned by low arch bridges. Pyramids of salt dry in the sun, beside the salt marshes.

credible left peak running back into the rip channel.

The next break is Aveiro, just 1 mile north of Costa Nova and has several top-to-bottom peaks across a 2-mile-long beach. These produce a high-performance wave with good walls. At half tide there is a middle section and a shore break. Aveiro is the place for beginners on days when it's only 1 to 2 feet. Costa Nova and Aveiro Beach breaks are ideal surf spots with waves to suit surfers beginner to expert, depending on conditions.

While Portugal may not hold the world's attention like some of the more powerful countries in Europe, it has been an independent kingdom since 1143 and is one of the oldest nations in Europe. Local industries include the preparation of sea salt and the catching and curing of fish. Portugal has a rich history tied to the sea and was once one of the world's greatest powers.

Photo R. Sumpter

I will always remember one set wave I had while struggling against the rip. I turned, took off, dropped into a clean face, carved a big right-hand turn, and lined up a barrel.

Rod Sumpter

Photo R. Sumpter

Peak | Beachbreak | NW Swell

Break: Beach break
Skill Level: Beginner to expert
Commitment: 3–10
Best Boards: Shortboard
Lifeguard: None
Hazards: Sandbars. Rips and currents start to form from waist-high surf and increase in danger in surf up to 18 feet.
Currency: Euro.
Going There: No visa is required by U.S., Canadian, Australian, British, Japanese, and EU citizens. All others require a visa.

Where to Stay: Hotel Arcada, +351 34 230 01, or fax +351 34 218 86. Hotel Afonso, +351 34 251 91, or fax +351 34 38 11 11. Residencial Alboi, +351 34 251 21. Portugal Tourist Office in the United States, (212) 354–4403. Tourist Office, Lisbon, +351 21 361 0350.
Finding the Break: From the Porto airport drive 50 miles south on the road to Lisbon, then take the coast road for Aveiro. Or from Lisbon take highway A8-ICI north as far as Leiria. You'll pass great dunes then come to Aveiro. Follow signs for Costa Nova and park at beach road, which runs for 2 miles along the coast.
Keep in Mind: Some crowded days.

Months	JF	MA	MJ	JA	SO	ND
Average Swell (feet)	6	5	4	3	4	6
Air Temp (C/F)	14/58	18/68	23/74	27/80	25/77	15/57
Water Temp (C/F)	13/55	14/57	16/60	20/68	18/64	14/58
Wetsuit	full	full	full	shorty	spring	full
Average Sunshine p/d (hours)	4	5	7	9	8	4
Average Rain p/m (inches)	4	3	2	1	1	3
Average Surfable Days p/m	20	19	17	15	17	22

57. SUPERTUBOS
Peniche, Portugal

Supertubos's waves are so steep to get into that they make you dizzy and can give you vertigo. This is cliff-hanging stuff. Once you're in, the solid cannon-firing action blows you out of the barrel and puts you in the cockpit of an F-16 fighter with guns firing at full throttle. Then off you go into oblivion. With board, or without? Depends on how strong that leash was.

Peniche, Portugal, is just 47 miles north of Lisbon, and is one of Europe's best left-hand beach breaks in an area that is a magnet to surfers. Peniche's many other nearby quality breaks are superb alternatives if Supertubos is flat.

Supertubos is on the south side of the Peniche peninsula, which at one time was a separate island. The island joined the coastline in the thirteenth century, forming the perfect surf peninsula that we all know and love today. Going south from Cape Carvoeiro is the fishing harbor called Molho Leste, which has a nice right peeling off a peak, and is often crowded with bodyboarders. The second break after this is the fantastic Supertubos, best with a 4-to-6-foot swell. It holds a south swell and is best with a northwest wind. The length of ride is short, but very intense and unforgettable. It's even heavier when it's over 6 to 8 feet.

Just a mile south is another classic break, Consolacao, which is a magic left and right point break on a small headland jutting out into the Atlantic. It's a fun wave on the right

Surfing started in Portugal around 1965 at the Costa del Sol area between Cascais and Estoril west of Lisbon, and quickly spread north to Peniche and Aveiro. Then Hank Williams, an American, began the manufacture of surfboards at Estoril from cork trees from local forests. These "cork tree surfboards" were cheap at $40–50 and were good to learn on. Today most modern surfboards are made in two locations—Peniche and Ericeira.

day, with its soft open-face waves on big days. Consolacao is also best in a south swell and northwest winds. From Consolacao the breaks farther south become more inaccessible, leaving most surfers with the no choice but to turn around and go back north, especially if there's a northerly groundswell running.

When there's a northerly groundswell, the other side of Peniche will be working best. The first north-side break is Praia do Baleal, a river-mouth and beach break. Next is Lagide, a left reef break, which stretches out as part of a beach break forming long lefts and mushy rights.

Portugal has 300 miles of coastline with surf from Moledo, Carinha, in the north to Sagres in the south. Peniche is one of the most picturesque places in Portugal, with its fishing village dating back to the fifteenth century. And at Peniche there is the faint smell of the fish-processing plant, an integral part of the surfing experience, as the salty taste of seawater in the Atlantic and the smells of the aquatic world surround you.

Worldwide, local scents reveal themselves in the surf. On Cornwall's south coast the smell of seaweed invades the break of Porthleven (Spot 45). In France the scent of the pine forests wafts over the break of Hossegor (Spot 53). And in western Australia, the fresh smell of eucalyptus permeates the senses at Gallingup. Here at Supertubos, it's the smell of the fresh fish on the air above the break that marks this unique spot. But what's a little fish smell when the waves are so perfect? Supertubos is ideal for the expert surfer and seafood lover.

Photo R. Sumpter

Photo R. Sumpter

Lefts

SW Swell

Break: Beach break

Skill Level: Intermediate to expert

Commitment: 6–10

Best Boards: Shortboard

Lifeguard: None

Hazards: Shallow shorebreak and outer sand bank with top-to-bottom breaking waves make this a challenging paddle-out, as well as a difficult ride at wave heights over 6 feet.

Currency: Euro.

Going There: No visa is required by U.S., Canadian, Australian, British, Japanese, and EU citizens. All others require a visa.

Where to Stay: Residencial Maritimo, +351 62 78 28 50. Residencial Vasco da Gama, +351 62 78 19 02, or fax +351 62 78 98 07. Camping Municipal de Peniche, +351 62 78 95 29, or fax +351 62 78 96 84. Portugal Tourist Office in the United States, (212) 354–4403; Lisbon, +351 21 361 0350.

Finding the Break: From the Lisboa airport drive 70 miles north. Take the road to Estoril and Cascais, then follow signs for Torres Vedras and then Peniche. Or from Lisbon take the A8-ICI north as far as Leiria. From Leiria take the N117 toward Queluz, then the IC19, which will take you to Sintra. From there, follow the N247 north to reach the N114, which takes you to Peniche.

Keep in Mind: Some crowded days when school's out and weekends.

Months	JF	MA	MJ	JA	SO	ND
Average Swell (feet)	5	5	4	3	4	4–6
Air Temp (C/F)	14/58	18/68	23/74	27/80	25/77	15/57
Water Temp (C/F)	13/55	14/57	16/60	20/68	18/64	14/58
Wetsuit	full	full	full	shorty	spring	full
Average Sunshine p/d (hours)	4	5	7	9	8	4
Average Rain p/m (inches)	4	3	2	1	1	3
Average Surfable Days p/m	20	14	12	9	15	18

58. LA SANTA
Lanzarote, Canary Islands

The whole reef surfing experience is rarely captured in any one spot, so it comes as some surprise that La Santa covers all the high and low points. From out the back you see sets arriving from halfway around the point, or the peak wells up out of nowhere and forms a perfect wall straight in your face. The takeoff is smooth, and a long drop sweeps you into a gliding rail turn. Cruising and directing maneuvers for hundreds of yards, the sections have a multitude of wave and swell formations to negotiate, with a windup of speed for the long downhill tube.

La Santa is situated on Lanzarote Island, in the chain known as the Canary Islands, south of Spain and east of North Africa (which can easily be seen from the island on a clear day). There are six neighboring islands: Tenerife, Fuerteventura, La Gomera, Gran Canaria, El Hierro, and La Palma. Five of the seven islands have surf, the fourth largest of which is Lanzarote, which derives its name from the thirteenth-century Italian explorer who settled here, Lancelloto Malocello.

La Santa is a world-class right-hand point break, with a sweeping barrel along the edge of the rocks. It has been made popular in the last decade by surfers from Europe discovering the island's warm climate and consistent surf. La Santa Point is the favorite, with its boulder-laid surf setup. Its length of ride, from 300 to 600 yards on a good day, is ideal. Known for its superb quality and speed, the point has a deep channel running the length of the break to aid paddling out, and which also improves the shape of the wave as it peels off close to the rocks.

When it comes to entering the water, accessing the break can take some time, because the lava rocks are very slippery and awkward to pass. Once you're past the shorebreak, where the waves are small (about 2 to 3 feet), it's easy enough to get into the channel and the calm water out back to the point surf, where it's breaking 6 to 8 feet. The water is blue, the barrels are many, and La Santa's waves work well from 4 to 12 feet. Ideal for the intermediate surfer in small surf, experts in the medium surf, and for big-wave riders if it's one of the huge days when the point is pumping 15 to 20 feet.

From the airport, the road takes you through tiny white painted villages, past extinct volcanic mountains, and leads through miles of barren wilderness to the other side of the island. Once on the other side, you must travel through a valley and over a hill to the beach, made mostly of boulders and black lava rocks—you may wish you'd brought your moon rover.

The scenery is entirely unique. With its fertile volcanic soil, small terraced farmyards create a checkerboard tapestry, nestling beside the villages. There is a thriving vacation trade, because the Canary Islands have beautiful warm weather when the rest of Europe is in the depths of winter.

Photo R. Sumpter

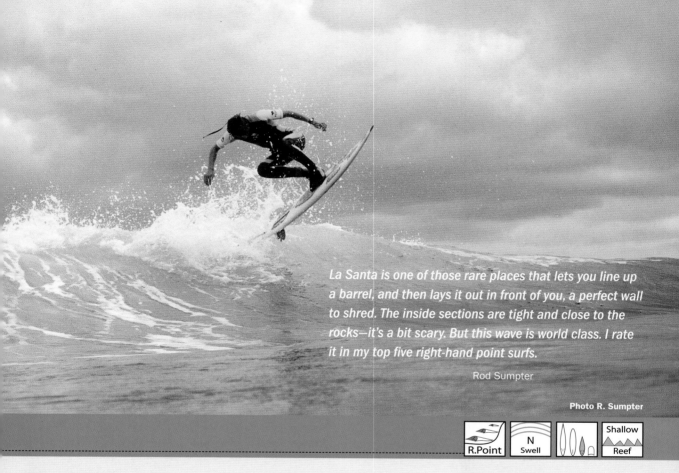

La Santa is one of those rare places that lets you line up a barrel, and then lays it out in front of you, a perfect wall to shred. The inside sections are tight and close to the rocks—it's a bit scary. But this wave is world class. I rate it in my top five right-hand point surfs.

Rod Sumpter

Photo R. Sumpter

| R.Point | N Swell | | Shallow Reef |

Break: Right-hand point break
Skill Level: Intermediate to expert
Commitment: 4–10
Best Boards: Shortboard
Lifeguard: None
Hazards: Rip currents, shallow rocks. Slippery boulders make the entry a tip-toe affair to a rocky shorebreak. The proximity of the surfing to rocks is the danger, and a wipeout could be fatal.
Currency: Euro.
Going There: No visa is required by U.S., Canadian, Australian, British, Japanese, and EU citizens. For vaccinations required, check with your doctor, health clinic, and embassy for up-to-date info.
Where to Stay: Club La Santa Sports (reception), +34 928 59 99 99, or fax +34 928 59 99 90. Lanzarote accommodations, info@lanzarote accommodation.com or +34 676 959 790. Faro Park The Gallery, +34 928 518 903. Santa Barbara, Costa Teguise. +34 928 592 148, or fax +34 928 591 801. Nautilus Costa Teguise, +34 928 592 148, or fax +34 928 591 801. Casa El Quinto, Tinajo, +34 928 529 232, or fax +34 928 529 839. Calima Surf Camp, info@calimasurf.com.
Finding the Break: Take the main road 3 miles to the capital, Arrecife; turn left for Tinajo, and from there take the road to La Santa. (Note the winding mountain roads.) Park at any of the beach trail roads from the cove to the point.
Keep in Mind: Crowded in December.

Months	JF	MA	MJ	JA	SO	ND
Average Swell (feet)	5	5	4	2	4	4–6
Air Temp (C/F)	22/72	23/73	24/75	28/84	26/79	20/70
Water Temp (C/F)	17/62	18/64	19/66	21/70	22/72	17/62
Wetsuit	full	full	full	shorty	spring	full
Average Sunshine p/d (hours)	7	8	9	10	9	7
Average Rain p/m (inches)	1	0.5	0	0	1	2
Average Surfable Days p/m	22	20	14	6	19	20

59. LA SANTA LEFTS
Lanzarote, Canary Islands

This extreme break is probably best to surf on a no-wind glassy day, as even a light offshore breeze will hold you at the top, beckoning disaster by rocketing you over the falls straight into a coral reef. This is a dicey wave by any description, and the fearsome drop and bottom turn give rise to over-stressed humming thruster fins and horrendous wipeouts.

Situated on the north coast of Lanzarote Island, a forty-five-minute drive from Arrecife, the capital, are the famous breaks of La Santa Lefts and El Quemao. Together they are known as the Pipeline of the Canaries. El Quemao—referred to as the Village Left—is the ultimate short-barreling left peak, with a length of ride of just 30 yards. It breaks on the reefs at the fishing village of La Santa, just to the left of the harbor, which is the best way out of this demanding break. The coastline here is made up of sharp lava reefs shelving steeply to the water's edge. Boulders, platforms, and craggy rock formations make for a lunar landscape, and a very difficult and slippery entry into the water. The waves of El Quemao are only a stone's throw from shore, and work best in a northerly swell and light southwest winds.

There is a strong local population of surfers here, and a good many are bodyboarders who find the short drop and tube of the Pipeline ideal. Big-gun surfboards aid early entry into these fiercely fast and hollow takeoffs.

Longboards, however, have no chance—the waves are too fast and steep. When La Santa Lefts are pumping, they are the finest-looking waves in the Canaries. The tube lines up as a down-the-line surf-out, comparable to Banzai Pipeline (Spot 2) in Hawaii, with a ride length of 150 to 300 yards on a good day. These breaks have only been surfed in the last two decades, since the arrival of hard-core European surfers.

If this demanding reef break isn't quite your style, there are a few beach breaks on the island, the best of which is at Famara, a twenty-minute drive east of La Santa. Famara has softer waves and is good for intermediate surfers. The Village Left and La Santa Lefts are both dangerous surf spots and are for expert surfers and big-wave riders only.

Looking inland from the roaring surf, you'll see that Lanzarote is an extinct volcano in the Atlantic Ocean; it's made up of sloping, clean, black volcanic plains and mountains. The main roads around the island are tarmac, and wind endlessly around hill and mountain passes with good views of distant surf breaks. There are quite a few fishing villages and farming areas, made fertile by the black volcanic ash that covers the island. Roll-on, roll-off ferries operate from Spain and all of the other Canary Islands, making island surf hopping hassle-free with good accommodations everywhere.

Photo R. Sumpter

The European equivalent of Pipeline. Both places are very sucky, very hollow waves, steep late takeoffs, and chances of incredible barrels—but very dangerous as well, because it's so shallow and close to the rocks. Definitely some of the more extreme waves in Europe.

John Sumpter,
1997 Ligger Bay Surfing Champion

Photo R. Sumpter

| Lefts | NW Swell | | Shallow Reef |

Break: Left-hand reef break
Skill Level: Expert
Commitment: 8–10
Best Boards: Shortboard
Lifeguard: None
Hazards: Waves break over sharp boulders and ledges. Rips and currents make this a death-defying shallow barrel to paddle into. Inside area has plenty of urchins.
Currency: Euro.
Going There: No visa is required by U.S., Canadian, Australian, British, Japanese, and EU citizens. For vaccinations required, check with your doctor, health clinic, and embassy for up-to-date info.
Where to Stay: Club La Santa Sports (reception), +34 928 59 99 99, or fax +34 928 59 99 90. Lanzarote accommodations, info@lanzaroteaccomodation.com or +34 676 959 790. Faro Park The Gallery, +34 928 518 903, or fax +34 928 518 903. Santa Barbara Costa Teguise, +34 928 592 148, or fax +34 928 591 801. Nautilus Costa Teguise, +34 928 592 148, or fax +34 928 591 801. Casa El Quinto, Tinajo, +34 928 529 232, or fax +34 928 529 839. Calmina Surf Camp, info@calimasurf.com.

Finding the Break: Take the main road 3 miles to the capital, Arrecife; turn left for Tinajo, and from there take the road to La Santa. (Note the winding mountain roads.) Park at any of the beach trail roads from the cove to the point.
Keep in Mind: Some crowds.

Months	JF	MA	MJ	JA	SO	ND
Average Swell (feet)	5	5	4	2	4	4–6
Air Temp (C/F)	22/72	23/73	24/75	28/84	26/79	20/70
Water Temp (C/F)	17/62	18/64	19/66	21/70	22/72	17/62
Wetsuit	full	full	full	shorty	spring	full
Average Sunshine p/d (hours)	7	8	9	10	9	7
Average Rain p/m (inches)	1	0.5	0	0	1	2
Average Surfable Days p/m	22	20	14	6	19	20

60. LOBOS ISLAND
Canary Islands

The extreme takeoff against the rocks starts hard up against the pit and pulls strongly at your fins. As wave sections boil, it throws and sucks the insides out of an overhead swell. The wall lines up way out ahead of you as you zigzag to avoid breaking wave sections, with the goal of making it all the way down that mixed hairy surf course and setting up a superdrive through the box.

Four miles northwest of Corralejo Fuerteventura, Lobos Island is the home to one of Europe's best right-hand point breaks, called Los Lobos. This is a surfers' and travelers' delight, a remote, barren island in the chain of seven. Los Lobos is accessed via the ferryboat that travels over from Fuerteventura morning and afternoon. The ferry ride is usually packed with bikers, walkers, and surfers and, although there's not much on Lobos, most people are attracted by the strange lunar landscape created by years of volcanic activity. The surfers, of course, are more intrigued by the island's classic waves.

When there's not much swell about, Lobos will be bigger than the other islands by as much as 4 feet. From the ferry there's a fantastic view of the right-hander peeling off at the harbor wall on Fuerteventura. This is the famous Lobos Right break. You can see a stripe of breaking swells and whitewater right along the view of the island, providing a fabulous insight into the forthcoming waves that peel the entire length of the shoreline. It takes twenty minutes to walk to the point, where entry is difficult over the million-year-old volcanic boulders. The barrels on the wave start right after takeoff and continue all the way through, making the walling sections and cutback connections superb. The ride lasts for about 0.25 mile, and on a good day runs 600 yards, leaving your legs tired but your brain stoked. A full day of surfing ends in the afternoon when you must catch the ferry back to the mainland.

This surf at Los Lobos is for experts only thanks to its break over shallow rocky ledges and its hollow, sucky, and gnarly characteristics. As you can imagine, the tubes also have a very demanding nature, none of which is for the fainthearted.

For those less inclined to take on Los Lobos's mean surf, take about a thirty-minute walk to the other side of the island, where you'll find a left break perfect for intermediates. The Lobos Left is a softer, well-lined-up cresting wave that needs a northerly groundswell and southerly wind to work best.

Photo S. Sumpter

Lobos is another one of the adventure spots. The wave's fine, and plenty of offshore wind. You have to walk to the far side of the island. It's a right about 6 to 8 feet, carving real down-the-line raciness.

Colin McPhillips,
2000–2002 World Longboard Surfing Champion

Photo R. Sumpter

| Rights | Lefts | R.Point | L.Point | NW Swell | NE Swell | | Shallow Reef |

Break: Right-hand and left-hand point break

Skill Level: Expert

Commitment: 7–10

Best Boards: Shortboard

Lifeguard: None

Hazards: The rocky shoreline and boulder-strewn line-up make this a demanding wave at waist-high to double overhead. The risky get-out becomes a nightmare. Beware of theft.

Currency: Euro.

Going There: No visa is required by U.S., Canadian, Australian, British, Japanese, and EU citizens. For vaccinations required, check with your doctor, health clinic, and embassy for up-to-date info.

Where to Stay: Apartments and Villas, OO +34 928 535 376. Costa Calma Beach, +34 928 875 046, or fax +34 928 875 544. Apartamentos Corralejo Beach, +34 928 866 315, or fax +34 928 866 317. Hotel Monica Beach, +34 928 547 214, or fax +34 928 547 318. Luxury Holiday Villas Agents, +44 (0) 870 443 2302.

Finding the Break: From the Fuerteventura airport take the road to Puerto del Rosario, then Puerto de Lajas to Corralejo. Continue to the harbor; the ferry to Lobos leaves daily at 10:00 A.M. and returns at 3:00 P.M.

Keep in Mind: Watch out for theft on Lobos.

Months	JF	MA	MJ	JA	SO	ND
Average Swell (feet)	5	5	4	2	4	4–6
Air Temp (C/F)	22/72	23/73	24/75	28/84	26/79	20/70
Water Temp (C/F)	17/62	18/64	19/66	21/70	22/72	17/62
Wetsuit	full	full	full	shorty	spring	full
Average Sunshine p/d (hours)	7	8	9	10	9	7
Average Rain p/m (inches)	1	0.5	0	0	1	2
Average Surfable Days p/m	22	20	14	6	19	20

61. THE BUBBLE
Fuerteventura, Canary Islands

When the Bubble breaks, watch out. This is the most challenging wave on the island. As the name implies, the Bubble bursts into a concave apex, and you're left strung up in a bottleneck canopy, about to drop like a stone. If you don't angle and put on speed down the face, you simply won't make it.

The Bubble is situated at the northern side of the island of Fuerteventura, also known as the North Shore. To get there you must first endure the drive over a potholed sand road along a reef-bound stretch of coastline. Fortunately, this coastline has some of the island's finest surf.

The Bubble is 10 miles west of Corralejo, a town of original design and local color. The island is a volcanic archipelago, located 71 miles off the northwest coast of the African continent. Fuerteventura is the second biggest island of the Canary Island chain, with 152 beaches and 160 miles of coastline. Of the seven islands, it's the longest at 62 miles, and it has the most surf of all the islands. The Bubble is the island's best and most famous surf break, often compared to Hawaii's Backdoor (Spot 1), with its steep, hollow drop-in and short, heavy-on-the-edge rides. This surf spot has a flat volcanic rock shelf 200 yards from shore, with rocks and spiky urchins from there to the shore, making entry quite difficult. The effort is duly compensated, however, as set after set towers in and the barrels seem to break endlessly in the same spot. This helps make possible very predictable positioning, providing more and more scary, hairy rides. The Bubble is a must-surf spot for experts.

Yarro, a nearby wave, is just a short paddle west of the Bubble. It's a long left and softer right, has a nice walling wave in the 4-to-6-foot range, and is the preferred fun wave of the area—a performance wave with rides of 250 yards on a good day.

If you've surfed the Bubble enough, Fuerteventura has waves all the way down its western coast. Access, however, can be quite difficult. On the south coast at Punta del Tigre is a peninsula with quality sand points. Driving here and elsewhere on the island can be dangerous, with narrow tracks and boulder-laden roads that wind around perilous cliff edges. Punta del Tigre is a good, fast right-hander on the eastern side of the peninsula. It's offshore in westerly winds, holding the waves well up to 8 feet in a southerly swell.

Photo R. Sumpter

The Bubble is good—probably the best wave I surfed there—hollow and a very steep drop.

Colin McPhillips,
2000–2002 World Longboard
Surfing Champion

Photo R. Sumpter

| Rights | Lefts | Peak | N Swell | |

Break: Right-hand reef break
Skill Level: Expert
Commitment: 6–10
Best Boards: Shortboard
Lifeguard: None
Hazards: Drifts and rip currents. Shallow rock bottom makes a steep throw-out wave dangerous. Flat platforms of rock and urchins hamper a clean get-out.
Currency: Euro.

Going There: No visa is required by U.S., Canadian, Australian, British, Japanese, and EU citizens. For vaccinations required, check with your doctor, health clinic, and embassy for up-to-date info. Where to Stay: Corralejo Beach, +34 928 866 315. Costa Calma Beach, +34 928 875 046, or fax +34 928 875 544. Apartamentos, fax +34 928 866 317. Hotel Monica

Beach, +34 928 547 214, or fax +34 928 547 318. Luxury Holiday Villas Agents, +44 (0) 870 443 2302.
Finding the Break: From the Fuerteventura airport take the road to Puerto del Rosario, then Puerto de Lajas to Corralejo. Go to the west side of the town and take the dirt road for Majanicho. This is the only road to the Bubble. About 4 miles along you will come to an open flat area with a good view of the surf—this is the Bubble. (Note that you'll pass five great unnamed reef breaks that are demanding to access and provide classic waves. If these are good, chances are the Bubble will be better.)
Keep in Mind: Rarely crowded, except on weekends.

Months	JF	MA	MJ	JA	SO	ND
Average Swell (feet)	5	5	4	2	4	4–6
Air Temp (C/F)	22/72	23/73	24/75	28/84	26/79	20/70
Water Temp (C/F)	17/62	18/64	19/66	21/70	22/72	17/62
Wetsuit	full	full	full	shorty	spring	full
Average Sunshine p/d (hours)	7	8	9	10	9	7
Average Rain p/m (inches)	1	0.5	0	0	1	2
Average Surfable Days p/m	22	20	14	6	12	20

62. ANCHOR POINT
Agadir, Morocco

If Agadir is the crown of this ancient and beautiful land, then Anchor Point is its jewel—a true testing ground for surfers wishing for high performance, long, clean point surf, and a hankering for the bazaar. Anchor Point has a steep hooking peak and a trough a mile deep. These silver waves get their rhythm from the rip currents that flow down from Mystery Point to Killer Point, so named because it's where the killer whales breach. Double overhead sets jack up with the curve of a Moroccan dagger. Then you stab at the wall and carve the face of the wave.

Anchor Point, discovered more than three decades ago, is situated in southern Morocco, 300 miles south of the capital of Rabat. This is the best and most famous of several world-class right-hand point breaks in Morocco. Anchor Point, in many ways, is a symbol of, and certainly the most admired, true point surf in Europe. But to get into this surf can prove to be as dangerous as a Moroccan saber.

Entering the water off rock slabs can be dangerous; timing is important. When the surf is big at 10 to 12 feet, strong north-to-south rips sweep down the lineup and a long paddle can be expected. Takeoff is a slide into a clean wall. But if there's a strong offshore wind, the desert sand can sting your face hard. Once you're launched in, the drop is steep and fast, the sections line up for a great wave, and your length of ride can be at 600 yards or more.

To get there from Agadir Al Massira International Airport, you must pass many fine surf spots. The first spot along the coast road is a mellow beach break called Main Beach. This break is at the southern end of Agadir Bay, where there are three huge rocks stuck out in the sea that help form good sandbars and have huge whitewater splash-ups on a big swell. These rocks can be indicators for the inside surf break that peels off the sandbars nicely. To the north the waves tend to close out in a barrel, but in the corner, toward the docks, there are gentle beginners' waves with soft, reforming swells in an area sheltered from big winter storms.

Past Agadir Bay the coast twists and turns past distant point surf and beckoning bays, all of which are difficult to get to; a four-wheel drive is well advised. Banana Beach can be a neat, fun wave, located just off the main road. So, too, is Tamghart. But it's not until reaching the town of Tarhazoute that the coast become a series of points, and the beach breaks stop. The main road then winds its way straight into the path of the first, the longest, and most classic wave of Anchor Point. Next is Mystery, a point reef break with several takeoff areas. Just around the winding road that hugs the coast is Killer Point. This is a big-wave spot with a big drop, close to the rocks, and a long wall that nearly connects with Anchor Point on a good day. This whole stretch of coastline northward oozes with breaks, especially for the four-wheel-drive vehicle in this rugged, colorful country. Ideal for the expert, but there are a few places to suit all grades of surfer. Morocco has it all.

The date of when surfing first started in Morocco has been lost to time. But in 1967 I took Wayne Lynch and Paul Witzig on a trip from France to explore the northern half of this country. They were making a surfing film called *The Hot Generation*. More surfers followed their lead while, at the same time, the first locals became interested in the sport as well. This led to the inception, in 1975, of the Royal Moroccan Surf Club. Since then local clubs have held regular championships among teams from Oudaya Surf Club, Cap Surf Morocco, and Agadir Surf Club.

The terrain of Morocco is harsh, bordering the western Sahara Desert and backed by the Atlas Mountains. The highest mountains in North Africa lie in the Toubkal National Park, and are popular for skiing through the winter.

The coastal city of Rabat, home to King Mohammad VI, also has some fine surf. His Highness took over power from his father in 1999, and, aside from being king, is also president of the local surf club.

Photo R. Sumpter

Anchor Point is the point break to change your life. This is a fast-down-the-line wave for a mile. There are six different sections on a good 6-to-8-foot swell. Race down the lineup and make an excellent barrel. It's not top to bottom, it's just down the line. In the pocket is amazing, hauling as fast as you can go.

Rod Sumpter

Photo R. Sumpter

| R.Point | NW Swell | | Shallow Reef |

Break: Right-hand point break
Skill Level: Expert
Commitment: 7–10
Best Boards: Shortboard
Lifeguard: None
Hazards: Rocky shelves and ledges; strong rip currents, jump-off entry
Currency: Moroccan dirham.
Going There: No visa is required by U.S., Canadian, Australian, British, Japanese, and EU citizens. All others require a visa. Vaccinations required—typhoid, polio, and malaria. Check with your doctor, health clinic, and embassy for up-to-date info.
Where to Stay: Vacation Villas, +44 (0) 7042 810 074. Sheraton Agadir Hotel, +212 48 843 232, or fax +212 48 844 379. Mecure Hotel, +212 972 894 1173, or fax +212 972 580 9225. Guest House and tours, bookings@purevacations.com.
Finding the Break: From the Agadir airport head to Agadir city center and follow signs to Agadir Bay. Then take the coast road north to Anchor Point, just north of the town of Taghazoute.
Surf Schools: Association Cap Surf Morocco, + 212 22 74 575. The Royal Moroccan Surfing Federation,and. Royal Moroccan Surfing School, +212 22 59 530.
Keep in Mind: Theft happens here. Be on guard.

Months	JF	MA	MJ	JA	SO	ND
Average Swell (feet)	5	5	4	2	4	4–6
Air Temp (C/F)	22/72	23/73	24/75	28/84	26/79	20/70
Water Temp (C/F)	17/62	18/64	19/66	21/70	22/72	17/62
Wetsuit	full	full	full	shorty	spring	full
Average Sunshine p/d (hours)	7	8	9	10	9	7
Average Rain p/m (inches)	2	1	0.5	0	1	2
Average Surfable Days p/m	15	12	10	3	14	19

Photo R. Sumpter

AFRICA

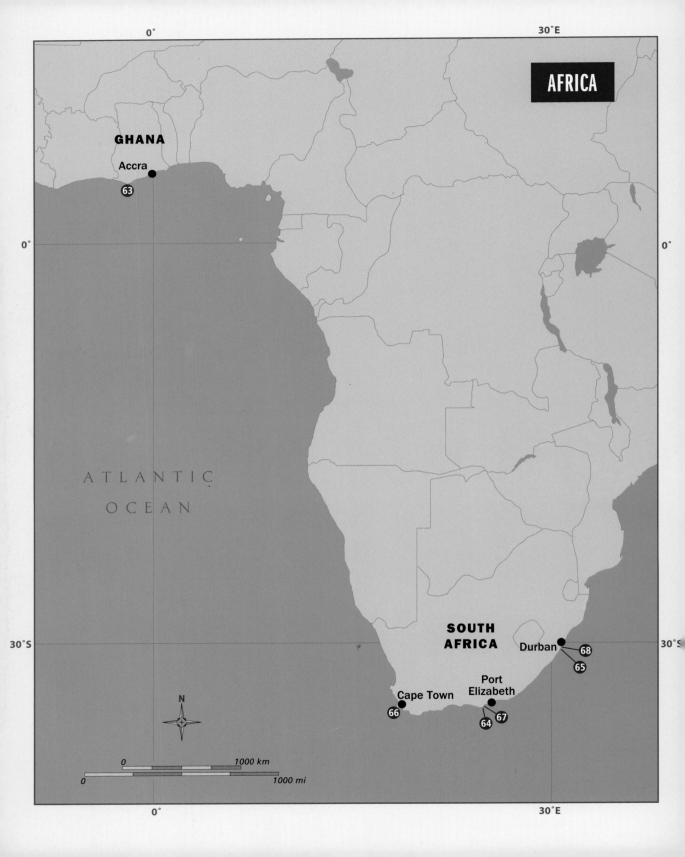

AFRICA

GHANA

Accra
63

ATLANTIC
OCEAN

SOUTH
AFRICA

Durban
68
65

Cape Town
66

Port
Elizabeth
64 67

N

0°   30°E

0°   0°

30°S   30°S

0°   30°E

0   1000 km

0   1000 mi

There's no richer surfing country to explore in the world than Africa. Two world-famous surf hot spots are Ghana on the west coast bordered by the Atlantic, and South Africa where the Atlantic and Indian Oceans converge.

You cannot go to Africa without coming away with some of its history. The west coast country of Ghana saw the bulk of slave-trade activity along the Cape Coast. Indeed, former trading posts can still be seen next to the surf. The mighty barreling point surf of Cape Three Points is an unforgettable area. Here slave ships stopped to pick up gold, ivory, slaves, and water before departing west—no doubt battling the huge surf on its arrival and departure.

Africa's west coast receives its surf from the Gulf of Guinea and low pressures off the Ascension Islands. Many coastal beaches, points, and reefs remain uncharted due to the inhospitable terrain. But Ghana's Cape Coast has plenty of waves, and good places to stay as well. Dixcove is the southernmost town with surf in Ghana; it's about 125 miles west of Accra. Still, the ultimate challenge and best spot is Cape Three Points, with its magic points lining up waves on the brow of the bays where the powerful Atlantic swells reach Africa. Cape Three Points holds a big swell and, although it's a lonely place to ride, it's also a perfect wave and a beauty spot. For the hardy traveler wanting waves worth riding, it is a must-adventure of beaches, villages, and points.

South Africa's east coast receives swell from the Indian Ocean, and the surf on its Atlantic west coast at places like Dungeons, Cape Town, can be 35 feet to 40 feet—some of the biggest waves in the world. This is also where the coast of Africa is a favored calving ground of southern right whales. During August and September these mammoths of the ocean can be observed close inshore. Indeed, the marine reserve of Walker Bay has been recognized by the World Wildlife Fund (WWF) as one of the world's top twelve whale-watching sites.

On the east coast there is a choice of fabulous breaks: Durban's Cave Rock, with heavy hollow barrels; North Beach, with its piers collecting and shaping sandbars to form great wedgy waves; Cape St. Francis, where the perfect wave has, for generations, been known to amaze surfers. At Jeffrey's Bay near Port Elizabeth, where the best tubes are at Super Tubes opposite the town dunes, surfers gather and wait for the ultimate test of speed and tube riding. Challenging the monster waves and harsh conditions of Super Tubes can be a surfer's most compelling dream, one that will long live in the memory of surfing tales.

There's no surfing place in the world quite like Africa. Its unique waves will always be special to photographers, surf filmmakers, and surfers alike. The sense of danger and wildness about the ocean only makes this continent all the more attractive to wave riders.

63. CAPE THREE POINTS

Ghana, West Africa

To find magic African point surf, look no farther than Ghana, at Cape Three Points. The place is, as its name implies, two bays and three points joined together to form probably the best point surf in all of West Africa. The waves swing in from behind the points and perform a hot, steamy tribal dance into the bays. A drumbeat of clean, glassy swell grows frenzied as the shore dump looms. Beads of sweat run down your face in anticipation. This place is hot!

Situated 125 miles west of Accra, the capital of Ghana, and 120 miles east of Abidjan, the capital of the Ivory Coast, is the fabulous surf break of Cape Three Points, the southernmost point in Ghana. Cape Three Points is a headland whose wave setup consists of three points and a beach break. First Point brings up a huge wall of green swell breaking over deepwater reefs, holding big surf of 10 to 15 feet. Then Second Point, which almost connects to the first, becomes a reforming takeoff peak This right-hand hotdog wall has a mighty wave face that lines up well. It holds best at 6 to 8 feet, and each point's length of ride is about 250 to 500 yards. The next break is Third Point, with its long lines of sweeping swell giving a fun mushy wave into the bay, as well as a beach break that can be downright harrowing. The wave dumps so hard, it's best to paddle in between sets. On occasion, however, the shorebreak can have a lot of shape and be a really good ride.

Ghana is one of Africa's most stable and developed countries, with 300 miles of coastline and several key surfing beaches. West of Accra is the tiny town of Busua Beach, with fine white sand and excellent bodysurfing lefts and rights. There's one hotel to stash your bags. A twenty-minute walk away is the beauty spot of Dixcove, which has the best beach break surfing for miles and is possibly one of the most picturesque beaches in Ghana. Here ace sandbars produce near-vertical, fast-walling waves with several sections ending in a high-performance hollow shorebreak.

The Ghanaian coast between Accra and Cape Three Points is also famous for its ocean-fresh lobster, available from the waterfront markets.

For flat surf days, there are numerous wildlife and game reserves in the area. These include the Kakum Nature Park, Owabi Wildlife Sanctuary, Bia National Park, Bui National Park, and Mole Game Reserve. These are all great for wildlife-watching and exploring the savannas.

Most of Ghana's road network is in decent shape, but as with many developing nations, some roads are in poor condition and badly potholed. However, if an award were given for the country with the friendliest people, Ghana would be a strong contender. A place of contrasts and surprises, the whole of the Cape Coast provides some good waves in the right conditions. This is a surf trip for the hardened traveler and the expert surfer only.

The best time to travel to the Republic of Ghana is from December to February, just after the second rainy season and before the humid heat when the Atlantic Ocean averages surfable swell.

Photo R. Sumpter

The whole idea of remote surfing locations appeals to me. It's a travelogue of adventures. I had some of my best waves just surfing beach breaks alongside dugout canoes. Really friendly people.

Rod Sumpter

Photo R. Sumpter

 Rights R.Point Beachbreak S Swell

Break: Point break
Skill Level: Expert
Commitment: 7–10
Best Boards: Shortboard, longboard
Lifeguard: None
Hazards: Rip currents, rocky outcrops, shallow sand-and-rock bottom
Currency: Cedi.
Going There: Visa required by U.S., Canadian, Australian, British, Japanese, EU, and all other citizens. Vaccinations required—yellow fever, cholera, typhoid, polio. Malaria risk. Check with your doctor, health clinic, and embassy for latest info.
Where to Stay: Busua Beach Resort, +233-31 21210. Raybow International Hotel, Dixcove Hill, +233 31 22072, or www.travel.yahoo.com/p-travelguide-588038-dixcove_busua_ghana. Cape Coast Hotel, +233 42 22755. Elmina Beach, +233 42 337 742. Savoy, +233 42 32805. Aggrey Palace, +233 42 33556. Excelsior, +233 42 33246. Biriwa Beach, +233 42 33333, or fax +233 42 33666. Accra Hotel, cudjoe1772@hotmail.com. Accra Guesthouses, +233 21 24006 or fax +233 31 22072. Official Ghana tourism Web site, www.ghana.com/republic/tourism. Ghana Tourism Network, www.ghanaonline.com.
Finding the Break: Cape Three Points lies five hours (125 miles) west from Accra on the Cape Coast road past Takoradi on West Africa's Gold Coast.
Keep in Mind: No crowds—you surf alone.

Months	JF	MA	MJ	JA	SO	ND
Average Swell (feet)	4–5	4	3	2	4	5
Air Temp (C/F)	26/79	27/81	23/74	28/84	28/84	24/76
Water Temp (C/F)	18/64	19/66	21/70	23/75	24/76	21/70
Wetsuit	shorty	shorty	vest	none	none	vest
Average Sunshine p/d (hours)	8–9	8	7	7–8	8	9
Average Rain p/m (inches)	0.5	2	5	7	2	1
Average Surfable Days p/m	10	12	14	12	12	11

It's a pumping, threshing, beating, manic right-hander that pulverizes the surfer's senses. It has been described, more than any other surf spot in the world, with the word *perfect.* And it's worth saying again. Cape St. Francis is perfect—a star spot for decades, once considered the best wave in the world. Surfers roll up, paddle out, and gravitate out through a pipeline-spitting shorebreak to the point break where the biggest, heaviest, and hollowest waves break. Cape St. Francis point looks easy, uniform and perfect, but beware the power and speed. This is where the waves can crush you into liquid, pour you into the curl, turn you into spray, wash you around, and spit you out the other end.

Situated 10 miles southwest of Jeffrey's Bay (Spot 67) and 30 miles south of Port Elizabeth, St. Francis Bay and the adjacent Cape St. Francis offer the quintessential right point break, with perfect tubes peeling off a sand dune point a couple of days a year. Called "the perfect wave" in the surfing film *Endless Summer,* Cape St. Francis became instantly famous in the early 1960s.

Today's Francis Bay, with Cape St. Francis point, beach, and the estuary of the Kromme River, form an aquatic playground for surfing, deep-sea fishing, whale-watching, and scuba diving.

Cape St. Francis waves start forming in the great Southern Ocean between the continent of Africa to the north and Antarctica to the south. The wind blows across the water, and the surface becomes ripples, then white horses. Over time, order appears, and long swell lines start marching across the sea. They catch on the rim of Cape St. Francis headland and sweep into St. Francis Bay as the perfect wave.

Another break of interest in the area is Seal Point, 3 miles west of Cape St. Francis. Its lighthouse marks the westernmost point on the eastern cape. Built in 1873, the lighthouse is now a national monument. Seal Point is a right-hand reef break running down a rocky boulder point. It is sheltered in gales, and is good for times when elsewhere is too big or blown out. Additionally, if Cape St. Francis and Seal Point should be flat, then a 150-mile trip northeast to the Sunshine Coast (if you're in a traveling mood) will bring you to the famous Nahoon Reef. This right-hand, big-wave reef point is a long 0.5-mile paddle out from the beach. This spot might just save the day, with a good 3-to-4-foot wave.

Photo R. Sumpter

How surfing started in South Africa and how Cape St. Francis became one of the world's most famous waves is largely a question of chance. It all started after World War II, when Australian surfers described to Durbanite Fred Crocker, who became the first board builder in South Africa, how surfboards were built, and how they rode standing up. This knowledge was passed on to Jon Whitmore from Cape Town, who went on to discover Cape St. Francis and its perfect waves. It wasn't until 1962 that Bruce Brown, a surf filmmaker from California, rediscovered the spot after talking with Jon Whitmore and decided to make a film called *Endless Summer.* The rest, as they say, is history.

Although length of ride has been shortened by the 1995 development of a commercial harbor at the point called Port. St Francis, top surfers say the wave is still world class.

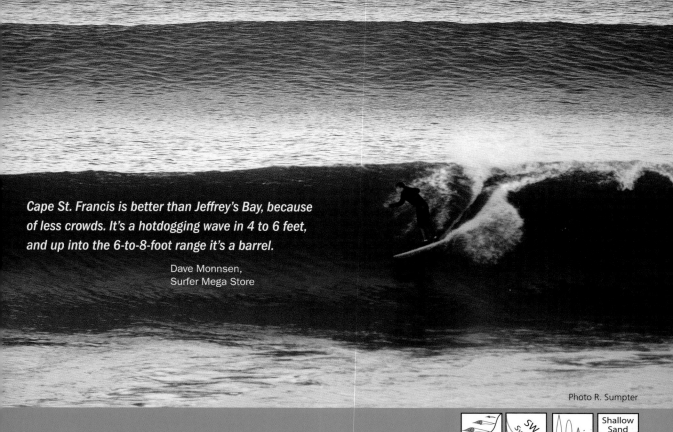

Cape St. Francis is better than Jeffrey's Bay, because of less crowds. It's a hotdogging wave in 4 to 6 feet, and up into the 6-to-8-foot range it's a barrel.

Dave Monnsen,
Surfer Mega Store

Photo R. Sumpter

R.Point | SW Swell | | Shallow Sand

Break: Right-hand point break
Skill Level: Expert
Commitment: 5–10
Best Boards: Shortboard
Lifeguard: None
Hazards: Shallow sand-bottom tubes; rip currents; powerful tubes and heavy waves
Currency: Rand.
Going There: No visa is required by British and Irish passport holders; all others should check with their embassy. Vaccinations required—tetanus, typhoid, polio, malaria, tuberculosis (children). Check with your doctor, health clinic, and embassy for the latest info.
Where to Stay: Cape St. Francis Resort, +27 (0) 42 298 0054. Seal Point Backpackers +27 (0) 42 298 00284, or www.capestfrancis.co.za.Waterways B & B, +27 (0) 42 294 0282. Thatch Cottage, +27 (0) 42 294 0082, or fax +27 (0) 42 294 1998. Safari.com, Jeffrey's Bay, +27 (0) 21 783 3622, or +27 (0) 21 783 3626.

Finding the Break: Located 400 miles east of Cape Town and 540 miles southwest of Durban. From the Port Elizabeth airport, follow the signs to the N2 motorway toward Cape Town and Humansdorp. Once you are on the N2, keep driving for approximately forty-five minutes until you see the R330 Humansdorp exit. Take this exit and follow the road into Humansdorp, looking for signs to St. Francis Bay. Park at the beach.

Keep in Mind: The perfect wave is rare.

Months	JF	MA	MJ	JA	SO	ND
Average Swell (feet)	1–2	3	4–5	5	4	2
Air Temp (C/F)	28/82	27/81	24/76	23/74	24/76	26/79
Water Temp (C/F)	24/76	24/76	23/74	22/72	22/72	23/74
Wetsuit	none	none	shorty	spring	shorty	none
Average Sunshine p/d (hours)	6	7	7	7	5	5–6
Average Rain p/m (inches)	5	4	3	1	2	5
Average Surfable Days p/m	1	2	3	6	3	1

65. CAVE ROCK
Durban, Natal, South Africa

One of South Africa's top three surf spots is Cave Rock. When the swell gets overhead at the "Rock" and the world-class waves explode across the shallow reefs, all hell breaks out at the summit. Loose leg rope tangles and you're down the wave face, clawing across the wall. In the face of doom, the middle section looms like a wall of glass. Sheer horseshoe peaks end the wave like a Mike Tyson fight: fast, nasty, and brutal. The final kick-out finishes in victory celebrations, foam and flying tinsel. Dream on.

Cave Rock is situated 3 miles south of Durban on the "Southside" (as it's known locally), on the way toward Brighton Beach and the Bluff. This gigantic rock headland that forms the southeastern arm of Durban's harbor is the spot that receives much attention on Cave Rock Beach. With its tubing, barreling waves, this hollow right-hander is the sought-after spot in the Durban area. Waves hit hard and heavy with huge gaping barrels, which, along with Jeffrey's Bay, has made South Africa famous in the surfing world.

South Africa is blessed with two coastlines to surf, the Atlantic's west coast and the Indian Ocean's east. On the east coast you'll find a string of beaches that includes breaks such as Cave Rock, Brighton Beach, Anstey's Beach, and Garvies Beach, all of which are just south of the Mkomazi River. On the north side of the river are Doonside, Warner Beach, Winkelspruit, and Illove. Cave Rock is world class and is known for its consistency and for the quality, speed, and power of its tubes, having a length of ride on a normal day of 50 yards and 100 yards on a good day. Cave Rock is a revered break respected by all those who have surfed this awesome wave. This is a must-surf spot for the expert if you're planning a trip to South Africa.

Cave Rock on a spring low tide looks like one flat slab of rock stretching out 200 yards from a tiny strip of sand. The nearest center of population is Durban, a bustling city and home to Seaworld, where they have a large population of sharks. Cave Rock is netted against sharks, as are all the beaches mentioned in the text. However, South Africa's coastline is 1,700 miles long, so the less popular and remote beaches are not always totally protected from these toothy carnivores.

Photo © ASP Tostee

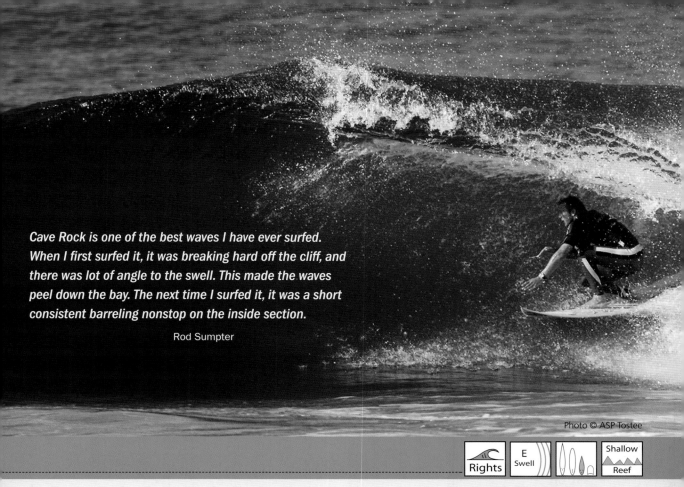

Cave Rock is one of the best waves I have ever surfed. When I first surfed it, it was breaking hard off the cliff, and there was lot of angle to the swell. This made the waves peel down the bay. The next time I surfed it, it was a short consistent barreling nonstop on the inside section.

Rod Sumpter

Photo © ASP Tostee

Rights | E Swell | | Shallow Reef

Break: Right-hand reef break
Skill Level: Expert
Commitment: 6–10
Best Boards: Shortboard
Lifeguard: None
Hazards: Rocky seabed, dangerous rip currents, tubing waves
Currency: Rand.

Going There: No visa is required by British and Irish passport holders; all others should check with their embassy. Vaccinations required—tetanus, typhoid, polio, malaria, tuberculosis (children). Check with your doctor, health clinic, and embassy for the latest info.
Where to Stay: Bluewater Beachfront

Hotel, +27 (0) 31 332 4272, or fax +27 (0) 31 337 5817. Albany Hotel, +27 (0) 31 304 4381 or fax +27 (0) 31 307 1411. Holiday Inn Garden Court North Beach, +27 (0) 31 32 7361 or fax +27 (0) 031 37 4058. Palace Protea, +27 (0) 031 32 8351 or fax +27 (0) 031 32 8307. Holiday Inn Crown Plaza, +27 (0) 031 37 1321 or fax +27 (0) 031 32 5527. Hostels, +27 (0) 031 467 1192 or ansteysbeach@mweb.co.za. .

Finding the Break: From the Durban airport take the M4 south, then take Bluff/Edwin Swales turnoff; follow the BEACH signs. Look for a sign on Ansteys Road/Foreshore Drive, then signs for Cave Rock.

Keep in Mind: Crowds in December.

Months	JF	MA	MJ	JA	SO	ND
Average Swell (feet)	2	4	5	5–6	3–4	2–3
Air Temp (C/F)	28/82	27/81	24/76	23/74	24/76	26/79
Water Temp (C/F)	24/76	24/76	23/74	22/72	22/72	23/74
Wetsuit	none	none	shorty	spring	shorty	none
Average Sunshine p/d (hours)	6	7	7	7	5	5–6
Average Rain p/m (inches)	5	4	3	1	2	5
Average Surfable Days p/m	10	4	3	2	6	9

66. DUNGEONS
Cape Town, South Africa

Big waves don't get much bigger than these. Tall, heavy, and pitching with the power of a stampede, the noise of the Zulu drums. You need your biggest rhino chaser to catch these moving mountains. They're bigger than 30 feet and grow fast. You have to be a big-wave rider to join this charge of the light brigade.

Dungeons is a right-hand reef break situated off Hout Bay, Cape Town, within a stone's throw of the Sentinel Mountain, Cape Town's famous landmark. This imposing surf spot is a storm-blasted collection of jagged rocks and reefs, wedged between cliffs of the Sentinel Mountain and Seal Island, a popular tourist attraction. This is the biggest and meanest surf spot in Africa, and is one of the most dangerous on earth, being surfed by extremely fit athletes only. They must have great upper-body strength and practice unique breathing techniques in the event they wipe out and are held under for several minutes. The equipment these big-wave surfers use is special, too; the surfboards are 8 to 10 feet long and known as rhino chasers or big-wave guns. Light and sleek and thicker than normal boards, these rhino guns provide the necessary speed down a big wave's face. Dungeons only starts to break when the swell gets above 15 feet, and is best in light northwesterly winds anywhere from half to low tide. At high tide the drop is Dungeons' main feature, as it fills to be a fat and short wave. At dead-low tide all the elements can produce a great wave, with a length of ride at about 100 to 200 yards.

Hout Bay is a fishing village with a superb restaurant that serves fresh fish caught behind the Dungeons surf break, where seals compete for the catch and surf in the waves performing a spectacular water ballet. Close to shore the harbor wall has some good waves in the right conditions, along with other breaks in the area such as the Hoek, Noordhoek Beach, a spectacular beach break stretching to Kommetjie Dunes with plenty of heavy, barreling waves. Dungeons is ideal for big-wave riders only, but is a fantastic spectacle to watch for surfers and gawkers of any level.

South of Hout Bay is the town of Hermanus Bay, built along the cliff shores of Walker Bay near the southernmost tip of Africa. Magnificent mountains watch over the town, which is home to 150 southern right whales that visit between July and December every year. Nature lovers from all over the world visit Hermanus to view these awesome creatures. This is one of the best land-based whale-watching destinations in the world, for, at times, these awesome creatures are as little as 30 feet away.

Photo © ASP Tostee

Dungeons only breaks a couple times a year. It's a big-wave spot, and so only when you get your big winter storms will Dungeons break.

Dave Monnsen,
Surfer Mega Store

Photo © ASP Tostee

| Rights | W Swell | | Shallow Reef |

Break: Right-hand reef break
Skill Level: Expert
Commitment: 10–10
Best Boards: Big-wave board
Lifeguard: None
Hazards: Dangerous rip currents, triple-overhead heavy waves, rocky outcrops, deep channels
Currency: Rand.

Going There: No visa is required by British and Irish passport holders; all others should check with their embassy. Vaccinations required—tetanus, typhoid, polio, malaria, tuberculosis (children). Check with your doctor, health clinic, and embassy for the latest info.
Where to Stay: Hout Bay Manor, +27 (0) 21 790 0116. Marine Hotel, +27 (0) 028 313 1000, or fax +27 (0) 28 313 0160. Windor Hotel, +27 (0) 28 313 0912. Hermanus Backpackers, +27 (0) 28 312 4293, or fax +27 (0) 28 313 2727. Hout Bay Hotel, +27 (0) +27 (0) 21 790 4730, or fax +27 (0) 21 790 4952. Peninsula Hotel, +27 (0) 21 439 8888, or fax +27 (0) 21 439 8886. Table Mountain Lodge, +27 (0) 21 423 0042, or fax +27 (0) 21 423 4983. The Cape Castle, +27 (0) 21 439 1016, or fax +27 (0) 21 439 1019. Holiday Inn Cape Town,+27 (0) 21 423 3664. Winchester Mansions Sea Point, +27 (0) 21 434 2351, or fax +27 (0) 21 434 0215.
Finding the Break: From the Cape Town airport, take the N2 to Cape Town. Follow the signs to M3 Muizenberg, then Kirstenbosch to Hout Bay.
Keep in Mind: Crowds at Christmas.

Months	JF	MA	MJ	JA	SO	ND
Average Swell (feet)	4-6	4-6	6	8	6	3-4
Air Temp (C/F)	27/81	27/81	26/79	24/76	25/78	26/79
Water Temp (C/F)	24/76	24/76	23/74	22/72	22/72	23/74
Wetsuit	none	none	short	spring	short	none
Average Sunshine p/d (hours)	11	9	7	6	7	10-11
Average Rain p/m (inches)	1	2	5	6	5	2
Average Surfable Days p/m	2	1	1	0	1	2

67. JEFFREY'S BAY
South Africa

Huge waves greet you as you watch the endless lines of swell break at the best spot in the world for long, fast waves. Like tin solders in a row, these lines peel down the rock-sand point. Legend has it that many years ago, a great Zulu king surfed Jeffrey's Bay, found it very much to his liking, and renamed it the Kingdom of the Waves.

Today small tribes of surfers come from all over the world to marvel at a wave that rides for 1,000 yards and spits like an angry cobra. There's more time here for tunnels, turns, head dips, and lightning speed rides. Dropping down to the Kingdom of the Waves in a tube that roars like a lion, you'll know how stoked that Zulu king was.

South Africa is one of the world's best surfing destinations with two coastlines to surf, the Atlantic's west coast and the Indian Ocean's east—nearly 2,000 miles to explore. Jeffrey's Bay is situated halfway down the east coast, 20 miles west of Port Elizabeth. It's the home of one of Africa's best surf spots, with waves in the world-class bracket. The point farthest out on this Atlantic oasis is called Super Tubes, with powerful, hollow waves. The next surf point down the chain is called Tubes, followed by the Point. Super Tubes is the best wave in the right conditions, followed by Tubes, and then the Point. They all come under the heading of Jeffrey's Bay, because on really good days you can surf right through each spot on one wave, making a ride length of about 1,200 yards.

Tubes is unique on many occasions for its tube combing close to the rocks. The Point's main attraction is as a performance wave with a superb wall to the beach break. Just passing the main parking area you can view all three locations peeling off, and pan 180 degrees to see perfect waves in each direction. The fabulous thing about "J Bay"—as it is fondly known—is that it provides the surfer with small,

> In the late 1960s local Port Elizabeth surfer Gavin Rudolf rode Jeffrey's Bay so often and so well that he got the nickname Mr. Super Tubes.

medium, and big waves, each of a world-class standard.

The township of Jeffrey's Bay has good facilities, and access to the Point is either from the beach break and out though a channel, or straight out from the main parking area through a sand rock pool alleyway to the shallow ledge, where timing is required to dodge the sets. For Super Tubes, access is a lot harder, basically involving rock-hopping to the ledge and jumping off at the right time in order to paddle across the bay. This is a must-surf spot for the intermediate surfer in 3-to-6-foot swell sizes, and for experts in the 6-to-15-foot range. It's for big-wave surfers over 15 feet.

The beach at Jeffrey's Bay is backed by huge sand dunes leading to scrub vegetation. Generally speaking the area is made of plateau escarpments, like raised tabletops, that fall to the coastal plain. Farther into this huge country are mountainous areas, the highest of which is Lesotho. This is often called the Kingdom of the Sky, because the peaks rise above 4,500 feet.

The national parks and animal reserves are the top attractions for many tourists visiting South Africa. This has led to greater protection for the endangered animals. The Addo Elephant National Park, just north of Port Elizabeth, protects the last remaining herds that once roamed the province; the nearby Mountain Zebra National Park is home to the Cape mountain zebra.

Photo R. Sumpter

Jeffrey's Bay, South Africa—oh, just a magnificent wave. It's just a tubing barreling wave. It's a long ride. . . . My son surfed Super Tubes, Tubes, and the point in one wave. I rate it as probably in the top five surf spots in the world.

Al Sehorn,
former vice president,
United States Surfing Federation

Photo R. Sumpter

Rights | R.Point | SE Swell |

Break: Right-hand reef break

Skill Level: Expert

Commitment: 6–10 and 9–10 when it's big

Best Boards: Shortboard up to gun

Lifeguard: None

Hazards: Grinding waves overpower the inside area, making timing all-important to squeeze between the sand and rock gullies or jump from the flat rocks into the very short channel before the heavy waves wash you away or pound you into the rock. Undertow varies; either it aids return to takeoff or hinders it.

Currency: Rand.

Going There: No visa is required by British and Irish passport holders; all others should check with their embassy. Vaccinations required—tetanus, typhoid, polio, malaria, tuberculosis (children). Check with your doctor, health clinic, and embassy for the latest info.

Where to Stay: Lazee Bay, +27 (0) 42 296 2090. Mount Joy Guest House, +27 (0) 42 296 1932. Jeffrey's Bay Backpackers, +27 (0) 42 293 1379. A1 Kynaston rooms, +27 (0) 42 296 1845. Island Vibe backpacker lodge, +27 (0) 42

293 1625. Port Elizabeth Beach Hotel, +27 (0) 41 583 6220, or fax +27 (0) 41 583 6220. Holiday Inns Garden Court, +27 (0) 41 52 3720, or fax +27 (0) 41 55 5754. Safari.com, Jeffrey's Bay, +27 (0) 21 783 3622 or +27 (0) 21 783 3626.

Finding the Break: From the Port Elizabeth airport, follow the signs to the N2 motorway toward Cape Town and Humansdorp. Once you are on the N2, keep driving for approximately forty-five minutes until you see the R330 Humansdorp exit. From the N2 (Cape Town or Port Elizabeth side) take the first turnoff that indicates Jeffrey's Bay. As soon as you reach town you will find yourself on Da Gama Road. This is the main road—everything in J Bay is on and along Da Gama Road. Park at the beach.

Contest: Billabong Pro (WCT), July.

Keep in Mind: When the surf's up to 6 feet, it can be crowded. Over 10 feet and it's usually uncrowded.

Months	JF	MA	MJ	JA	SO	ND
Average Swell (feet)	4	3-4	5-6	6	4-5	3
Air Temp (C/F)	28/82	27/81	24/76	23/74	24/76	26/79
Water Temp (C/F)	24/76	24/76	23/74	22/72	22/72	23/74
Wetsuit	none	none	shorty	spring	shorty	none
Average Sunshine p/d (hours)	6	7	7	7	5	5-6
Average Rain p/m (inches)	5	4	3	1	2	5
Average Surfable Days p/m	15	9	6	6	6	14

68. NORTH BEACH
Durban, South Africa

Good waves don't come easy when you're fighting off the crowds, the fishing lines, and waiting for swell. But there are three right-handers along the piers of Durban's marine parade all firing in barreling wedgy waves that make the fight worth the trouble. They form running down the piers, then fan out. These are tough, hooky, sand-bottomed waves that churn like a cement mixer, and you can ride from pier to pier three times as stoked.

The seaside resort city of Durban lies at the northern end of South Africa's east coast and just an hour's flight from the capital of Johannesburg. Since the early 1940s and 1950s, Durban's beaches have been a haven for surfing, and the National, International, and Professional Surfing Championships are held here each year. Today this is a vibrant surf center boasting more surf shops, board builders, and surfers than the rest of South Africa's many surfing locations and cities put together.

Durban has only a few reefs and point breaks, but it enjoys many fine beach breaks and sandbank groins. On the south side of Durban, nearby, is Cave Rock with its famous barreling breaks and unbelievable right-hand tube rides, which are world class on the right day. Durban's premier surf breaks are the Bay of Plenty, North Beach, and the Wedge along Durban's seafront, where the piers focus the waves.

> It was 1947 when Ernie Thomson and Brian van Biljon started putting style into Durban's surfing, and by 1948 guys like Leith Jardine were starting to "go for it" on steep, late takeoffs. In 1951 the South Beach Surfboard Club was formed, the first official surfboard club in South Africa.

North Pier and New Pier turn the waves into superb shapes and make this an ideal surf destination. Anglers fishing from the piers do put their lines across the surf at times, but usually give surfers the waves and try to fish the outer deep water from the end of the pier instead.

More than 20 miles of surfing beaches are netted to keep sharks out and provide safe bathing for swimmers all around Durban. Durban is a city blessed with many fabulous sea views. It also gets more than its share of awesome wedging sand pit barrels and high-performance waves. Durban is world class in power, form, and length of ride on the right day. Ideal for any surfer on small days and for the expert when the waves are over 5 feet.

Photo © ASP Tostee

North Beach is a sand-bottomed wave, and a 150-yard right-hand break, which is similar to that of a point break. You're going to be able to get three barrels on a wave. For a city beach break, it's one of the best in the world.

Dave Monnsen,
Surfer Mega Store

Photo © ASP Tostee

Rights | Beachbreak | SE Swell

Break: Beach break
Skill Level: Beginner to expert
Commitment: 4–10
Best Boards: Shortboard
Lifeguard: In season
Hazards: Rip currents, shallow sand bottom, sharks, wedgy waves, murky water. Fishermen, pier pylons, and fishing lines make a lively surf session. It can be dangerous if you're not careful.
Currency: Rand.
Going There: No visa is required by British and Irish passport holders; all others should check with their embassy. Vaccinations required—tetanus, typhoid, polio, malaria, tuberculosis (children).

Check with your doctor, health clinic, and embassy for the latest info.
Where to Stay: Holiday Inn Garden Court North Beach, +27 (0) 31 32 7361, or fax +27 (0) 31 37 4058. Palace Protea, 031 32 8351, or fax +27 (0) 31 32 8307. Holiday Inn Crown Plaza, +27 (0) 31 37 1321, or fax +27 (0) 31 32 5527.
Finding the Break: From Durban International Airport take the M4 to Durban. Take the Victoria Embankment turnoff and continue along the embankment. Turn left onto Stanger Street, then right onto Somtseu Road. Follow the road, turning right at the traffic circle and parking at beach parking lot.
Keep in Mind: Crowds in December.

Months	JF	MA	MJ	JA	SO	ND
Average Swell (feet)	3	4	5	5–6	3–4	2–3
Air Temp (C/F)	28/82	27/81	24/76	23/74	24/76	26/79
Water Temp (C/F)	24/76	24/76	23/74	22/72	22/72	23/74
Wetsuit	none	none	shorty	spring	shorty	none
Average Sunshine p/d (hours)	7	7	7	7	5	5–6
Average Rain p/m (inches)	5	4	3	1	2	5
Average Surfable Days p/m	10	4	3	2	6	9

Photo D. Sumpter

PACIFIC

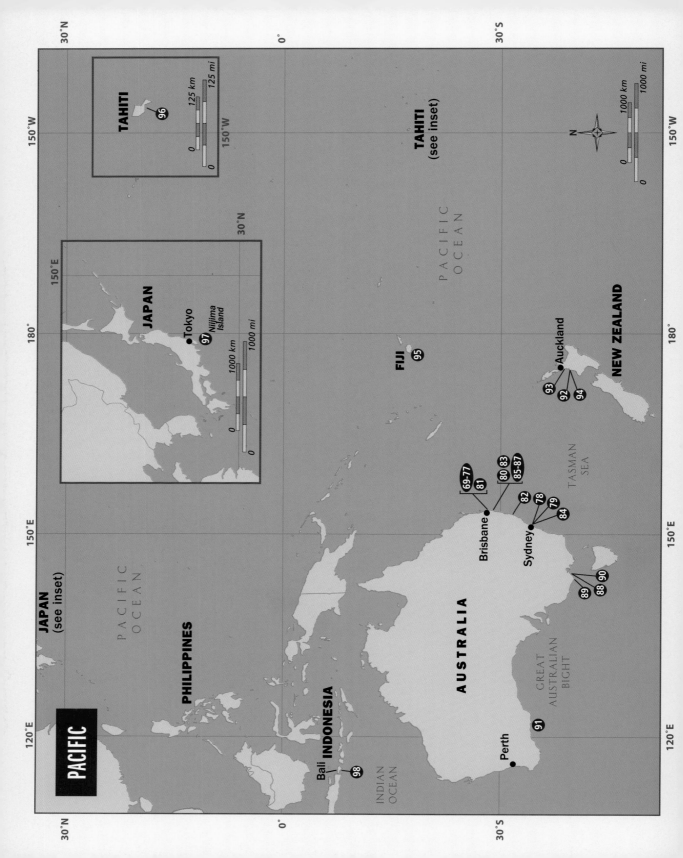

The Pacific is the largest and most exciting ocean in which to surf, with more famous destination spots than anywhere on the planet. Australia is the lucky country, the young country with surf on the east, west, and south coasts and weather systems perfectly designed to make waves year-round.

The Pacific and the Coral Sea cover the area of Australia's Gold Coast, with world-famous breaks like Kirra, Burleigh Heads, and Duranbah pumping beautifully throughout the year. Queensland waves can be the greatest surf location in the Pacific, especially if a cyclone passes nearby in the eastern Coral Sea combined with a high-pressure system over the Tasman Sea to create offshore wind across Australia's east coast. And northern New South Wales has the ripping surf spots of Cabarita, Lennox Head, and the famed point surf of the Pass, Byron Bay. Sydney has the popular Manly Beach with frequent clean, demanding beach break barrels. Bondi and Avalon Beach are home to much of Australia's surf history, fine headland reefs, and beach break waves.

Victoria's Bells Beach, a tiny bay sandwiched between two small headlands, receives swell from the Southern Ocean in huge proportions, giving waves 25 feet to form Bell's outstanding surf. The big swells that travel from New Zealand at Eastertime make big surf at Bells Beach, Winkipop, and Johanna, making Victoria an exciting destination for surfers on the prowl for big-wave riding.

Across the Tasman Sea, New Zealand's North Island is an exciting surf location with breaks such as Raglan and Indicators holding some of the rarest long lefts in the world.

In the middle of the Pacific Ocean is Tahiti. Summer surf from November to March comes from swell from the Christmas Island Ridge, and from April to October from big winter southerly storms in Antarctica and New Zealand that send up plenty of swell. The famous Teahupoo waves are super heavy for those advanced surfers dreaming of surfing this big-wave challenge. They will be stoked, no doubt. West, across the Kermadec Trench, is beautiful Tahiti where encircling reefs and long paddles are required if you don't have a guide with a boat. Surf spots are usually named for the local villages or island, such as Tavarua with its magic left-hand reef break.

Just east of the South Honshu Ridge is Japan's Niijima Island, where superb thick heavy beach break waves form, and where the friendly culture and hospitality make this location any traveler's dream spot. The scenic island of beaches, headlands, and coves is the perfect surfing destination.

69. BURLEIGH HEADS
Gold Coast, Queensland, Australia

Burleigh Heads is a level above the rest. Its waves are so much more powerful, its point surf is epic, and the beach break is grinding. The curved beach runs out to a right-angled point, and it's a swell magnet. Paddling out can be an awesome experience. From the beach you have to negotiate the pounding shorebreak. From the point, the dredging dry mix of sand and rock that explodes around you requires timing to pass safely.

Situated 50 miles south of Brisbane and a fifteen-minute drive north from the New South Wales border are the sparkling sands of one of Australia's best beaches, Burleigh Heads. This spot is the center of the Gold Coast's 30-mile stretch of coastline and is one of the thirty-five beaches patrolled by lifeguards in season. It's also a national wildlife park, a beauty spot with spectacular Norfolk pines fringing the beach, and is a short drive from the subtropical hinterland.

Burleigh Heads is a near-flawless surf setup. It can be fast and hollow with long tubing sections from out at the sand and boulder point, or right through to the beach, about a 300-yard ride on a good day. The waves seem almost machine-made as they sweep around the point with such consistency and precision. On a good southerly swell with south to southwest winds, you will get the ride of your life.

The headland walk reveals deeper, hollower wave sections and a breathtaking view of quality surf on a good day. Burleigh Heads is best at 6 to 8 feet in a southeast swell and southwest to west winds, and can be a fun wave in smaller conditions. An ideal longboarder's hotdog wave when conditions are small, Burleigh picks up swell first when other places are flat and—at the other extreme—when other point breaks are closed out. In cyclone conditions at 10 to 12 feet plus, Burleigh will still be ridable. The waves hold their shape in almost any size swell and create one of Australia's big-wave spots, like Currumbin and Lennox Head (Spot 83). Burleigh Heads is a demanding wave over 5 feet for the expert surfer, and on big days ideal for the professional surfer or big-wave rider. The site of many professional surfing championships, Burleigh can be ideal for the longboarder on the right small day.

Burleigh Heads can boast of a fine beach and a superb boulder-laid point, fringed with pines. There is a park and picnic area, showers, restrooms, and a small township of many shops. It was in 1959 that the famous surfer Bob Evans from Sydney made regular business trips to the Gold Coast and one Sunday stopped off at Burleigh Heads to try a few curlers. After a ride or two, he commented to local surfers "of the extra speed attained." Amazed at this, he wrote an article for the *Sydney Morning Herald*. Burleigh became the "in" spot to surf in Queensland.

Photo R. Sumpter

Burleigh Heads is a world-class wave, for sure, in my top five. My favorite maneuver is to get barreled there. You can get a ten- to fifteen-second tube ride at Burleigh with no problem.

Joel Parkinson,
2001 World Junior Surfing Champion

Photo D. Sumpter

R.Point | Beachbreak | SE Swell | Shallow Sand

Break: Beach break and right-hand point break

Skill Level: Beginner to expert

Commitment: 6–10; 8–10 over 8 feet

Best Boards: Shortboard

Lifeguard: In season

Hazards: Rip and sweep currents; shallow sand bottom; heavy, fast waves.

Bone-dry sand barrels firing thick green and blue lips await you on a good overhead day and require total respect. Timing a lull to get out at the point is all-important. A long paddle around from the beach might be wiser.

Currency: Australian dollar.

Going There: Visa required except by Australian and New Zealand citizens. Vaccinations required except by Australian and New Zealand citizens—tetanus. Check with your doctor, health clinic, and embassy for up-to-date info.

Where to Stay: Burleigh Heads International Motor Inn, +61 (0)7 5535 0035. Oceanside Cove Apartments, +61 (0)7 5538 4300. Le Beach, +61 (0)7 5500 5059. Luxury Apartments, +61 (0)7 5535 0855. Camp Burleigh, +61 (0)7 5535 1324

Finding the Break: Easy to find. From the NSW border take the Pacific Coast Highway (M1) north 11 miles and turn right at the Burleigh Heads traffic lights. Follow the coast road to the point and parking area.

Keep in Mind: Crowded when the surf's up.

Months	JF	MA	MJ	JA	SO	ND
Average Swell (feet)	2–3	3–4	4–5	5	3–4	2–3
Air Temp (C/F)	29/85	27/82	23/74	20/69	25/77	28/83
Water Temp (C/F)	24/75	23/76	21/70	18/65	19/67	22/72
Wetsuit	none	shorty	spring	spring	shorty	none
Average Sunshine p/d (hours)	8	7	6–7	7–8	8	8
Average Rain p/m (inches)	6	3	2	3	2	4
Average Surfable Days p/m	15	17	19	22	20	17

70. DURANBAH
Gold Coast, Queensland, Australia

The logarithms of this surf spot are precise. You can set your watch by the waves at Duranbah. This great A-frame peak wells up and sails in off undulating sandbars. Its thundering barrels and consistently surfable conditions make it famous, and it's often considered to have the best surf on the coast. The crunch of the meaty waves feels as hard as nails against the tightly packed sand of the shorebreak, and the blow of the curl on a wipeout will bounce you off the bottom more often than not.

Situated next to the Tweed River, north of the New South Wales border and 500 yards south of Point Danger, the superconsistent beach break of Duranbah awaits. Point Danger overlooks the Duranbah beach as it sweeps south to the Tweed River and Fingal Head, and toward the northern New South Wales beach of Cabarita (Spot 81).

With its backdrop of towering hills, 250-foot cliffs, and sloping bluffs to the north and south, the coastline here is very scenic. Going west there are valleys, hinterland, and eucalyptus trees that edge on to Pittwatter Bay. This huge waterway backs on to the beach and feeds the mighty Tweed River that runs alongside Duranbah, with a breakwater separating the surf from the river. Duranbah Beach lies under the towering hills and cliffs of Point Danger, just on the north side of the Tweed River breakwater. The waves on the Duranbah beach side are some of the best during strong southeast swells and easterly winds, sheltered at the brow of the breakwater at low tide. The waves here take on an amazing shape, peeling off from the rocks and spreading out to the

> Duranbah has a history of rescue. The Surf Academy was formed as an associated project within the Volunteer Marine Rescue Point Danger Association for surfer rescue programs, competitions, and education.

middle of the beach as fantastically good ridable waves. Although never as good as the A-frame peaks down the beach, they are still worthy in mean, fast, nasty onshore conditions to help shake the cobwebs from flat spells.

Duranbah is famed for its powerful waves, back-door barrels, and great peaks.

It's rare for "Bah," as it is locally called, not to have some sort of wave. Duranbah is reliable for picking up any swell going, and is usually breaking when other places are too small or flat. Always crowded when conditions are good, this is a super beach break of consistent quality, but it's best in 4 to 8 feet in a northeast to southeast swell and southwest and southern winds.

At the south side of the beach is the rip that flows back out against the breakwater. This aids the paddle out, and also forms a right peak halfway along the breakwater wall. The middle beach break has several sand-peak bank formations and can hold surf up to 12 feet. This is a big-wave riders' spot when it's 15 feet plus and is a dangerously heavy, thick-lipped wave from takeoff to hairy inside finishes on closeout. Best for the expert if it's over 6 feet. Best for the intermediate surfer if it's 3 to 4 feet. Good for beginners if it's 1 to 2 feet.

Over on the rocky northern end of Duranbah Beach are boulders known as Lovers Rock and the famous Point Danger, named by Captain Cook. The currents here are dangerous and could sweep you on the rocks or around to Snapper Rocks (Spot 75).

To the south, the large pipe structures that can be seen are the Sand Bypass Project. Don't be surprised to see a red dredger barge out the back of Duranbah digging up sand and carting it off. This is part of the Tweed River Entrance Sand Bypass Project (TRESBP) formulated between New South Wales and Queensland to overcome the sand buildup in the mouth of the River Tweed. This project supplies a shortage of sand to the Duranbah, Snapper Rocks, and Kirra beaches.

Photo © ASP Tostee

Duranbah is my favorite surf spot. It's my home beach, just because it's home. It barrels and I love it. It's a beach break, world class, an A-frame peak, and nothing down the beach but barrels.

Mark Occolupo,
1999 World Surfing Champion

Photo D. Sumpter

| Rights | Lefts | Peak | Beachbreak | SE Swell | |

Break: Beach break
Skill Level: Beginner to expert
Commitment: 3–10 at 4 feet; 8–10 over 8 feet
Best Boards: Shortboard
Lifeguard: In season
Hazards: Dangerous rip currents, shallow sand bottom. Heavy waves in an east swell. Shifting peaks crush in on shallow sand, strong rips sweeping north at half to low tide make this one of the hardest waves in Australia.
Currency: Australian dollar.
Going There: Visa required except by Australian and New Zealand citizens. Vaccinations required except by Australian and New Zealand citizens—tetanus. Check with your doctor, health clinic, and embassy for up-to-date info.
Where to Stay: Wangaree Homestead Duranbah, +61 (0)2 6677 7496. Richard Carter Realty, +61 (0)7 5599 5000. Coolangatta YHA, +61 (0)7 5536 7644, or fax +61 (0)7 5599 5436. Sunset Strip Budget Resort, +61 (0)7 5599 5517. Twin Towers Resort, +61 (0)7 5536 2277

Finding the Break: From Coolangatta's Main Street head south past Twin Towers Resort where the road becomes the official border between NSW and Queensland. Go straight on. This road becomes Boundary Street; and 0.5 mile on up the hill, you will overlook Duranbah Beach and Danger Point.
Keep in Mind: Crowded in summer and when everywhere else is flat.

Months	JF	MA	MJ	JA	SO	ND
Average Swell (feet)	2–3	3–4	4–5	6	4–5	3
Air Temp (C/F)	29/85	27/82	23/74	20/69	25/77	28/83
Water Temp (C/F)	24/75	23/76	21/70	18/65	19/67	22/72
Wetsuit	none	shorty	spring	spring	shorty	none
Average Sunshine p/d (hours)	8	7	6–7	7–8	8	8
Average Rain p/m (inches)	7	4	3	2	3	5
Average Surfable Days p/m	18	24	25	26	23	17

71. GREENMOUNT

Gold Coast, Queensland, Australia

This is a sun-blasted, salt-brushed, air-sprayed, postcard-perfect wave. Greenmount is classic. Nowhere else can claim as clean an endless line of swell on glassy days with offshore conditions as sheltered Greenmount Bay. Like water rats, the surfers pile into the blue lines of see-through waves and spend all day performing ripping stuff, until the sunset smothers them in slow-motion crimson curls.

Low tide is blessed with phenomenal surf at Greenmount, breaking on sandbars between Rainbow Bay (Spot 73) and Coolangatta, at the heart of Queensland's Gold Coast. This series of point breaks and beach breaks is loosely described as a chain of classic right-hand point breaks. Captain Cook sailed past these breaks in 1770, naming the outermost headland Point Danger. This is the southernmost headland in Queensland, and gateway to the waterways of the mighty Tweed River.

The beaches of Greenmount and Coolangatta have some of the Gold Coast's best surfing conditions and most picturesque scenery. Greenmount Beach and neighboring Rainbow Bay are the Gold Coast's only north-facing beaches, providing sheltered conditions during southeast storms and strong winds. A walk around to the point at Snapper Rocks (Spot 75) throughout the months of April to August improves your chances of seeing whales on their annual migration.

At Greenmount well-lined-up waves breaking softly for beginners is the norm most of the time, but the swells that arrive in spring and autumn turn on some fantastic barrels. The wave size can be overhead, and the length of ride from

> **Michael Peterson is Greenmount's most famous surfer, a surfing legend, surf guru, and great surfer. He learned his trade at Greenmount's shorebreak as a schoolboy, went on to ride the point, and inspired a generation with his radical cutbacks and style.**

Rainbow Bay through to Greenmount can be 700 yards on a perfect day if you're lucky. Another great break south of here is the big-wave riding spot of Danger Point, a river mouth surfed by lifeguards from Greenmount, Coolangatta, and Snapper Rocks Surf Life Saving Clubs, as well as big-wave surfers. The use of a personal watercraft is a must if you're interested in surfing here. But make sure that you're not only an expert but that the conditions are right.

Greenmount is a must-surf spot for beginners to intermediate surfers and has some of the best longboarding in Queensland. Bigger swells arrive April through September, providing solid tubes, and January through March can be a perfect time, ideal for the expert on the right day.

Beautiful Greenmount beach is fringed by 100-foot-tall Norfolk pines and backs onto the small town of Coolangatta. There are several surf shops, and the annual Surfers Exhibition is held in the shopping mall, displaying products from all over Australia. The Greenmount hills stretch out into the hinterland and the vast tropical rain forest of the Gold Coast.

Photo D. Sumpter

Greenmount is so beautiful, just so picturesque it makes the perfect postcard. It's got a lovely little wave that peels down a sand bottom. It's a soft wave—it doesn't have a lot of power—it's a good fun wave.

Mark Richards,
1979–1981 and
1983 World Surfing
Champion

Photo D. Sumpter

| R.Point | Beachbreak | E Swell | |

Break: Beach break

Skill Level: Beginner to expert

Commitment: 1–10 under 3 feet; 4–10 over

Best Boards: Longboard up to 3 feet; shortboard over 4 feet

Lifeguard: In season

Hazards: Dangerous sweep current, shallow sand bottom. Mostly gentle in 2 to 4 foot surf but becomes a lion in sheep's clothing in surf larger than double overhead.

Currency: Australian dollar.

Going There: Visa required except by Australian and New Zealand citizens. Vaccinations required except by Australian and New Zealand citizens—tetanus. Check with your doctor, health clinic, and embassy for up-to-date info.

Where to Stay: Greenmount Beach Resort, +61 (0)7 5536 1222. Rainbow Place, +61 (0)7 5536 9144. Eden Tower, +61 (0)7 5536 8213. Colonial Tweed Caravan Park, +61 (0)7 5524 2999. The Bay Apartments, +61 (0)7 5536 2988. Richard Carter Realty, +61 (0)7 5599 5000. Coolangatta YHA, +61 (0)7 5536 7644, or fax +61 (0)7 5599 5436. Sunset Strip Budget Resort, +61 (0)7 5599 5517. Coolangatta Sands Hotel, +61 (0)7 5536 3066.

Finding the Break: Easy to find. From Coolangatta town center walk 300 yards through the Coolangatta Mall, then turn right (south) and walk 300 yards to Greenmount Surf Life Saving Club.

Keep in Mind: It's crowded here from December through Australia Day and on weekends.

Months	JF	MA	MJ	JA	SO	ND
Average Swell (feet)	1–2	3	3	3	2	1–2
Air Temp (C/F)	29/84	27/81	21/70	20/68	23/72	28/82
Water Temp (C/F)	23/74	20/68	19/66	19/66	20/68	22/72
Wetsuit	none	vest	spring	spring	shorty	none
Average Sunshine p/d (hours)	7	7	6	5	7–8	8
Average Rain p/m (inches)	7	4	3	2	3	5
Average Surfable Days p/m	22	24	25	26	23	19

72. KIRRA

Gold Coast, Queensland, Australia

Rows of awesome swells pass the breakwater, then suddenly steepen and jackknife into barreling turbo gunships. Long green-blue breaking waves with the deepest takeoffs spit like a blowpipe with lightning speed. To make the drop you need to be fast—the drop is always radically tight—and the suck-out at the bottom and down the line is Kirra's most prized feature. The wave is probably the fastest and hollowest in Australia. From the farthest point to the clubhouse, rides are only makable by going through at least one tube.

Situated at the southern end of Queensland's Gold Coast, Kirra is next to Greenmount (Spot 71) and 9 miles south of Surfers Paradise (Spot 77).These beaches are surrounded by the Coral Sea, as part of the Pacific Ocean. Kirra derives its name from the Aboriginal word for "spirit" and "peace," and is rated by many top surfers as the best surf spot in Australia—some say the world. What makes it so special is its unique sand-bottomed bars stretching from the first breakwater groin to the Kirra Surf Life Saving Club. A total of 800 yards, and surfable for this distance on a good day. On its best days, the waves are a perfect down-the-line tube, created when sand is swept around from the New South Wales beaches of Duranbah and Danger Point. This forms sand point sections across the ocean floor and has built one of the greatest surf lineups in the world.

From the hill above Kirra you can see the wave sections joining up to make one long, fast, incredible ride. Sand is deposited by the strong rip current known as the sweep. The same rip currents encourage surfers to get out of the water and walk back to the takeoff area, because the rip can be too fierce to paddle against. It's best here in a strong southeast swell and light southwesterly wind. This is an ace surf spot not to be missed when the conditions are right—for the expert surfer.

Drift surfing is a must on big days when the sweep is too powerful to hold position. During the cyclone season from February to April, the waves are best and the crowds are the biggest—spectators vying for position to watch and surfers packing the lineup. This happens whenever the word is out that there's a pumping swell, with many other surf breaks closed or too big to surf. The scenic path that connects Kirra to Coolangatta, Greenmount, Rainbow Bay, and Snapper Rocks has vantage points where you can check out the waves.

Kirra's surfing popularity really got a boost in the early 1960s when California photographer and kneeboarder George Greenough took pictures of Russell Hughes in the tube from the water at Kirra. It became known as the ultimate place for extreme hollow waves.

Photo © ASP Tostee

When I die I've told them to scatter my ashes at Kirra.

Peter Townend,
1976 World Surfing Champion

Photo © ASP Tostee

Rights | E Swell | | Shallow Sand

Break: Beach break and right-hand sand-bottomed point break

Skill Level: Intermediate to expert

Commitment: 6–10

Best Boards: Shortboard

Lifeguard: In season

Hazards: Strong tides, and rip and sweep currents, shallow sand bottom. It's just so perfect that danger seems a far off thing until you feel the rip into the groin suck you out, past where you want to wait. There is also the power of a 6-foot barreling turbo-charged wave that sends your head spinning. Locals have it wired, but even for the best it's demanding.

Currency: Australian dollar.

Going There: Visa required except by Australian and New Zealand citizens. Vaccinations required except by Australian and New Zealand citizens—tetanus. Check with your doctor, health clinic, and embassy for up-to-date info.

Where to Stay: Aloha Surf Motel, +61 (0)7 5598 1145. Kirra Beach Motel, +61 (0)7 5536 3311. Kirra Beach Hotel, +61 (0)7 5536 3311. Motel and Holiday units, +61 (0)7 5536 3599. Kirra Beach YHA, +61 (0)7 5536 7644.

Finding the Break: Easy to find. From Coolangatta town center's Main Street, go north for 1 mile. Park by the Kirra Surf Life Saving Club (you will pass Kirra groin, the first and second points, and then come to the beach break).

Contest: Quicksilver (WCT), March.

Keep in Mind: Crowded whenever it's good. Dawn is the best time.

Months	JF	MA	MJ	JA	SO	ND
Average Swell (feet)	2–3	3–4	4–5	5	3–4	2–3
Air Temp (C/F)	29/85	27/82	23/74	20/69	25/77	28/83
Water Temp (C/F)	24/75	23/76	21/70	18/65	19/67	22/72
Wetsuit	none	shorty	spring	spring	shorty	none
Average Sunshine p/d (hours)	8	7	6–7	7–8	8	8
Average Rain p/m (inches)	7	4	3	2	3	5
Average Surfable Days p/m	3	4	6	8	7	5

73. NOOSA HEADS
Sunshine Coast, Queensland, Australia

It's honking and all the bells are ringing. Fast waves are peeling off for what seems like an endless ride. Last night the storm swooped past, and now all the waves are here. It's like a steamroller knocking holes in the ocean—swells become tubes and growing lines back up to the horizon. There are sections pounding on the rocks, splash-ups 20 feet high, and wave upon wave coming in and spinning curls. This is Noosa Heads. When a new swell hits and the long flat period is over, it's that much more exciting. Noosa's surf sends a buzz around the entire town. It's an event. It's special. And people flock to the beach to watch.

This sunbaked stretch of Queensland's coast from Noosa to Moolooaba is known as the Sunshine Coast, and is blessed with warm, crystal-clear waters and the best of Australia's right-hand point surf. Noosa's long line of breaking waves are made up of swells wrapping around five points and bays, one being an Australian national park, the break being called National Park. This eucalyptus-tree-lined bay is one of the most favored spots in this chain, with its sandbars, reefs, and rocky boulders strung together to cre-

Noosa Heads is just one of three towns that make up the community of Noosa. Two miles inland along the Noosa River is Noosaville, a small town that is the access point for trips to the Teewah Colored Sands. This area features multicolored sands that were created by natural chemicals in the soil. Dating back to the ice ages, some of the seventy-two hues of sand form wave patterns on the cliffs up to 600 feet tall. The third Noosa community, 4 miles upriver, Tewantin has a unique Bottle Museum with more than 5,000 bottles on exhibit, inside a house made from bottles!

ate the ideal longboarding conditions. Noosa Heads has become a magnet within the surf industry and is famous for its cafes, restaurants, bistros, and hotels, providing a vacation haven with plenty to do.

The swell at Noosa Heads is reliant on low-pressure systems and storms passing through here to generate waves of sufficient magnitude, which then enter the series of bays to produce the famous classic point surf conditions. Noosa has five bays and beaches joined together, each of which connects in a chain to form Noosa Heads. The first is Granite, a demanding, secluded bay for the expert surfer. Tea Tree is the most popular break; it has an excellent takeoff and classic performance waves, and walls all the way to the cobblestone shorebreak. Boiling Pot is a fast wave with a string of breaking sections that, on a good day, join up to Noosa National Park for a ride of more than 500 yards. Johnson's, a beautiful point surf and beach, is next in line; it also connects to the National Park and could increase a ride to 800 yards. Finally, there's First Point with superb sandbanks. It joins at its eastern end to Main Beach, which also has good breaks, including a breakwater groin and several peaks produced from rip currents. In all, the variety here at Noosa Heads is amazing—a truly world-class mix of waves and locations. This is a must-surf spot for the longboarder from 2 to 8 feet and the shortboarder at 8 feet plus, depending on the conditions.

Photo D. Sumpter

Noosa Heads must be one of the most picturesque locations to go surfing in the world. There are three or four perfect points that peel along the edge of the National Park, and you've got world-class waves.

Mark Richards,
1979–1981 and 1983 World Surfing Champion

Photo R. Sumpter

 R.Point E Swell

Break: Beach and right-hand point breaks

Skill Level: Beginner to expert

Commitment: 3–10

Best Boards: Longboard

Lifeguard: Beach in season

Hazards: Slippery boulders make entry hard but a few rocky outcrops and rip currents do aid getting out in places. The dangers are then mainly from bouncing off the bottom during a wipeout and hitting your head.

Currency: Australian dollar.

Going There: Visa required except by Australian and New Zealand citizens. Vaccinations required except by Australian and New Zealand citizens—tetanus. Check with your doctor, health clinic, and embassy for up-to-date info.

Where to Stay: Sheraton Noosa Resort, +61 (0)7 5449 4888. Noosa Crest, +61 (0)7 5447 2412. Caribbean Noosa Motel, +61 (0)7 5447 2247. Noosa Blue Resort, +61 (0)7 5447 5699. Netanya Beachfront +61 (0)7 5447 4722. The Noosa North Shore Wilderness Camp, +61 (0)7 5449 7955.

Finding the Break: From Brisbane head north on the Bruce Highway until you pass the Caloundra/Landsborough turnoffs. Two hundred yards past the intersection you'll see the Ettamogah Pub on the left. Travel another 500 yards and take the Sunshine Motorway exit on the left. Continue on and you will see an exit on the left for Noosa Heads. There is a road that goes halfway out to the point, with parking in the national park. The coast is edged by a coastal track.

Surf Schools: Merricks Learn to Surf, +61 (0)4 1878 7577. Wavesense Surf Coaching, +61 (0)7 5474 9076.

Event: Festival of Surfing, March.

Keep in Mind: Weekdays on a good swell out of season is the best time. Weekend crowds.

Months	JF	MA	MJ	JA	SO	ND
Average Swell (feet)	2–3	3–4	4–5	5	3–4	2–3
Air Temp (C/F)	29/85	27/82	23/74	20/69	25/77	28/83
Water Temp (C/F)	24/75	23/76	21/70	18/65	19/67	22/72
Wetsuit	none	shorty	spring	spring	shorty	none
Average Sunshine p/d (hours)	8	7	6–7	7–8	8	8
Average Rain p/m (inches)	7	4	3	2	3	5
Average Surfable Days p/m	11	17	19	22	14	10

74. RAINBOW BAY

Gold Coast, Queensland, Australia

Rainbow Bay is a right-hand sand-bottomed point, superbly situated adjacent to the golden sands of some of Queensland's finest surfing beaches, complete with spectacular views of the entire Gold Coast. This breathtakingly fast right-hand point break gets very hollow when sandbar conditions are ripe, but it can be a fun wave regardless.

The wave has an excellent takeoff, starting from where the waves of Snapper Rocks (Spot 75) leave off. The re-forming swell rebuilds again as a point wave at Rainbow Point and peels across the beach. The wave is fast and hollow past a rocky outcrop of coral strung across its path. You'll need to corner hard past this. Then the sandbanks twist and turn, making it line up as a beach break. From the beach break the surf is generally a beginners' wave. The middle section winds on down pushing forward, and keeps the power on as the wave peels down the bay and sweeps well toward Greenmount. The total ride can be 500 yards long.

Rainbow Bay is a curved horseshoe-shaped beach facing north. It's best in a south to southeast swell, and west to southwest winds, holding waves of 6 to 8 feet. Sometimes when the banks are shallow just off the rocky out-

> **Rainbow Bay Surf Life Saving Club was established in 1962, and it now offers its members accommodations, surf-training boats and patrols, and an ocean deck, where nonmembers have a low-cost restaurant and bar overlooking the spectacular views of Rainbow Bay to Kirra and Surfers Paradise.**

crops, it becomes a top-to-bottom tube for 30 yards and turns into a total performance wave. This spot has many different condition setups to suit the beginner to intermediate surfer, and on bigger days in the right conditions, it's ace for the expert longboarder.

The bay was probably named for the rainbow lorikeets, thousands of which roost each evening in the giant Norfolk pine trees fringing the beach. These brightly colored birds arrive at sunset, performing aerial displays until they settle in at nightfall.

Photo D. Sumpter

I have never seen a better little sandy bay than Rainbow. It spells out tubes and can hold big days.

Rod Sumpter

Photo D. Sumpter

R.Point Beachbreak SE Swell

Break: Beach break and sand point
Skill Level: Beginner to expert
Commitment: 2–10
Best Boards: Longboard, shortboard
Lifeguard: In season
Hazards: Sweep and rip currents, shallow sand bottom make the big days over 10 feet pounding. Coral clusters protrude on the right side of the beach and you surf very close to them on a good wave from the point.
Currency: Australian dollar.
Going There: Visa required except by Australian and New Zealand citizens. Vaccinations required except by Australian and New Zealand citizens—tetanus. Check with your doctor, health clinic, and embassy for up-to-date info.

Where to Stay: Rainbow Place, +61 (0)7 5536 9144. Eden Tower Phone, +61 (0)7 5536 8213. Colonial Tweed Caravan Park, +61 (0)7 5524 2999. The Bay Apartments, +61 (0)7 5536 2988. Richard Carter Realty, +61 (0)7 5599 5000. Coolangatta YHA, 07 5536 7644, or fax +61 (0)7 5599 5436. Sunset Strip Budget Resort, +61 (0)7 5599 5517. Coolangatta Sands Hotel, +61 (0)7 5536 3066.

Finding the Break: Easy to find. From Coolangatta town center head for the beach, turn right (south), and go 1 mile, following the coast roads—or take the scenic footpath around Greenmount Point to Rainbow Bay. You can't miss it; it's before Snapper Rocks.

Keep in Mind: Crowded during school vacations.

Months	JF	MA	MJ	JA	SO	ND
Average Swell (feet)	2–3	3–4	4–5	5	3–4	2–3
Air Temp (C/F)	29/85	27/82	23/74	20/69	25/77	28/83
Water Temp (C/F)	24/75	23/76	21/70	18/65	19/67	22/72
Wetsuit	none	shorty	spring	spring	shorty	none
Average Sunshine p/d (hours)	8	7	6–7	7–8	8	8
Average Rain p/m (inches)	7	4	3	2	3	5
Average Surfable Days p/m	17	22	24	26	21	19

75. SNAPPER ROCKS

Gold Coast, Queensland, Australia

Snapper Rocks has the ultimate takeoff area behind a string of worn and jagged lava rocks, known as Snapper Rocks. It breaks over a sand bottom where an epic combination of backwash and incoming swell meet to produce a mighty wedge on a long wall that catapults you into a racing start. You won't forget the snap-judgment decision needed to make this spinning-top wave work for you at first—you can easily spin out and bail, or rip.

The Gold Coast has the best group of beaches connected as right-hand point breaks from Snapper Rocks to Kirra (Spot 72). Snapper Rocks is the southernmost surf point, and is at the start of a sequence of classic Gold Coast point breaks. Steeped in longboarding traditions dating back to the early 1960s, and a strong Surf Life Saving Club, Snapper Rocks is a premier longboarder destination. After takeoff, the drop and the wall speed along tight curling faces, where off-the-top setups and endless carving off clean sections is a barrel of fun with razor-edge sections.

Snapper Rocks cannot be beaten on its day and continues to be the best longboarding performance wave in Queensland, with the Australian National Longboarding Championships held here. Perfect rides are possible for the adventurous with the skill to trim fast and beat the tube. Rides up to 700 yards are possible here.

After a long ride or after drift surfing with the undercurrent that sweeps north past the surf spots of Snapper Rocks, Rainbow Bay, and Greenmount, which are strung together on a good swell, it's best to then walk or jog the 1.5-mile scenic path back to Snapper Rocks and jump in off the rocks for more. The best surfing conditions are a strong southeast swell and a light southwest to west wind. It's always been imagined that Snapper Rocks "Point" can launch you into surfing a dream ride to Rainbow Bay (Spot 74) and on to Greenmount (Spot 71), and then to Kirra (Spot 72). This may happen one day, but to date there are only anecdotal local yarns saying that a surfer has gone all the way. Conditions up to the present show a fade-out dead-water gap of 50 yards between the four locations that would require some paddling. But it just needs the right sand conditions to one day join the breaks at low tide. This is a must-surf spot for the longboarder, and an excellent wave for the shortboarder.

Swell swings in from around the headland just 0.25 mile away from where Captain Cook discovered and named Danger Point in 1770. This is where many vessels have been shipwrecked by the area's awesome waves and where whales breach in winter. (It took Captain Cook another eight years to discover, witness, and record surfing in Hawaii in 1778, in his voyage of discovery.)

Photo D. Sumpter

Early surfing was known as the sport of kings, and Australian surfing got a big boost from two quarters. First, the great Hawaiian Duke Kahanamoku gave surfing exhibitions up and down the east coast during three trips to Australia, in 1951, 1956 and 1957. And second, the Surf Life Saving movement popularized water sports in the same period through its network of surf clubs. Snapper Rocks is now the location for one of the finest longboarder clubs in the world. It's where former World Junior Surfing Champion Joel Parkinson lives, and where ASP President Wayne "Rabbit" Barthomew learned to rip waves.

My favorite surf spot in the world has to be Snapper Rocks to Kirra. That whole area—Snapper Rocks, Rainbow Bay, Greenmount—is a long right-hand point, and when it's good it goes the whole way through to Kirra.

Joel Parkinson,
2001 World Junior Surfing Champion

Photo © ASP Tostee

 R.Point SE Swell   Shallow Sand

Type of Break: Beach break and sand point break

Skill level: Beginner to expert

Commitment: 5–10

Best Boards: Longboard, shortboard

Lifeguard: In season

Hazards: Rip and sweep currents, shallow sand bottom, and rocky outcrops all combine to make the bigger days dangerous. Getting in to ride a 12-foot day requires waiting till the splash up beside Snapper Rocks has calmed, and then paddling like hell before the snaking swell appears around the rocks to blast you smack in the mouth.

Currency: Australian dollar.

Going There: Visa required except by Australian and New Zealand citizens. Vaccinations required except by Australian and New Zealand citizens—tetanus. Check with your doctor, health clinic, and embassy for up-to-date info.

Where to Stay: Carool Holiday Apartments, +61 (0)7 5536 7154. Rainbow Place, +61 (0)7 5536 9144. Eden Tower, +61 (0)7 5536 8213. Colonial Tweed Caravan Park, +61 (0)7 5524 2999. The Bay Apartments, +61 (0)7 5536 2988. Richard Carter Realty, 61 (0)7 5599 5000. Coolangatta YHA, +61 (0)7 5536 7644, or fax +61 (0)7 5599 5436. Sunset Strip Budget Resort +61 (0)7 5599 5517. Coolangatta Sands Hotel, +61 (0)7 5536 3066.

Finding the Break: Brisbane Airport to Snapper Rocks. Turn left onto the Gateway Arterial Road and pass through the toll gate to the Gold Coast. Follow the Pacific Highway for approximately 32 miles (50 km). You will see Coolangatta Airport on your right. Follow the sign left to Kirra, Coolangatta. Go straight through the center of town onto Boundary Road (where the main road turns right). Go straight for 0.3 mile. Turn left at the shops and right at the beach front. Parking along the roadside is free.

Keep in Mind: Summer crowds on weekends.

Months	JF	MA	MJ	JA	SO	ND
Average Swell (feet)	2–3	3–4	4–5	5	3–4	2–3
Air Temp (C/F)	29/85	27/82	23/74	20/69	25/77	28/83
Water Temp (C/F)	24/75	23/76	21/70	18/65	19/67	22/72
Wetsuit	none	shorty	spring	spring	shorty	none
Average Sunshine p/d (hours)	8	7	6–7	7–8	8	8
Average Rain p/m (inches)	7	4	3	2	3	5
Average Surfable Days p/m	14	18	22	26	22	17

76. STRADBROKE ISLAND

Gold Coast, Queensland, Australia

If there ever was a place to surf the way you want to, Stradbroke Island is it. Its peaks are like curvy racetracks, perfect for those of you who drive a surfboard like an Indy car, whipping around a hairpin bend, then out past the bowl and on to the straightaway. This is where bold blue skies meet crystal-clear water and powerful Pacific swells. The waves at Stradbroke shimmer in the heat like diamonds, the perfect prize for those entering the race.

This island, with its many surf spots, is remote, and is ideal for getting away from the crowds and finding good waves.

Located just south of the Great Barrier Reef on Queensland's east coast, just fifteen miles southeast of Brisbane's city center, both North and South Stradbroke Islands were once a single landmass. In 1896 a cyclone swept away the sandbank between the two islands, leaving a channel now called Jumpinpin. North Stradbroke Island, where most of the surf is found, is best with an east to southeast swell and southwest to west winds. One of the main surf focus points is at Point Lookout, a beach bay point with outstanding lefts. The surf break of Cylinder on the northeast coast of North Stradbroke is also amazing, with its long, fast, powerful tubes and its spectacular views. Heading south on North Stradbroke Island is Deadmans—good waves and the last of the notable northeast coast waves. There is also an excellent caravan campsite there.

To get to South Stradbroke, you'll need to take a boat ride, and must carry with you all of your supplies, including mosquito repellent. There are no stores or doctors on the

Set in Morton Bay, North Stradbroke Island is popularly known as Straddie. The bay has seen heavy sand mining to the south of the island, and this shifting of sand has produced human-made shapes along the coast. Apart from a few rocky headlands, Stradbroke is all sand, with Mount Tempest towering to 275 feet, the highest coastal sand hill in the world.

island, so be prepared and be self-sufficient. The benefit to this remoteness is the island's uncrowded beach breaks and waves. Here on South Stradbroke, there are many unnamed sandy coves, sand points, lonely sandbars, and shorebreaks to surf that peel off nicely in the right conditions. South Stradbroke is famous for angled swells, creating a neat wave, best in a south swell and light west winds.

The bush drops down to the narrow beaches, where the boating facilities and surf access are tackled best in small to midsized 4-to-5-foot surf. If the surf is 6 to 8 feet or bigger, entry will be hampered, and mooring will be well offshore and away from the breaks. For the experienced boatman, this barren and remote surf coastline has a lot to offer. North Stradbroke Island is a must-surf spot for the surfer who wants to get away from it all, in the right conditions. South Stradbroke is more for the "adventure" surfer.

Photo R. Sumpter

North Stradbroke Island—good summer fun.

Bob McTavish,
former Australian Surfing Champion

Photo R. Sumpter

Peak	Beachbreak	E Swell

Break: Beach break

Skill Level: Beginner to expert

Commitment: 4–10

Best Boards: Longboard, shortboard

Lifeguard: None

Hazards: Dangerous rip currents, shallow sand bottom

Currency: Australian dollar.

Going There: Visa required except by Australian and New Zealand citizens. Vaccinations required except by Australian and New Zealand citizens—tetanus. Check with your doctor, health clinic, and embassy for up-to-date info.

Where to Stay: Ocean Beach Resort Lookout Point, +61 (0)7 3409 8555 or (800) 450–004. Stradbroke Island, Lookout Point, +61 (0)7 3409 8888, or fax +61 (0)7 3409 8588. Dolphin Holiday, +61 (0)7 3409 8455, or fax +61 (0)7 3409 8606. South Stradbroke Island Campgrounds, +61 (0)7 5577 2849. Minjerribah, +61 (0)7 3409 9445

Finding the Break: Just one hour from Brisbane International Airport and Brisbane city, North Stradbroke Island is easily accessible by vehicular ferry from Cleveland or Redland Bay. All townships are linked with sealed roads, which are accessible by conventional vehicles, but a four-wheel drive is required for driving on beaches and inland sand tracks.

Surf Schools: North Stradbroke Surf Rider Association, +61 (0)7 3409 8524. Straddie Adventures, +61 (0)7 3409-8414.

Keep in Mind: Rarely crowded, except school vacations.

Months	JF	MA	MJ	JA	SO	ND
Average Swell (feet)	2-3	3-4	5	4-5	3-4	3
Air Temp (C/F)	29/84	27/81	21/70	20/68	23/72	28/82
Water Temp (C/F)	23/74	20/68	19/66	19/66	20/68	22/72
Wetsuit	none	vest	spring	spring	shorty	none
Average Sunshine p/d (hours)	7	7	6	5	7-8	8
Average Rain p/m (inches)	7	4	3	2	3	5
Average Surfable Days p/m	17	18	19	22	26	20

77. SURFERS PARADISE
Gold Coast, Queensland, Australia

Ride the golden mile of Surfers Paradise and witness a fiery place of steep, short, sexy waves, glamorous sunsets, and more peaking waves than can be found at any other real estate in Australia. The beaches are right in front of high-rise hotels, packed with shopping malls, nightlife, and restaurants. Get surfed out, check out the nightclubs, have some drinks, and get ready for the dawn patrol.

Surfers Paradise is a top destination for international surfers attracted by quality facilities and the brilliant turquoise ocean that pumps barrels onto the pure white sand. The Gold Coast coastline is packed with famous breaks. But to choose "Surfers" is to choose Australia's most unique wave experience.

Situated 10 miles north of Burleigh Heads (Spot 69), and 10 miles south of South Stradbroke Island (Spot 76) is Australia's "Golden Mile of Surf." At first the choices appear similar to other surf spots on the Gold Coast. But upon closer inspection, the south-end breaks are fantastic for longboarding, and the north end has fierce tubes for the shortboarder. Bodyboarders find their own great sandbar wedge to surf right in the middle, below the huge apartment tower blocks. Nearby breaks to the south include Broad Beach, Mermaid Beach, Nobby Beach, and Miami. To the north you'll find Narrow Neck and the Spit.

The first hotel was built on the Gold Coast in 1923 at Surfers Paradise, and it's now Australia's number one tourist destination. If the waves are 2 feet plus, with light offshore winds, chances are it's good for beginners from half to low tide. If it's 3 or 4 feet, it should be good for intermediates. This counts for most of the tidal stages, except for the dead-high tide, as the steeply sloping beach creates

> In 1921 the Royal Life Saving Society placed some safety equipment, a reel and line, on the beach at Surfers Paradise to assist any struggling surfers. It turned out to be very successful, and in 1925 the Life Saving Club of Surfers Paradise was formed.

a pounding shorebreak and backwash. At 4 to 6 feet and bigger, it's for experts when, at low tide, the right-hand barrels suddenly start to show themselves. Over 8 to 10 feet and its surf becomes huge closeouts; rip currents abound, with a heavy and pounding set-line wave. These are dangerous conditions, and the lifeguards will surely fly the red flag.

The best surf conditions for longboards are on head high days when the breaking swells are soft, and down-the-line cover-ups are possible. This doesn't happen all the time, but when it does, this is an excellent longboarding wave. Surfers Paradise is a lively tourist destination, and for surfers it's one long line of quality beach breaks, picking up any swell, often breaking when elsewhere is flat. Surfers Paradise is a must-surf spot for all surfers on the right day.

If you need an escape from the beaches, there are numerous activities to choose from, including horse riding in the beautiful rain forest of the Numinbah Valley, as well as day tours of the Springbrook National Park and Tambourine Mountains. Carnivals, street parades, and sporting events are always a part of Surfers Paradise, the most famous being the Indy car race through the center of town in mid-October.

Photo R. Sumpter

When it's good, it's great. It's one of the few wave locations where you can drift-surf a variety of beach breaks in a couple of hours, and get a drink on the walk back.

Rod Sumpter

Photo R. Sumpter

NE
Swell

Break: Beach break
Skill Level: Beginner to expert
Commitment: 3–10
Best Boards: Bodyboard, shortboard, long-board
Lifeguard: In season
Hazards: Dangerous rip currents, shallow sand bottom in all surf conditions. Generally a tough wave with plenty of power over 4 feet. Some shark sightings.

Currency: Australian dollar.
Going There: Visa required except by Australian and New Zealand citizens. Vaccinations required except by Australian and New Zealand citizens—tetanus. Check with your doctor, health clinic, and embassy for up-to-date info.
Where to Stay: Oceanside Cove Apartments, +61 (0)7 5520 0040. Breakfree Beachcomber resort, +61 (0)7 5570 1000. Biarritz Apartments, +61 (0)7 5570 1377. Main Beach Surfers Paradise Tourist Park, +61 (0)7 5581 7722. Backpackers Resort, +61 (0)7 5592 4455.
Finding the Break: From the Coolangatta airport follow the Gold Coast Highway north to Beach Road, Surfers Paradise. From the Brisbane airport follow the Pacific Highway to Gold Coast and the Gold Coast Highway south to Beach Road, Surfers Paradise. There's beachside parking to the north and to the south (not in center of town, and note the one-way traffic loops to the surf).
Surf School: Cheyne Horan School of Surf, +61 (0)1 800 22 7873.
Keep in Mind: Summer crowds on weekends.

Months	JF	MA	MJ	JA	SO	ND
Average Swell (feet)	2	3	4–5	5	3–4	2
Air Temp (C/F)	29/85	27/82	23/74	20/69	25/77	28/83
Water Temp (C/F)	24/75	23/76	21/70	18/65	19/67	22/72
Wetsuit	none	shorty	spring	spring	shorty	none
Average Sunshine p/d (hours)	8	7	6–7	7–8	8	8
Average Rain p/m (inches)	7	4	3	2	3	5
Average Surfable Days p/m	15	17	19	20	19	16

78. AVALON BEACH

Northern New South Wales, Australia

Clean, monolithic lines hit the headlands on both sides of Avalon Bay, shattering a boomerang-bending breaker out into the abyss of South Avalon. So heavy are these waves that on big days, the beach has to be closed. But the crowds stay on to watch this huge surf crashing in. It's days like this that some Surf Life Saving members will venture out, hoping to stand up and slide down the wave's apex, gliding into the arms of these giants. The best sight of all, however, is to watch the champion bodysurfers fly, twist, and do somersault turns on the shoulders of these monsters, going to places only a bodysurfer dares go.

Avalon Beach is situated in one of the prettiest areas of Sydney, 3 miles south of Whale Beach and 24 miles north of Bondi (Spot 79). There are sixteen beaches on the north side of Sydney, and Avalon (also meaning "an island paradise") is one of the best.

There are four famous surf breaks within Avalon Bay, the first of which is Little Avalon. This is a radical rock-ledge point break at the beach's southeast corner, with nearly impossible-to-make hollow tube rides of 50 yards and very fast even for expert surfers. The 200-foot cliffs, which tower over this break, provide shelter from southwesterly winds and are a

> Surfing in Australia really picked up a boost when Dick Van Straland invented the first foam board in 1959, and I had the privilege of testing it at North Avalon. It was a 3-to-4-foot day, and the waves were just right for a little hot-dogging. It turned, trimmed, and cornered well, and felt like a magic carpet—a new, better material for sure. But I didn't think it rode the whitewater as well as balsa wood.

spectacular viewing place if you want a great view from above.

North Avalon Rocks is famous for its superb left reef point with boulders of various sizes making up the surf lineup. This is often a powerful, glassy, walling wave, breaking over patchy boiling currents into a rip. The outer takeoff area is closest to the rocks, but the inside section is the shallowest—the submerged boulders almost show themselves on some waves. North Avalon Rocks is a real treat of a wave, however, when you kick out in the rip, having made it. It's best on a northeast swell and light westerly winds.

It was at the Surf Life Saving Club end of South Avalon that the great Duke Kahanamoku Team from Hawaii gave a display of surfing in 1957 that set alight Australia's passion for the sport. His cornering, turning left and right, and holding trim was the first time that most modern-day maneuvers were shown. South Avalon Surf Life Saving Club surf spot has a sandbar peak that still pumps excellent surf in the 6-to-8-foot range and is also good for small surf, picking up any swell going. Then there's North Avalon, the famous right-hander beach break that peels off into the corner rip beside the rocks. The rip current here circulates, aiding paddling for a really fast return to the takeoff area. This is a classic right-hand beach break when it's 4 to 6 feet.

Avalon Beach is an all-around classic surf spot with something to suit everyone, on the right day.

There are a string of oceanfront Sydney suburbs stretching north along the coast, from Manly to the picture-perfect Palm Beach. There are many beaches along the way, and one of the greatest is beautiful Avalon Beach.

Photo D. Sumpter

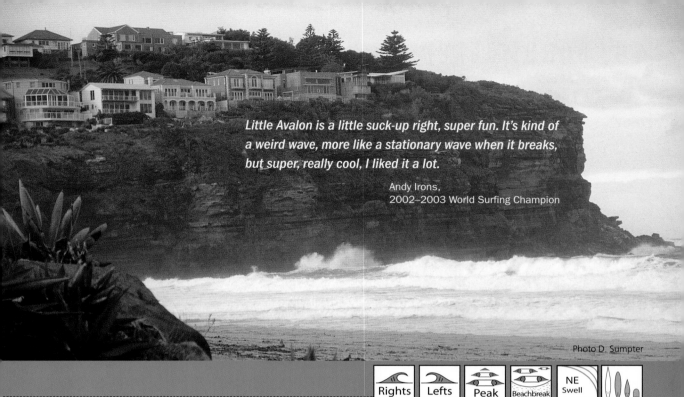

Little Avalon is a little suck-up right, super fun. It's kind of a weird wave, more like a stationary wave when it breaks, but super, really cool, I liked it a lot.

Andy Irons,
2002–2003 World Surfing Champion

Photo D. Sumpter

| Rights | Lefts | Peak | Beachbreak | NE Swell |

Break: Beach break, left-hand point break and right-hand reef break

Skill Level: Beginner to expert

Commitment: 3–10; 8–10 for Little Avalon

Best Boards: Shortboard, longboard, bodyboard

Lifeguard: In season

Hazards: Boulders spaced a foot apart make access difficult at north Avalon rocks, but it is the preferred access point for advanced surfers as the barrels quicker to surf. Further out the area known as "The Man with Hat On"
has an entry point used on double overhead days. The beachbreak at north Avalon has a regular rip beside the rocks making access easy. Farther south Little Avalon, a dangerous wave with inside-out, top-to-bottom curls, breaks low off shallow ledges. The beachbreak at south Avalon has variable rips to hinder or aid, but on double overhead days these grinding waves are brutal to paddle through.

Currency: Australian dollar.

Going There: Visa required except by Aus-
tralian and New Zealand citizens. Vaccinations required except by Australian and New Zealand citizens—tetanus. Check with your doctor, health clinic, and embassy for up-to-date info.

Where to Stay: Avalon Beach North B&B, +61 (0)2 9918 3323. Avalon Beach Backpackers Hostel, +61 (0)2 9918 9709. Avalon Beach RSL, +61 (0)2 9918 2201. Holiday Apartments, +61 (0)2 9918 2763. Pelican Rest B&B, +61 (0)2 9918 8696

Finding the Break: From the Sydney airport go over Sydney Harbor Bridge heading north and follow the coast highway to Avalon Beach. Park at the Surf Life Saving parking area for South Avalon and Little Avalon (to the right behind the rock pool, 300 yards next to the cliff), or head for Palm Beach and take the right-hand turn 3 miles along for North Avalon; follow signs for the beach.

Keep in Mind: Summer and weekend crowds when the surf is good.

Months	JF	MA	MJ	JA	SO	ND
Average Swell (feet)	2	3–4	5	6	3–4	2–3
Air Temp (C/F)	26/80	21/70	18/65	19/66	20/68	16/79
Water Temp (C/F)	21/70	19/68	17/62	16/61	17/62	18/68
Wetsuit	none	shorty	spring	spring	shorty	none
Average Sunshine p/d (hours)	8	7	6	6	8	8
Average Rain p/m (inches)	5	6	5	4	3	3
Average Surfable Days p/m	14	23	20	26	18	17

79. BONDI BEACH

Sydney, New South Wales, Australia

The huge waves curl over like the shell shapes of the Sydney Opera House. Bondi's waves are bright blue-eyed bombshells; head-high waves that zigzag and carve around. Glassy offshore days are pure performance days, and can be very sweet. Hot, hot sand, the bluest ocean, and waves that regularly thrill, Bondi can get big, but it's mostly just right. "No worries," as they say around here.

Bondi is Sydney's closest beach and easily its best. Despite being very crowded on weekends, it is one of the most picturesque beaches in the heart of the city and a lifeline to the many hyped-up city workers, suffering from the Aussie heat, in need of a lunchtime dip and an escape from the city.

Situated 24 miles north of Avalon Beach (Spot 78) and 2 miles from Sydney's city center with its Opera House and Harbour Bridge, Bondi is a beautiful white sand beach with a long history of "Bronzed Aussie" events, such as the Surf Life Saving Club's march and the Surf Carnivals. Many of the National Surfing Championships are held here as well, thanks to this spot's superfine surf. And I am proud to say that I am a former champion of Bondi, winning the Junior National Surfing Championships here in 1963.

Bondi is in the municipality of Wavely in East Sydney, its name derived from the area's Aboriginal tribal leader's name. There are several distinct surf breaks along this mile-long beach, one of Sydney's largest, all of them sheltered by headlands at both the north and south ends. At the southern end of the beach, the sandbars are best, giving perfect walling peaks continually shaped by rips and currents. The peak nearest the cliff is called the Pit, a right-hand peak with very hollow sections, especially at low tide. The most famous sandbar breaks are more toward the middle of the south end, straight out from the promenade called South Bondi. This is where most surfers check out the waves, park up, and paddle out.

As a popular city beach, the "dawn patrol" gets the pick of the waves. Eyes scan the waves from apartment buildings and dwellings right around the shoreline early each morning as part of the daily surf-check ritual. On a good day when the surf's up, you'll enter down through the terraced gardens, across the huge lawns, onto the massive sands, which, in summer, are packed with sun-baking Aussie crowds. Bondi is ideal for everyone from beginners to experts on the right day with its full spectrum of conditions.

Ever since English explorer Captain James Cook claimed the eastern half of Australia as British territory in 1770 and named it New South Wales, Sydney and the surrounding areas have been at the forefront of Australian life. Almost all Australians live within a two-hour drive of the coast, and during the summer months it is almost second nature to make for the water and cool off. It was for this reason that, in 1906, the world's first lifesaving club was set up here on the shores of Bondi.

On flat days take a trip to the nearby mountains, something certain to cool the body and freshen the mind. Just two hours west of Sydney you'll find the truly spectacular cliffs, canyons, and eucalyptus forests of the Blue Mountains. Here you'll discover such wonders as cooling waterfalls, spectacular climbing, and a cliff drive that skirts the 200-foot drop into the valley below. While it isn't surfing, this freshwater diversion should have you hankering for another day at Bondi's spectacular sets.

Photo D. Sumpter

Bondi is a great beach for beginners and experts alike, a great city beach, like Waikiki, a worthy symbol of Australia's greatness.

Rod Sumpter

Photo D. Sumpter

Beachbreak

E Swell

Break: Beach break
Skill Level: Beginner to expert
Commitment: 2–10
Best Boards: Shortboard
Lifeguard: In season
Hazards: Side rip currents and out-flowing channels make returning to the same peak easy, but getting in the right position after a long left or right is impossible; better to drift surf.
Currency: Australian dollar.

Going There: Visa required except by Australian and New Zealand citizens. Vaccinations required except by Australian and New Zealand citizens—tetanus. Check with your doctor, health clinic, and embassy for up-to-date info.
Where to Stay: Bondi Sands, 1 (800) 026 634. Bondi Beach Guesthouse, +61 (0)2 9300 9310. Bondi Beach Homestay B & B, +61 (0)9 624 0700. Beach Road Hotel, +61 (0)2 9130 7247.

Bondi Hotel, +61 (0)2 9130 3271. Bondi Junction Hotel, +61 (0)2 9389 5726. RSL Club, +61 (0)2 9389 5333. Indy's Bondi Beach Backpackers, +61 (0)2 9365 4900. Noah's Bondi Beach, +61 (0)2 9365 7100.

Finding the Break: Bondi Beach is the inner-city beach of Sydney. It's only 2 miles from the heart of Sydney, and only twenty minutes by taxi from Sydney Kingsford Smith Airport. From Sydney International Airport, take the Eastern Distributor Road and exit before the toll. Turn right onto Cleveland Street, which becomes Lang Road. Turn right onto Oxford Street, which become 5 Bondi Road. Follow this until it turns into Campbell Parade and Beach Road near the beach.
Surf School: Let's Go Surfing, +61 (0)2 9365 1800.
Keep in Mind: Vacations and summers are crowded; best in winter.

Months	JF	MA	MJ	JA	SO	ND
Average Swell (feet)	2	3-4	5	6	3-4	2-3
Air Temp (C/F)	26/80	21/70	18/65	19/66	20/68	16/79
Water Temp (C/F)	21/70	19/68	17/62	16/61	17/62	18/68
Wetsuit	none	shorty	spring	spring	shorty	none
Average Sunshine p/d (hours)	8	7	6	6	8	8
Average Rain p/m (inches)	5	6	5	4	3	3
Average Surfable Days p/m	17	19	20	26	24	18

80. BROKEN HEAD
Northern New South Wales, Australia

I was staying with my son and a team of international surfers at the Broken Head campsite. The waves here were made famous by George Greenough's surf films, *The Inner Most Limits of Pure Fun* and *Crystal Voyager*. These films feature Broken Head's classic tubing waves, which can be described as round, oblong, or square-shaped barrels. The movies were filmed from George's kneeboard. The film gives a bird's-eye view of surfing, with the use of a fish-eye lens—very realistic.

I woke up at 5:30 A.M. while it was still dark. I watched the sun rise over Broken Head with the surf pouring in—it was an amazing sight. Then I decided to slip into a shore-break and paddle out to take on some of the heavy barrel waves. A few blasts from thundering lips soon got me fully awake and ready for the day's adventure. I found that the Point break was magic, the forerunner to the heavy hollow middle and inside sections, where shallow sandbars became finally a dry barrel on the beach. After a long tube ride like that, the thrill was immense. I rate it in my top five barrel rides in the world.

Situated on the north coast of New South Wales, 7 miles north of Lennox Head (Spot 83) and 3 miles south of Byron Bay (Spots 86 and 87), is a curved-shaped 100-yard-wide beach surrounded by bush and scrubland called Broken Head. This great right-hand point surf break is world class and packs a punch on the right day.

There are four beaches in the Broken Head Reserve area: Broken Head, Kings Beach, Brays Beach, and Whites Beach. The coast then continues south with the mammoth Seven Mile Beach, it is largely a deserted beach with beach breaks backing onto the Australian wilderness that runs all

> The northern New South Wales coastline is known for its mixture of natural beauty, mild climate, and good resorts. Clean isolated beaches abut rain forest, with national parks and reserves holding World Heritage status.

the way to Lennox Head. The headland has two prominent rock outcrops called the Cocked Hat Rocks, both of which are good location finders in the surf lineup forming the Point. The Point surf is famous for its easy takeoff into a long straight walling wave that hollows and tubes to a top-to-bottom barrel off the sand bottom, becoming oververtical on the shorebreak, which often doubles up and can be a mighty, gnarly wave when over 6 feet.

The beach slopes steeply, and the sand dunes are eroded by tide and waves, making access down steep tracks to the beach. The horseshoe-shaped coastal profile then fans out from the inside shorebreak to the Point which forms one of the world's greatest breaks. This is a must-surf spot for any surfer on small soft days, and ideal for an expert surfer on hollow days whenever the tubes and barrels are running.

In the winter Broken Head, part of the Broken Head Nature Reserve, becomes a great place for whale-watching. You could be lucky enough to see dolphins surfing and white-breasted sea eagles plunging into the ocean and snatching up fish. Broken Head is one of the few places in New South Wales where the beach is fringed by rain forest.

Photo D. Sumpter

Thin upper perfection.

Bob McTavish,
former Australian Surfing Champion

Photo R. Sumpter

Rights | R.Point | Beachbreak | SE Swell

Break: Beach break
Skill Level: Beginner to expert
Commitment: 3–10; up to 8–10 if over 6 to 8 feet
Best Boards: Shortboard, longboard if small
Lifeguard: In season
Hazards: Rip currents, shallow sand bottom, gnarly waves. The waves are so hollow they're square-shaped more than round. Dangerous wave crests and breaking lips make duck diving impossible and the paddle out arduous over 8 feet.
Currency: Australian dollar.
Going There: Visa required except by Australian and New Zealand citizens. Vaccinations required except by Australian and New Zealand citizens—tetanus. Check with your doctor, health clinic, and embassy for up-to-date info.
Where to Stay: Beachside, +61 (0)2 6685 3805. Broken Head Caravan and Camping Park, +61 (0)2 6685 3245. Caravan Park Suffolk Park, +61 (0)2 6685 3129. Park Hotel Motel, +61 (0)2 6685 3621.
Finding the Break: Easy to find. From Lennox Head go north on the coast road, following signs for Byron Bay. Three miles before Byron Bay, turn right at the sign for Broken Head and park in the campsite. The caravan park (which is the hub of Broken Head) is situated about 5 miles south of Byron Bay.
Keep in Mind: Summer crowds and at weekends.

Months	JF	MA	MJ	JA	SO	ND
Average Swell (feet)	3	4–5	5	4–5	3–4	3
Air Temp (C/F)	29/84	27/81	21/70	20/68	23/72	28/82
Water Temp (C/F)	23/74	20/68	19/66	19/66	20/68	22/72
Wetsuit	none	shorty	shorty	shorty	vest	none
Average Sunshine p/d (hours)	7	7	6	7	8	8
Average Rain p/m (inches)	6	3	2	3	2	4
Average Surfable Days p/m	19	22	24	26	20	18

81. CABARITA BEACH
Northern New South Wales, Australia

This is where you get connected to your board, to the ocean. When you've surfed a few waves, you get stoked, and there's no place like it—a place to knock down performance barriers. A good spot to melt into some aquamarine waves, where spiky pandanus palms fringe the headland as lines of waves break like arrowheads across the beach.

Cabarita is situated 20 miles south of the Queensland–New South Wales border, east of Murwillumbah, and 30 miles north of the Pass, Byron Bay (Spot 86). Blessed with a classic surf sand point headland, this unique tropical break is a sought-after point break when the conditions are right. Best in light southwesterly winds and a southeasterly swell, if it's pumping at 4 to 8 feet and everything is right, this is a magical wave. On days of little to no swell elsewhere, Cabarita will pick up almost any swell going, and is world class in every respect once the waves get over 6 feet.

The main focus is on the Point Surf, a walling, barreling wave that starts lining up from around the headland and runs down the surf line onto layered sandbars lying across its path. This produces excellent sections, mostly rights, with the occasional wedgy left.

Norries Headland stands proud as the main geographic feature in the area. With Cabarita Beach on the northeast side of Norries Headland, it is ideally placed to collect swell. Cabarita is a beautiful location and is the quintessential surf spot for combining point surf and beach break waves together in one location. Cabarita Beach is often referred to as Bogangar, an Aboriginal word meaning "place of many pippies," the ancient ceremonial shell found on the beach at Cabarita, more commonly called middens. This remote, uncrowded surf spot, with its world-class right-hand waves, is a magnet for surfers, and many professional surf championships are held there each year.

Deciding which is the best length of short surfboard to ride and which shape will work best at Cabarita is often a science unto itself. The decision generally depends on the stage of tide. Generally, the choices follow this basic formula: At low tide a pin tail thruster, at half tide a swallowtail thruster, and at high tide a fish or squash tail three-fin thruster. The sweep and rip current can be strong. This is a must-surf spot for any surfer on small days and for the experts when the waves are 6 to 8 feet.

Just a thirty-minute drive from Coolangatta and an hour from Byron Bay, this stretch of northern New South Wales has other beaches as well, such as Hastings Point and Kingscliff, as well as Fingal Point to the north with lonely, scary surfing, fishing, and sun-baking opportunities. The major populations live in Murwillumbah, a town that also houses Australia's biggest shark tank and breeding program of gray nurse sharks.

The great outback starts with miles of hinterland and Mount Warning's stone spire looks like a gigantic thumb pointing toward the heavens. It was named by Captain Cook in 1770 (eight years before he first documented seeing surfing in Hawaii) in an effort to warn mariners of the dangerous offshore reefs. It was known to the Aboriginal people as Wollumbin, meaning "fighting chief of the mountains." Today Mount Warning National Park attracts hikers, tourists, and geology enthusiasts alike, enjoying some of the finest natural beauty Australia has to offer. The famous Mt. Warning can be seen clearly from Norries Headland at the southwest end of Cabarita Beach. Only a twenty-minute drive away, Mount Warning National Park is a popular place to explore on flat days.

Cabarita is a really fun wedge beach break . . . kind of a wedge with a little more point break to it—a really fun wave. It's a right off the point, but there can be lefts in the middle of the beach as well going against the right.

Andy Irons,
2002–2003
World Surfing
Champion

Photo D. Sumpter

Rights | Beachbreak | SE Swell

Break: Beach break and right-hand sand point
Skill Level: Beginner to expert
Commitment: 4–10
Best Boards: Shortboard
Lifeguard: In season
Hazards: Strong rips, deep gullies, and sandbars. Big southeast swells produce huge point surf with a grinding beach break.
Currency: Australian dollar.
Going There: Visa required except by Australian and New Zealand citizens. Vaccinations required except by Australian and New Zealand citizens—tetanus. Check with your doctor, health clinic, and embassy for up-to-date info.
Where to Stay: Emu Park Lodge, +61 (0)2 6676 1190. Holiday Rental, +61 (0)2 6676 1666. Cabarita Beachfront Motel, +61 (0)2 6676 1444. Cabarita Beach Front Hideaway, +61 (0)2 6676 1444. Diamond Beach Resort, +61 (0)2 6676 3232
Finding the Break: From Queensland take the Pacific Coast Highway south, exiting for the Tweed Coast. Follow the coast road to Cabarita Beach.
Keep in Mind: Only crowded on weekends.

Months	JF	MA	MJ	JA	SO	ND
Average Swell (feet)	3	4–5	5	4–5	3–4	3
Air Temp (C/F)	29/84	27/81	21/70	20/68	23/72	28/82
Water Temp (C/F)	23/74	20/68	19/66	19/66	20/68	22/72
Wetsuit	none	shorty	shorty	shorty	vest	none
Average Sunshine p/d (hours)	7	7	6	7	8	8
Average Rain p/m (inches)	7	4	3	2	3	5
Average Surfable Days p/m	15	19	22	24	15	12

82. GRASSY HEAD
New South Wales, Australia

If you'd like to surf on a huge impressive beach with oodles of stoking peaks and breaks, then Grassy Head is the place for you. From the first sight of breaking waves to the first splash in the face, the deep-driving rides are mighty. You can paddle into a wave at any part of the lineup and drop in or take off out by the farthest headland, where the sets come off the point and ride all the way back to the beach. From the beach break or from the point, the waves are wedgy right-hand peaks that pack a punch if you come unstruck. The surrounding grassy hill and green valleys around the deserted white sandy beach make this an ideal countryside to surf with no crowds.

Grassy Head is a small seaside village, situated 20 miles south of Coffs Harbor on the central coast of New South Wales. It's approximately 320 miles north of Sydney at the southern edge of Nambucca Valley—fondly referred to as the Valley. It boasts 14 miles of true surfing inspiration. Having so many beaches and points to surf, the choices and diverse locations in the Nambucca Valley are amazing.

Of the many named breaks in the area, the best choice is often Grassy Head. This is located 10 miles north of South West Rocks and 20 miles southeast of Macksville. Grassy Head, a sand-bottomed right-hander with rocky outcrops, a big barrel, and a long powerful wall, holds waves up to 12 feet, challenging even for the expert. The deep sand channels produce staggered peaks out to the point, and the numerous inside waves re-form.

If it's small, it can be a fun performance wave, with a peak beside the point, and classic midway tubes though to the shorebreak. On the other side of Grassy Head is Trial Bay, a beach break with four-wheel-drive access and a huge number of sandbar peaks from which to choose. Trial Bay is good in a northwest wind.

Grassy Head sits in the middle of this surf playground and is the best wave in most conditions. But there are other wonderful and magic locations nearby to surf in a day—or maybe surf two or three in a morning. Going north, the next major surf spot is Scott's Head, a right-hand point break with a sandy bottom and a ride as long as 100 to 300 yards. Scott's Head hosts many surfing events, including the New South Wales State Masters and Women's Championships. Scott's Head is composed of Little Beach, Main Beach, and the main focus break, the Point, a well-lined-up right-hander. Farther north is Nambucca Heads, which has many barrel sections spread across long white sandy beaches with good peaks on the right day. *Nambucca* comes from the Aboriginal word *gumbaynggir,* meaning "entrance to the waters." Going 2 miles farther north is Valla Headland, North Valla Beach, the best wave around for bodyboarding. The short, hollow peaks and good wedgy waves on the right day are definitely worth checking out. Head south from Grassy Head for the fantastic longboarders' wave of Crescent Head, made famous in the 1960s, where the right-hand point pumps in pure peeling surf. These breaks can produce the perfect wave. It's only a question of being there at the right time. This is an ideal location for everyone from beginner to expert with waves to suit all skill levels.

Nambucca Valley is at the heart of Australia's banana country, with plantations lining the highway all the way up to Coffs Harbor. There are 512 growers harvesting more than 1,300 kilograms per year in the area—25 percent of Australia's produce.

The Dorrigo Plateau has tropical rain forest and many waterfalls, and the Nymboida River is famous for whitewater rafting, a good diversion for those flat surf days.

Photo D. Sumpter

Grassy, Scotts, Nambucca, and Crescent Heads: This whole coast is just amazing. Anyone can be perfect on any given day. My favorites are Grassy and Crescent Head with their perfect walls for thirty seconds of nose riding, head dips, and cover-ups. This coastline just abounds with possibilities.

Rod Sumpter

 Rights Lefts R.Point E Swell

Type of Break: Beach break

Skill Level: Intermediate to expert

Commitment: 6–10

Best Boards: Shortboard; longboard on small days

Lifeguard: None

Hazards: Rips and currents, rocky outcrops, shallow sand bottom

Currency: Australian dollar.

Going There: Visa required except by Australian and New Zealand citizens. Vaccinations required except by Australian and New Zealand citizens—tetanus. Check with your doctor, health clinic, and embassy for up-to-date info.

Where to Stay: Grassy Head Hideaway Villas, +61 (0)2 6569 0811. Sandcastle Holiday Apartments International, +61 (0)2 6652 6599. Stone Haven Farmstay, +61 (0)2 6652 2663. Grass Trees Escape, +61 (0)2 9907 1440. The Seabreeze Hotel, +61 (0)2 6566 6205. Trial Bay Lodges, +61 (0)2 6566 6594. Horseshoe Bay Beach Park, Livingstone Street, South West Rocks, +61 (0)2 6566 6370. The Bay Motel, +61 (0)2 6566 6205. Cape Smoky Lighthouse B&B, +61 (0)2 6566 6301. South West Rocks Motel, +61 (0)2 6566 6330.

Finding the Break: Turn off the Pacific Highway 10 miles north of Kempsey (onto Tourist Drive 14) and follow the road a further 4 miles through banana plantations, forests, and farmland to Stuarts Point. Proceed north, following signs to Grassy Head.

Surf Schools: Loggerheads Malibu Club, +61 (0)2 6568 7314. East Coast Surf School, +61 (0)2 6651 5515. Tezza's Surf School, +61 (0)4 0885 3788.

Keep in Mind: Crowds on a good swell in summer.

Months	JF	MA	MJ	JA	SO	ND
Average Swell (feet)	3–4	4–5	5–6	5–6	2–3	3–4
Air Temp (C/F)	28/82	27/81	23/74	22/72	21/70	28/82
Water Temp (C/F)	21/70	20/68	19/66	18/64	17/64	21/70
Wetsuit	none	shorty	shorty	long	long	none
Average Sunshine p/d (hours)	7	6	5	6	7	8
Average Rain p/m (inches)	7	4	3	2	3	5
Average Surfable Days p/m	16	17	18	19	17	14

83. LENNOX HEAD
Northern New South Wales, Australia

There's nothing quite like a riproaring point wave, protected by a huge green sloping crescent-shaped hill, to find all the offshore winds. Add to this a scalloped rock-sediment seafloor to pull in the swell. This is where Australia's barrels are often biggest and best.

Situated at the southern end of Seven Mile Beach, 8 miles south of Broken Head (Spot 76) and 6 miles north of Ballina, Lennox Head is shaped like the profile of a sitting lion, with the head dominating this part of the coastline. Lennox is known for its quality point surf and ultrahollow waves. It's a beauty spot with awesome views of the surf lineup. When there's a clean 6-to-8-foot swell, it's good to walk along the track from the village that follows the coast south, passing the seated shelters, and on along the coast rising up to the headland until you're high enough to look back at the great view of surf and swell lines marching in. It's a classic "surf pic" to remember as you look north along Seven Mile Beach.

Looking south are more surf breaks, including Boulder Beach with its heavy, hollow beach break waves, Sharpers Beach and Flat Rocks, best with an east swell and west winds, and on to the waterways of Ballina.

Lennox Head beach break is a fine wave, often working

> The rocks at Lennox Head are very slippery and are almost as famous as the surf for being difficult. You need to use a special wedged footstep to walk over them to access the waves—this needs practice to perfect. It's worth trying out your technique on flat days, when the snorkeling is excellent and the point's rock ledges are clearly visible.

when the point is not, and best in a southeast swell and light southwest winds. This area is called the Moat, and has a consistently fine peak whenever there is a 4-to-6-foot swell. This is a magic setup, with point and beach breaks close at hand. From the headland parking area you can make your way down through the grassy track to the rock-strewn water's edge of slippery boulders and round stones and enter the fantastic waves of Lennox Head. This is a must-surf spot for advanced to expert surfers.

Photo D. Sumpter

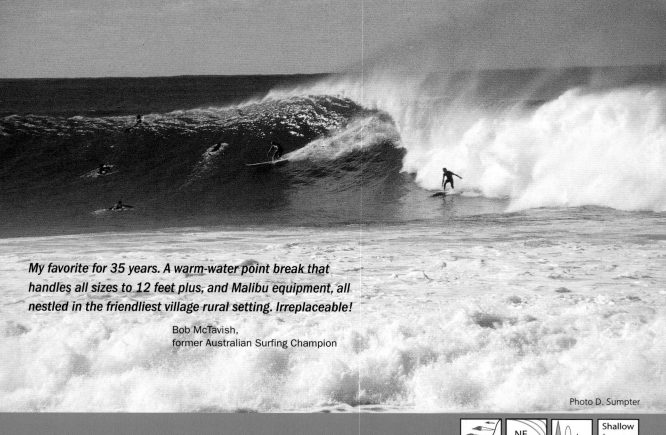

My favorite for 35 years. A warm-water point break that handles all sizes to 12 feet plus, and Malibu equipment, all nestled in the friendliest village rural setting. Irreplaceable!

Bob McTavish,
former Australian Surfing Champion

Photo D. Sumpter

Break: Beach and right-hand point break
Skill Level: Intermediate to expert
Commitment: 3–10 at the beach; 8–10 if big at the point
Best Boards: Longboard, shortboard, bodyboard, big-wave gun
Lifeguard: Beach in season
Hazards: Rip and sweep currents, rock ledges, pounding set waves. Slippery rocks about a foot round on the walk out.

Currency: Australian dollar.
Going There: Visa required except by Australian and New Zealand citizens. Vaccinations required except by Australian and New Zealand citizens—tetanus. Check with your doctor, health clinic, and embassy for up-to-date info.

Where to Stay: Santa Fe Motel, Lennox Head, +61 (0)2 6687 7788. Bomboras Lennox Head Apartments, +61 (0)2 6618 0000. Newalls Apartments, +61 (0)2 6687 5144. Beachfront Apartments, +61 (0)2 6687 7209. Lennox Hotel, +61 (0)2 6687 7312.
Finding the Break: Easy to find. From Byron Bay head south on the coast road for Ballina; after driving for ten minutes, you will be at Lennox Head town. Go straight ahead to the junction and up tourist drive. Park at the top on Lennox Head Point on your left to see the panorama.
Keep in Mind: Summer crowds on weekends.

Months	JF	MA	MJ	JA	SO	ND
Average Swell (feet)	2–3	3–4	4–5	5	3–4	2–3
Air Temp (C/F)	29/85	27/82	23/74	20/69	25/77	28/83
Water Temp (C/F)	24/75	23/76	21/70	18/65	19/67	22/72
Wetsuit	none	shorty	spring	spring	shorty	vest
Average Sunshine p/d (hours)	8	7	6–7	7–8	8	8
Average Rain p/m (inches)	7	4	3	2	3	5
Average Surfable Days p/m	11	16	20	21	16	9

84. MANLY BEACH

Sydney, New South Wales, Australia

Manly's beach breaks are like a clap of thunder, dark blue and lightning fast. The sets seem to wander in for a long time from far out, and finally break as crunchy, creamy waves that drain dry on the sandbanks. At high tide the fast-walling sections join up to a neat shorebreak.

Situated on the north side of Sydney 10 miles from the Sydney Harbour Bridge and 20 miles north of Avalon Beach (Spot 77), Manly has a reputation for solid beach break waves that peak like spires off multiple sandbars. These wedgy waves tread their way over a seascape to break as peaks across the beach. Half a mile to the south end of the beach is the big point surf of Fairy Bower, and the rare breaking wave of the Bombora lies a mile out to sea to the north.

Manly Beach is where most of today's barrel riding is done, because there are good sandbars producing quality lefts and rights off a dozen breaks. One is in the flag lifeguard area, and is a good bodysurfing and handboard peak. In all there are 4 miles of surfing coastline, starting with the headland point surf of Fairy Bower, the first break to the south of Manly, which is best in a swell from 8 to 18 feet. This is Manly's most famous break. To the north there are some great waves at South Steyne and North Steyne.

Around the headland to Queenscliff there are some nice waves with some rock-sediment ledge takeoff areas that produce some walling rights and bowling lefts. Manly has a lot to offer; it's suitable for the beginner on small days and ideal for the intermediate and expert when bigger.

About 0.5 mile out to sea, between Queenscliff and North Steyne, is the epic break known as the Bombora. This was made famous in 1961 when Dave Jackman first surfed it at 30 feet. He paddled into the peak bowl and outsurfed the collapsing curl to ride under the face of this monster wave to the shoulder. Since then, it has become a surf spot ridden on rare big days.

Manly is one of Australia's most famous surf spots thanks to hosting the first World Surfing Championships in 1964. The event was a great success, with superb 4-to-6-foot surf consistently throughout the weeklong championship. Manly was chosen for its central location with plenty of facilities and reliable beach break waves. The world press reported it with great acclaim. The event still captures the minds and hearts of most Australians as the moment when the sport became a world fraternity. A global body of people evolved, caught in the apex of a common goal—surf fever.

Photo D. Sumpter

Manly is a great beach break and a neat place. Fairy Bower is my favorite point wave in Australia.

Rod Sumpter

Photo D. Sumpter

Beachbreak

E Swell

Break: Beach break

Skill Level: Beginner to expert

Commitment: 3–10

Best Boards: Longboard and shortboard

Lifeguard: In season

Hazards: Surf larger than double overhead makes the paddle out against heavy sand bar closeouts difficult if not impossible. In overhead surf it's still a race against thick lips and inside closeouts as mid-tide channels and gullies cause strong rips. A strong high tide shore break, dangerous rip currents, shallow sand bottom.

Currency: Australian dollar.

Going There: Visa required except by Australian and New Zealand citizens. Vaccinations required except by Australian and New Zealand citizens—tetanus. Check with your doctor, health clinic, and embassy for up-to-date info.

Where to Stay: By the Beach B&B, +61 (0)2 9979 1711. Pacific Park Royal, +61 (0)2 9977 7666. Beach House, +61 (0)2 9938 5899. Manly Holiday Apartments, ++61 (0)2 9981 6891.

Manly Backpackers Bungalow, +61 (0)2 9977 5494. Tepee Adventure Tours camping, +61 (0)4 1490 5127. Quintin House, +61 (0)2 9977 3607. Manly Beach Hut Hostel, +61 (0)2 9977 8777.

Finding the Break: Easy to find. From Sydney Kingsford Smith Airport, head north on Southern Cross Drive and then turn left onto Anzac Parade. Drive straight and turn right on Crown Street; travel north across the Sydney Harbour Bridge and follow off-ramp directions to Manly Beach. Alternatively, take the ferry from Sydney at Circular Quay; to Manly it takes about thirty minutes, or fifteen minutes by Fastcat.

Surf Schools: Manly Surf School, +61 (0)2 9977 6977. Australian Surf School +61 (0)2 9970 6813.

Keep in Mind: Crowded in summer and on weekends.

Months	JF	MA	MJ	JA	SO	ND
Average Swell (feet)	2	3–4	5	6	3–4	2–3
Air Temp (C/F)	26/80	21/70	18/65	19/66	20/68	16/79
Water Temp (C/F)	21/70	19/68	17/62	16/61	17/62	18/68
Wetsuit	none	shorty	spring	spring	shorty	none
Average Sunshine p/d (hours)	8	7	6	6	8	8
Average Rain p/m (inches)	5	6	5	4	3	3
Average Surfable Days p/m	12	19	20	26	24	11

85. TALLOW BEACH
New South Wales, Australia

You can't imagine your luck when you survey the scene. There's surf the size of sugarcane fields wafting in the offshore breeze; towering cliffs hang over clear-water sandbars, where schools of fish and pods of dolphin play. Once you've seen a wave break perfectly, there's no stopping the adrenaline rush.

Tallow Beach is situated 125 miles south of Brisbane and 500 miles north of Sydney, approximately 1 mile south of "Cape Byron" and 2 miles from the town center of Byron Bay. It's known for its wide variety of surfing conditions, and there are a lot of peaks from which to choose, including everything from soft, fun longboarding waves to steep and heavy waves. There's always an off-the-beaten-track peak with your name on it along this stretch of coast that curves southward, with no one else around for what seems like miles.

Tallow Beach is 4 miles long and starts at the far northerly break, which is called Cosy Corner. Tucked into the headland at Cape Byron, this is a superb long left and shorter right peak. This develops some top-to-bottom challenging waves, in almost any swell. The shape and hollowness depends on the sandbanks of the day and the state of the tide. This is a well-lined-up, steep-sectioning, barreling wave, breaking out beside the headland rocks, and is also the most sheltered. It can resemble a sand point at low tide and is often the best wave on the beach, getting very busy on weekends. On big-surf days, when it's 10 to 15 feet, tow-in surfing is a must because the rip currents are so strong.

Then there's Dolphins, named for the frequent visiting pods that choose this peak to surf. This beach break has a single long sandbar stretched across the face of the beach for 50 yards; at each end a deep channel forms the most perfect right and left. The takeoff in the middle of this bar allows the timing of an extremely deep barrel. Some of the best beach breaks occur past Tallow Creek, and there are plenty of waves peaking all the way south to Suffolk Parks. This is a must-surf spot for the intermediate surfer on 2-to-3-foot days, and for the advanced and expert over 6 feet.

The New South Wales government has created the Cape Byron Marine Park covering the Tallow coast as an important contribution to the Australian way of life. This huge beach is backed by sand dunes, and has cliffs at the Byron Bay end going northward. It can get crowded on the weekends, especially if the surf's good. Nearby Byron Bay is a magnet for backpackers and surfers alike, with plenty of accommodations, and an easy lifestyle.

Photo D. Sumpter

A very pretty, lovely beach. Excellent surf with lots of different peaks, from up in the corner at Cosy Corner, a good left-hander, very sucky. . . . It can have strong rips, beautiful water, dolphins, and stuff. Often very busy; a good beach, fantastic beach break surf.

John Sumpter,
1997 Ligger Bay Surfing Champion

Photo D. Sumpter

| Lefts | Peak | Beachbreak | SE Swell | |

Break: Beach break
Skill Level: Beginner to expert
Commitment: 5–10
Best Boards: Shortboard
Lifeguard: None
Hazards: Dangerous rip currents, shallow sand bottom, and changing sand bars produce radically different line-ups. Dolphins appear from nowhere, often at speed, and surf the waves.

Currency: Australian dollar.
Going There: Visa required except by Australian and New Zealand citizens. Vaccinations required except by Australian and New Zealand citizens—tetanus. Check with your doctor, health clinic, and embassy for up-to-date info.
Where to Stay: Tallow Beach Houses, +61 (0)2 6685 4533. Byron Lakeside Holiday, +61 (0)2 6680 9244. Aman Byron, +61 (0)4 1486 2684. Dolphin Motor Inn, +61 (0)2 6680 9577. Byron Bay Guest House, +61 (0)4 2100 8886. Aquarius Backpackers, +61 (0)2 6685 7663, or fax +61 (0)2 6685 7439. Arts Factory Backpackers Hostel, Byron Bay, +61 (0)2 6685 7709. Byron Bay Camping Park, +61 (0)2 6685 6751. Cape Byron Hostel, +61 (0)1 1800 652 627. Bruddhas Beach House, +61 (0)4 1621 8869

Finding the Break: From Byron Bay town center, take the Cape Byron Lighthouse road for 1 mile and watch for Tallow Beach. Turn to the right after 0.5 mile and park under eucalyptus trees at the beach parking area.
Keep in Mind: Summer crowds on weekends.

Months	JF	MA	MJ	JA	SO	ND
Average Swell (feet)	2–3	3–4	4–5	5	3–4	2–3
Air Temp (C/F)	29/85	27/82	23/74	20/69	25/77	28/83
Water Temp (C/F)	24/75	23/76	21/70	18/65	19/67	22/72
Wetsuit	none	shorty	spring	spring	shorty	none
Average Sunshine p/d (hours)	8	7	6–7	7–8	8	8
Average Rain p/m (inches)	7	4	3	2	3	5
Average Surfable Days p/m	23	25	26	27	22	21

86. THE PASS
Byron Bay, New South Wales, Australia

With dynamite nose rides, flashy roundhouse cutbacks, sparkling tubes that breathe out liquid gold in the shape of a longboarder's tailblock spray, this is a dreamlike wave. It's called Byron Bay's the Pass. The break starts with the takeoff opposite a 30-foot-high craggy rock that forms one side of the Pass; the other side is where the fishermen's boat ramp gives access to the ocean from the steep beach and bush. The closer you are to the rock on takeoff, the bigger the swell bounces up. It jumps a 4-to-5-foot wave into a 7-to-8-foot drop as it reflects from the rock face. The sidewash adds to a hairy takeoff. The wave's shape is a loop just after takeoff all the way to the shore. It's a dream first section whether you take off wide at the point or tuck in close to the craggy rock.

From here the shallow water runs out over sandbars toward Clarks Beach, and the hollow waves wall up fast, swinging and bending and making for a long, exciting ride. On big days when a cyclone swell arrives, it's a different matter. Swells build up out back 300 yards north of the Pass. These big groundswells arrive, crashing into Cape Byron's headland, splashing up and billowing spray hundreds of feet into the air. At the Pass these wave trains of swell are a mighty sight. Here you see the waves side-on. A big-wave surfer waits for the right sloping peak to crack the wave left. The onlooker views these swanlike moving mountains in awe as towering waves head north down to Byron Bay to feed the beaches and reefs toward Mount Warning. A beautiful sight.

Situated 10 miles south of New Brunswick Heads and 6 miles north of Broken Head (Spot 79), on the north coast of New South Wales is the quintessential point surf of the Pass. Few places have such perfect sandbars angled across an incoming swell, as is the setup at Cape Byron's the Pass. Located halfway out on the peninsula on the northeast side

of Cape Byron, Australia's easternmost landfall, this is one of the best point surf beach breaks in the world. It is famous for its consistent tubes and long right-hand breaking waves, with a possible length of ride up to 500 yards. It's the perfect longboarders' wave that combines a nice takeoff and drop into a hollow tubing and cutback section. As it re-forms its barreling halfway in, it then speeds along for performance surfing to a diminishing shorebreak, where more often than not you end up on dry sand.

On a good day the swells continue to the next break called Clark's Beach, which can be nearly as good on the right day. The Pass is the sought-after wave in Australia, with nothing quite like it. With fine yellow sand and tall gum trees lining the coastline, this sand-bottomed break surpasses all others in the area.

First ridden by longboarders, the Pass is ideal nose riding that can last for 150 yards and a tube ride 50 yards. Best in a southeast to east swell, and south to southwest winds, the Pass can have strong rip currents if the swell is big, and on strong tidal days a 1-to-3-mile-per-hour sweep can be running. On weekends it is likely to be very crowded, because the whole area is a beauty spot. This is a must-surf spot for any surfer on small days, and best for experts when there is an offshore wind and waist-high or greater waves.

On Byron Bay's west there's Belongil, a beach break, then the Wreck, an old shipwreck that forms its own quality left and right peaks and solid tubes. Beach breaks for the beginner are at Main Beach, mostly soft peaky lines of swell peeling off fast and good. The beach stretches up to the Pass along the horseshoe-shaped beach with fun and fluffy waves. Next is the Recreation Centre Park's break, with fast lefts and rights, as well as good amenities for a day out at the beach when there are mostly closeout waves.

Byron Bay is at the center of an Australian alternative lifestyle, with a unique shopping center of surf shops, opal stores, clothes shops, and remedy shops. There are several backpackers' hostels, hotels, and bars. By all accounts it's one of the friendliest towns and one of the most laid-back places in Australia.

Photo D. Sumpter

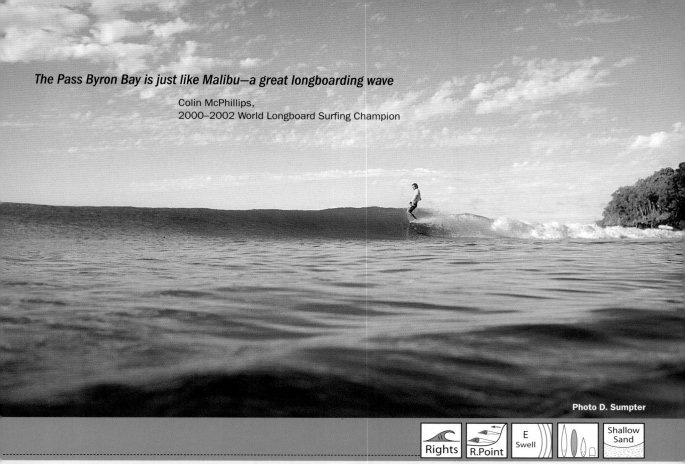

The Pass Byron Bay is just like Malibu—a great longboarding wave

Colin McPhillips,
2000–2002 World Longboard Surfing Champion

Photo D. Sumpter

Rights | R.Point | E Swell | | Shallow Sand

Type of Break: Point break
Suits Surfers: Intermediate to expert
Commitment: 5–10
Best Boards: Longboard
Lifeguard: In season, November to March
Hazards: The undertow is generally against the paddle out. From low to high tide the undertow makes it hard to keep position on 4-to-6-foot waves. At dead high tide it's best and the low tide barrels are the most hollow and perfect up to and over 6 feet. In 15-foot surf, it's the paddle that's a challenge.

Currency: Australian dollar.
Going There: Visa required except by Australian and New Zealand citizens. Vaccinations required except by Australian and New Zealand citizens—tetanus. Check with your doctor, health clinic, and embassy for up-to-date info.

Where to Stay: Aman Byron, +61 (0)4 1486 2684. Dolphin Motor Inn, +61 (0)2 6680 9577. Byron Bay Guest House, +61 (0)4 2100 8886. Aquarius Backpackers, +61 (0)2 6685 7663, or fax +61 (0)2 6685 7439. Arts Factory Backpackers Hostel, Byron Bay, +61 (0)2 6685 7709. Byron Bay Camping Park, +61 (0)2 6685 6751. Cape Byron Hostel, +61 (0)1 800 652 627. Bruddhas Beach House, +61 (0)4 1621 8869

Finding the Break: From Byron Bay center take the coast road signposted for Cape Lighthouse. As you wind up Cape Byron Head, the first turn left takes you to good parking and the Pass (the Pass waves run past the restaurant.)
Keep in Mind: Busy to crowded on weekends.

Months	JF	MA	MJ	JA	SO	ND
Average Swell (feet)	2–3	3–4	4–5	5	3–4	2–3
Air Temp (C/F)	29/85	27/82	23/74	20/69	25/77	28/83
Water Temp (C/F)	24/75	23/76	21/70	18/65	19/67	22/72
Wetsuit	none	shorty	spring	spring	shorty	none
Average Sunshine p/d (hours)	8	7	6–7	7–8	8	8
Average Rain p/m (inches)	7	4	3	2	3	5
Average Surfable Days p/m	9	12	17	21	18	14

87. WATEGOS
Byron Bay, New South Wales, Australia

It's summer and you're at the top of Wategos Bay. This eye-catching scene sweeps out to sea before you. The gum trees are shedding seeds in the offshore wind, and they settle on the shoulders of waves marching in, just about to break. Like surfers paddling into a set, they turn and twist on a crashing barrel. Punch hard into the green part of the wave and push your fins down under the curl. Leave the inner edge to splash rocks behind you as you travel down the line. There are split seconds to lift or drop the rail, to trim and carve a straight line out to the middle bay, or to spin out in the curl.

Wategos Beach is situated 2 miles east of Byron Bay in the tropical far north of New South Wales, and 50 miles south of the Queensland border. Set amid stunning scenery, there are two classic surf breaks at Wategos Beach. To the east is Little Wategos, a right-hand point break with the takeoff close to the rocks. The wave quickly peels off sandbars reeling away from the point and out into the bay, making this is a fast, down-the-line, freight train of a wave. The middle of the bay walls up and backs off, or breaks into a peak depending on the size of the swell, with a nice left. This, in turn, enters the bay proper and fades out to rebuild again at the beach break.

Wategos Beach break is the most popular and considered the primary break, and a unique feature separates it from a regular beach setup and puts in into a class of its own: When conditions are right, the swell raps in across the beach, and the right-hander becomes an inside-out sand point like Kirra (Spot 72), superhollow and extreme. When this happens, and the word is out that the swell is up and the banks are right, it gets crowded. As a beach break it has everything you could want, shifting white sand and turquoise clear warm water, with lefts and rights changing with the tides. Little Wategos is ideal for the expert surfers, and Wategos Beach is perfect for beginners on most days, except when the swell is up over 4 feet, the sandbars are perfect, and the waves are pumping. Then it's for experts only.

This is a beauty spot and great surf spot, with the chance to see dolphins surfing the swells and whales off the point from May through October. The Aboriginal people called this point of land Walgun, which means the Shoulder. It gave them sandy beaches, seafood, wildlife, and springwater and was a good place for telling daytime stories.

Photo D. Sumpter

This is my favorite wave in the world for turns. I first heard about it from Phil Edwards when he was making Surfing Hollow Days. *I learned Johnny Fain's forehand turn and mastered Phil's drop knee cutbacks here.*

Rod Sumpter

Photo D. Sumpter

R.Point | SE Swell | Shallow Sand

Break: Beach break
Skill Level: Beginner to expert
Commitment: 5–10
Best Boards: Shortboard
Lifeguard: In season
Hazards: A short shelving beach with a strong north-flowing sweep current makes returning to take-off difficult. The point has shark sightings, and dolphins surf the waves to perfection. Holds a big swell but requires a lot of paddle power. Tow-in surfing over 15 feet.
Currency: Australian dollar.
Going There: Visa required except by Australian and New Zealand citizens. Vaccinations required except by Australian and New Zealand citizens—tetanus. Check with your doctor, health clinic, and embassy for up-to-date info.
Where to Stay: Wategos Panorama, +61 (0)4 0818 7877. Aman Byron, +61 (0)4 1486 2684. Dolphin Motor Inn, +61 (0)2 6680 9577. Byron Bay Guest House, +61 (0)4 2100 8886. Aquarius Backpackers, +61 (0)2 6685 7663, or fax +61 (0)2 6685 7439. Arts Factory Backpackers, Hostel Byron Bay, +61 (0)2 6685 7709. Byron Bay Camping Park, +61 (0)2 6685 6751. Cape Byron Hostel, 1800 652 627. Bruddhas Beach House, +61 (0)4 1621 8869.
Finding the Break: From Byron Bay town center, take the coast road signposted for Cape Lighthouse. As you wind up the Cape Byron Headland road, the first left turn goes to the Pass. Carry on, following signs for the Cape Lighthouse, and you will see the next left turn for Wategos Beach. There is good parking and picnic tables.
Keep in Mind: Summer crowds on weekends.

Months	JF	MA	MJ	JA	SO	ND
Average Swell (feet)	1-2	2	3	3-4	3	2
Air Temp (C/F)	29/85	27/82	23/74	20/69	25/77	28/83
Water Temp (C/F)	24/75	23/76	21/70	18/65	19/67	22/72
Wetsuit	none	shorty	spring	spring	shorty	none
Average Sunshine p/d (hours)	8	7	6-7	7-8	8	8
Average Rain p/m (inches)	7	4	3	2	3	5
Average Surfable Days p/m	7	9	11	12	14	6

88. BELLS BEACH
Victoria, Australia

When is a great surf break considered great? When you're at Bells Beach and the ground shakes as waves break like bombs on the shore, and guys fly like falcons across the wall of water. You'll know Bells Beach is special in the first moments when you feel yourself dropping down the face of the wave and crank your first turn to negotiate through its bowl at 25 miles per hour. You then disappear as the greenroom covers you in glass. You wonder if you're ever going to come out. Great moments like these have made Bells famous.

This is Victoria's premier surf spot and Australia's big-wave town, with bags of barrels and one of the best waves you could ever wish for. This is a rugged area with towering cliffs and a South Pacific swell lunging into the lineup, making perfect lines of swell.

Situated 3 miles southwest of Torquay and 44 miles south of the city of Melbourne is the quintessential surf break of Bells Beach, a rock-sediment reef and point break. Victoria's most famous surf spot is named for the Bell family, who lived and farmed here in the mid-1800s. The location is unusual for holding everything from good small surf on up to big waves with perfection, and it doesn't matter what the tide is— only the wind is important, working best in a northwest wind.

The Rip Curl Pro Surfing Championships, the world's longest-running professional surf championships, are held here every Easter. Bells first became famous for hosting the 1970 World Surfing Championships, where Ralph Arness of the United States won the event (I came in seventh), with my team winning the World Relay Paddle Race. It was here also that Rip Curl Wetsuits and Quiksilver were created, where Peter Troy first surfed the site in 1949, and where the first Victorian championships were held in 1962.

Bells Beach regularly receives 15-to-20-foot surf around April. The huge swells are produced when cyclone-forming low-pressure systems sweep down Australia's east coast and around Cape Otway in the south, bringing with them massive swells that rise up from very deep water, ultimately arriving at Bells Point surf.

The Victorian branch of the National Trust now lists Bells Beach as a Site of Historical Significance, and a road has been carved out of the bush to make for easy access. The beach is narrow, and the bay fans outward toward the sea in a half-moon shape. There is a right-hand reef break called Rincon (after the classic break in California), a shorebreak that dumps a midsection bowl, and a far right-hand point. From the cliffs you can see how consistent the waves are, the lines of swell filling the bay and peeling off as if made by a machine.

There are other breaks nearby, including Winkipop (Spot 90), the famous Australian break with its super right-hand barrels and fast walls. Bells Beach is ideal for the intermediate surfer when it's 3 to 5 feet and best for the expert when it's 6 to 20 feet and bigger.

Victoria geography is about as diverse as it gets, with semiarid deserts, mountain ranges, fern-filled rain forests, river wetlands and floodplains, lakes and forests, salt plains, and sand dunes. Many of these ecosystems are spread over Victoria's thirty-four national parks and forty state parks, all of which are now protected areas once watched over by the spiritual beings of the Aborigines who came here from Asia some 50,000 years ago. It was believed that the spirits of the Dreamtime traveled the land, forming the area's many natural features.

The Australia Surfing Museum and Surfworld at Torquay, the town next to Bells Beach, both house surfing artifacts documenting the history of Bells—from the days when Peter Troy first rode the wild coast of Victoria, on up to the history of surfboard design, such as the original V-bottom by Bob McTavish, the Nose-Riders by Scott Dillon, and the Triple Stringer by Gordon Woods. Both the Australia Surfing Museum and Surfworld contain a host of pictorial surf history and are well worth the visit.

Photo D. Sumpter

Bells Beach, big cold thunder, gets better and better with modern boards.

Bob McTavish,
former Australian Surfing Champion

Photo R. Sumpter

 Rights R.Point S Swell   Shallow Reef

Break: Right-hand reef and point break

Skill Level: Expert

Commitment: 4–10; 9–10 when it's 15 feet plus

Best Boards: Shortboards from 6 feet, 4 inches, to 8 feet, 10 inches; big-wave guns if it's huge

Lifeguard: In season, November to February

Hazards: Big waves, wave bowl, shallow point inside section of wave, rip currents, rocky ledges, fierce shorebreak.

Currency: Australian dollar.

Going There: Visa required except by Australian and New Zealand citizens. Vaccinations required except by Australian and New Zealand citizens—tetanus. Check with your doctor, health clinic, and embassy for up-to-date info.

Where to Stay: Beach Cottage, +61 (0)3 5261 4010. Nomads Bells Beach Backpacker, +61 (0)3 5261 7070. Point Break Packers, +61 (0)3 5261 5105. Surf City Motel, +61 (0)3 5261 3492. Zeally Bay Caravan Park, +61 (0)3 5261 2400. Bellbrae Motel, +61 (0)3 5261 3777.

Finding the Break: Easy to find. From Torquay follow the signs for Lorne along the Great Ocean Road. Three miles on you'll see the Bells Beach Reserve parking lot. Park here and walk the remaining yards to the top of Bells Beach.

Contest: Easter Rip Curl Pro (WCT).

Keep in Mind: Summer crowds on weekends.

Months	JF	MA	MJ	JA	SO	ND
Average Swell (feet)	3	6–7	5–6	5–6	3–4	2–3
Air Temp (C/F)	26/79	18/65	15/60	16/62	17/63	23/74
Water Temp (C/F)	18/64	17/62	16/60	13/55	14/57	15/59
Wetsuit	full	full	full	full	full	full
Average Sunshine p/d (hours)	8	5	3	4	6	7
Average Rain p/m (inches)	2	1–2	2	2	2	2
Average Surfable Days p/m	9	14	18	22	20	11

89. JOHANNA
Victoria, Australia

This remote section of Australia's coastline is sheer paradise to a surfer, with consistent swells from the Southern Ocean and its resulting waves, pounding on miles and miles of white sand beaches. On glassy, no-wind flat days, you can hear a pin drop at the nearby campsite, but on surf days the crashing waves are so loud, you won't be able to sleep. This headstrong beach and reef break lets you drive curvy turns, both hard and fast. It's like flicking on a trail of lights as the sun glints through glassy walls and you fly across the verticals.

Situated 50 miles southwest of Bells Beach (Spot 88) and 125 miles south of Melbourne in Otways National Park, Johanna is a superb beach break of world-class waves with peaks the length of the entire beach. These waves are formed by riptides, sandbars, and rocky reef outcrops placed just right to produce quality breaks. Johanna is a changeable spot, and famous for increasing its size without warning. Raw swells arrive from the Arctic regions and can double or triple the height of waves—from 5 to 15 feet—in just a few hours.

Johanna Beach itself is 5 miles long, with Sutherlands

> The Mella Gully Park is nearby Johanna Beach, known for its glow worms, best seen in summer. Also consider checking out the Big Tree, a huge, 300-year-old messmate eucalyptus tree measuring 27 feet in circumference.

> To stay close to the surf at Johanna Beach, you can't beat the state park campground near the beach. This is the place to stay for maximum surf. If you want some fishing as well, there are cottages to rent along the Johanna River.

Beach at the eastern end and Dinosaur Cove at the western. The area is famous for its fossils, including those of the dinosaurs that roamed here more than 150 million years ago. Aboriginal communities once hunted the coastal woodlands near Johanna Beach using fire, dingoes, and spears, but today you can bush camp near the beach and waves without fear of being trampled by wandering dinosaur.

Most visitors to Johanna are traveling south from Melbourne on the Great Ocean Road. This spectacular, scenic road provides access to plenty of surf spots worth checking out on your journey to Johanna, so allow some time for additional stops along the way. As a primer to some of the stops along the way, you'll pass Winkipop (Spot 90) and Bells Beach, Lorne, Wye River, Apollo Bay Foreshore, Glenaire, Bay of Islands, Warrnambool, Port Fairy Foreshore, Narrawong, Portland, Yellow Rock, and Bridgewater Bay Foreshore—just to name a few. Johanna is a must-surf spot for the expert. So if you're short on time, pass up some of the other spots and come here first.

Photo D. Sumpter

Johanna's a wonderful series of beach breaks on a long open beach in . . . one of the most beautiful areas of Victoria. Peaks along the beach, and a very powerful, hollow, fast-breaking beach break.

Mark Richards,
1979–1981 and 1983
World Surfing Champion

Photo D. Sumpter

Rights	Lefts	Peak	Beachbreak	S Swell	

Break: Beach break and right- and left-hand reefs

Skill Level: Intermediate to expert

Commitment: 6–10

Best Boards: Shortboard

Lifeguard: None

Hazards: Sandbars between takeoff and the shorebreak cause heavy closeout waves and side currents. Rips are powerful when the waves are overhead. Rocky outcrops.

Currency: Australian dollar.

Going There: Visa required except by Australian and New Zealand citizens. Vaccinations required except by Australian and New Zealand citizens—tetanus. Check with your doctor, health clinic, and embassy for up-to-date info.

Where to Stay: Red Johanna Holiday Apartments, +61 (0)3 5237 4238. Blue Johanna Cottages, +61 (0)3 5237 4224. Beacon Resort Holiday Park, +61 (0)3 5258 1133. The Light Keepers Inn, +61 (0)3 5289 6666. Apollo International Motel, +61 (0)3 5237 6100

Finding the Break: Traveling south from Bells Beach, follow the Great Ocean Road to Glenaire and watch out for a left turn 2 miles on, signposted JOHANNA BEACH.

Keep in Mind: Expect crowds in summer.

Months	JF	MA	MJ	JA	SO	ND
Average Swell (feet)	3	6	6	5–6	3	2
Air Temp (C/F)	26/79	18/65	15/60	16/62	63/17	23/74
Water Temp (C/F)	18/64	17/62	16/60	13/55	14/57	15/59
Wetsuit	full	full	full	full	full	full
Average Sunshine p/d (hours)	8	5	3	4	6	7
Average Rain p/m (inches)	2	1–2	2	2	2	2
Average Surfable Days p/m	9	15	18	22	20	10

90. WINKIPOP
Torquay, Victoria, Australia

The best view of Winkipop is either from under the green curl canopy, or riding down the long wall as if on a roller coaster. These bowling waves roll and peel off in a line down the point, all the way to beneath the cliff face. It's fast and furious and hectic to the very end.

Winkipop is a right-hand point wave that fits the criteria of consistent, sweet perfection mixed with gnarly cutting-edge performance. It's situated at the western end of the Great Ocean Road, which runs for 50 miles from Torquay in the north of Victoria to Johanna (Spot 89) in the south. This road is ranked as one of world's most scenic coastal drives and is certainly one of the best avenues on which to explore for quality waves.

Winkipop Bay is located next door to Bells Beach and receives the same big swells that create the world-renowned surf at Bells (Spot 88). Winkipop is below the parking area at Bells Beach with a good public access path and a short walk down the slope and cliff path to this fabulous right-hand point break.

This is one of Australia's ultimate peaks, a long-walling right point break with speed and multiple sections, each becoming faster and tighter the farther down the point you go. The length of ride on average is 200 yards to a maximum of 400 yards on a good day.

Winkipop is not for the fainthearted. It's a demanding, barreling wave with rocks, cliffs, and heavy inside sections. This is a must-surf spot for the expert.

The Great Ocean Road travels past miles of beautiful bays and beaches with huge cliffs and raging surf, all receiving the big swells from the Tasman Sea and Southern Ocean. In the summer lifeguards patrol many of the beaches along this drive, but at Winkipop you surf at your own risk. Other surf breaks close by are Torquay beach break, which is always smaller than Winkipop and considered a beginners' wave. It requires a south swell to make it work well. Lorne Point and beach break, which is fantastic on a big southwesterly swell and light northeasterly winds, is also a good alternative.

Photo R. Sumpter

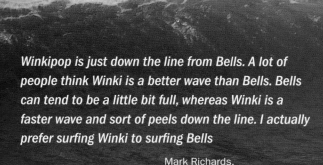

Winkipop is just down the line from Bells. A lot of people think Winki is a better wave than Bells. Bells can tend to be a little bit full, whereas Winki is a faster wave and sort of peels down the line. I actually prefer surfing Winki to surfing Bells

Mark Richards,
1979–1981 and 1983
World Surfing Champion

Photo R. Sumpter

 R.Point
 S Swell

 Shallow Reef

Break: Point break
Skill Level: Intermediate to expert
Commitment: 5–10
Best Boards: Shortboard
Lifeguard: None
Hazards: Shallow rock bottom, rocky shorebreak, steep takeoffs to fast walling waves like lightning. Narrow path from high cliffs.

Currency: Australian dollar.
Going There: Visa required except by Australian and New Zealand citizens. Vaccinations required except by Australian and New Zealand citizens—tetanus. Check with your doctor, health clinic, and embassy for up-to-date info.

Where to Stay: Cottage, +61 (0)3 5261 4010. Nomads Bells Beach Backpacker, +61 (0)3 5261 7070. Point Break Packers, +61 (0)3 5261 5105. Surf City Motel, +61 (0)3 5261 3492. Zeally Bay Caravan Park, +61 (0)3 5261 2400.
Finding the Break: Fairly easy to find. From Torquay follow the signs for the Great Ocean Road. Three miles on you'll see the Bells Beach Reserve parking area. Park here and walk the remaining 500 yards to the top of Bells Beach. Then, facing the sea, find the coastal track to your left (toward Torquay). Walk west 300 yards. This takes you to the point at Winkipop.
Keep in Mind: Summer crowds and busy weekends.

Months	JF	MA	MJ	JA	SO	ND
Average Swell (feet)	3	6–7	5–6	5–6	3–4	2–3
Air Temp (C/F)	26/79	18/65	15/60	16/62	17/63	23/74
Water Temp (C/F)	18/64	17/62	16/60	13/55	14/57	15/59
Wetsuit	full	full	full	full	full	full
Average Sunshine p/d (hours)	8	5	3	4	6	7
Average Rain p/m (inches)	2	1–2	2	2	2	2
Average Surfable Days p/m	9	14	18	24	20	12

91. OCEAN BEACH
Denmark, Western Australia

There's no time to wonder how or from where the wave sprang. It could have been that distant cyclone or the local storm in the night. But now it's pumping and it's time to go slide into the pocket, launch out, and pull in tight, face to face with the crystal maze. Check the stance and boldly go where there's space, tapping the hollow room.

Ocean Beach is situated 180 miles south of Perth and 15 miles east of Albany. It's at the entrance to Wilson's Inlet, a long sandy cape. A walk takes you out to this superb surf spot, which is a beach break as well as a famous right-hand sand point river-mouth break. Only breaking perfectly a few times a year, this is the sought-after wave in the area when it's working. On an average size swell of 3 to 4 feet, the beach break is a powerful fun wave with great left and rights peeling off over nicely shaped sandbars. When it's over 6 feet, the sand point may start to perform if the banks are right. The length of ride can be 100 to 300 yards, entering the river mouth. Sheltered from southwesterly gales and storms, it's best generally in a south to southwest swell and light northerly winds.

Bordered largely by desert to the east, Western Australia has a lot to offer by way of many more surf spots. There's Anvils Beach at the other end of Ocean Beach, with a peak left and right off sandbanks, and there's Lowlands

> The peaceful and inviting beaches and bays of the southern region happen also to be the southern right and humpback whales' choice for birthing their young year after year. The whales can be seen from shore from July to October. There are also whale-watching cruises that leave from Albany.

Beach just off Torbay Head. Dingo Beach and Muttonbird Island are all beach breaks, and Sand Patch is a reef break with lefts and rights. It is here, among granite ranges more than one million years old, that you will find some of Western Australia's best surf. This is a great coastline for surfing, suitable for beginners and experts, depending on wave size.

Western Australia covers one-third of the Australian continent, with two different climate zones—temperate to the west, and desert on the eastern border. Aboriginal tribes inhabited the area for perhaps 40,000 years. When the first Europeans visited in 1829, however, they named the township for Dr. Alexander Denmark, the first explorer of the area.

Photo R. Sumpter

It should be classed as a desert, the beach area is so big. The barrels are mostly right-handers from the river-mouth sandbar off the headland.

Rod Sumpter

Photo R. Sumpter

Rights | Beachbreak | SE Swell

Break: Beach break and river mouth
Skill Level: Beginner to expert
Commitment: 4–10
Best Boards: Shortboard

Lifeguard: In season
Hazards: Deep channels, eddies, rip current, shallow sand bottom, river-mouth
Currency: Australian dollar.

Months	JF	MA	MJ	JA	SO	ND
Average Swell (feet)	3	4	5	5–6	3–4	2–3
Air Temp (C/F)	26/80	21/70	18/65	19/66	20/68	25/78
Water Temp (C/F)	21/70	19/68	17/62	16/61	17/62	20/68
Wetsuit	none	vest	spring	spring	shorty	none
Average Sunshine p/d (hours)	10	9	6–7	5	6	10
Average Rain p/m (inches)	0	1–2	6	7	3	1
Average Surfable Days p/m	9	14	21	24	22	10

Going There: Visa required except by Australian and New Zealand citizens. Vaccinations required except by Australian and New Zealand citizens—tetanus. Check with your doctor, health clinic, and embassy for up-to-date info.
Where to Stay: Kind Park Farm B & B, +61 (0)8 9848 1147. Spring Bay Villas, +61 (0)8 9848 2456. Waterfront Motel, +61 (0)8 9848 1147. River-mouth Caravan Park, +61 (0)8 9848 1262. Gum Grove Chalets Ocean Beach, +61 (08) 9848 1378.
Keep in Mind: Rarely very crowded.

92. INDICATORS
North Island, New Zealand

It's a heart-stopping moment when you paddle out and ride your first blue-black wave and see human-sized wave trains grinding by, and wonder at the boulders resting on ledges against a jungle-covered mountain. This greater left peels off and crushes everything in its path. You either ride or get the rub. Surfboards break here on a regular basis, the waves are so strong, but for the adrenaline rush, this wave is worth it. Going one step better even than Indicators is Outer Indicators, where thunderous peaks peel on a good swell, and rip-sucking sets, like monsters, clean up.

Situated 1 mile west of Raglan (Spot 94) and 30 miles west of Hamilton is Indicators, one of New Zealand's best surf spots. This is a classic left-hand point break, located 0.25 mile west of Whale Bay. Raglan's four breaks—Indicators, Whale Bay, Manu Bay, and Wainui Beach—all share the same swells in this picturesque bay and headland setting. Raglan's top spot is known as Indies for short, and is a world-class wave set in a landscape of curving coastline that spreads out west from Raglan Harbor.

To the east is the outermost surf break called Outer Indicators, a fierce wave close to the headland that peels off well, is very gnarly, and is rarely crowded. This is a left reef point break, the most remote and wild in appearance of all the nearby surf spots, but it has days when a fine swell builds just right even if elsewhere is failing. Staying in the surf lineup is difficult, and you will need to paddle against the strong current. There are plenty of markers to line up with in order to keep in the right spot; there are a few houses, a prominent stack of boulders on the point, caves, and trees.

When you finish the ride, you have a choice: You can either take the short walk to Whale Bay Village center and follow the coastal path down through beautiful wild flora and fauna to the point, or you can paddle around to Whale Bay, a deep-water version of Raglan, with several takeoff areas. The best waves swing in from around Indicators Point, being too wide to break there. The waves then pick up on the steeply shelving rock bottom at Whale Bay and produce a fabulous left-hand clean takeoff area. This soft wave is fun and a unique feature is a big rock in the middle of the break where bystanders have a good view of which way a surfer will go around the rock. The best swell is a northwest to north, and with a light southerly to southeasterly wind. Indicators is a must for expert surfers.

With epic views, Indicators is the westernmost point on the Raglan peninsula. It has commanding views of the countryside, rivers, and mountains, and distant views of all the north coast toward Piha. There are hosts of activities to do here as well, such as kayaking, climbing, and trekking through the rain forest on numerous coastal trails.

New Zealand has about 2,300 miles of coastline, and an average of about one surf spot every 5 miles, so there's no way of getting to them all. Indicators is a good place to start.

Photo D. Sumpter

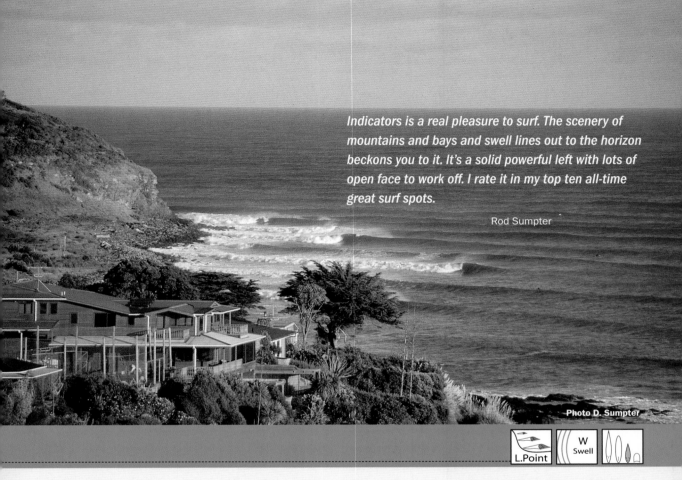

Indicators is a real pleasure to surf. The scenery of mountains and bays and swell lines out to the horizon beckons you to it. It's a solid powerful left with lots of open face to work off. I rate it in my top ten all-time great surf spots.

Rod Sumpter

Photo D. Sumpter

L.Point | W Swell

Break: Left-hand reef break

Skill Level: Intermediate to expert

Commitment: 5–10

Best Boards: Shortboard

Lifeguard: None

Hazards: Boulders in surf lineup, big gnarly waves

Currency: New Zealand dollar.

Going There: Visa required except by Australian and New Zealand citizens. Vaccinations required except by Australian and New Zealand citizens—tetanus. Check with your doctor, health clinic, and embassy for up-to-date info.

Where to Stay: Indicators Surf and Beach House, +64 (0)7 825 8818. Whale Bat Villas, +64 (0)7 825 6831. Raglan Cottages and Cabins, +64 (0)7 825 6892.

Magic Mountain Farm Lodge, +64 (0)7 825 6892. Waters Edge B & B, +64 (0)7 825 0567. Solscape Backpackers Raglan, +64 (0)7 825 8268. Campsites Raglan,+64 (0)7 866 0072. Raglan Information Center, +64 (0)7 825 0556

Finding the Break: Indicators and Raglan are situated in Waikato, on the North Island of New Zealand, approximately 20 miles west of Hamilton and 40 miles from Auckland International Airport. From Raglan's town center take Wainui Road around Raglan's coastline. One mile past Raglan is Indicators Point.

Keep in Mind: Not easy to access into the water and paddle out. Gets crowded with only a few in the lineup.

Months	JF	MA	MJ	JA	SO	ND
Average Swell (feet)	3	4	5–6	5–6	3–4	2–3
Air Temp (C/F)	24/75	20/68	13/57	15/60	17/63	20/69
Water Temp (C/F)	18/64	17/62	16/60	11/52	12/54	15/59
Wetsuit	full	full	full	full	full	full
Average Sunshine p/d (hours)	6	4–5	4	5	5	7
Average Rain p/m (inches)	8	11	13	15	12	9
Average Surfable Days p/m	8	10	12	14	12	8

93. PIHA
North Island, New Zealand

Piha's waves are like a cold piece of inky-blue glass, horse-shoe shaped, thick, and gnarly. You're more like a skate-boarder on a hard wall than a surfer at one with the waves here at Piha, a spot with continuous side rips, big holes, and blobby peaks smashing down and crushing the black sand into iron dust. You must confront this wave as the Maori warrior faces his enemy—full of power and ready for the ride of your life.

Situated among many other surf spots along the west coast on the North Island of New Zealand is Piha, home of New Zealand surfing. Piha is considered by some to be the place where it all started here back in 1956, when two Californians brought over Malibu longboards from the United States and demonstrated their skill and maneuver-ability to the local surf club members. Since then surfing at Piha has grown in popularity, and its challenging beach break has become synonymous with surfing drama. There are constant rescues—the surf can be dangerous, and all New Zealanders know that this is a break to be respected above all others.

The beach is divided in the middle by 150 yards of rock called Lion Rock, which does indeed look like a huge lion in profile, lying proudly on his very own beach. He is covered in vegetation, and you can climb to the top, gaining a spec-tacular view out to sea and the beautiful scenery of Piha. The south end is known as South Beach, and the north as Piha Beach, which is about forty minutes from the capital city of Auckland. Piha is a place of power and beauty, with a long beach of fine black iron sand and a spectacularly

rugged coastline. The beach adjoins a wildlife sanctuary and park, and is well known for its ecological beauty. The waves here can be heavy pounding curls and have gnarly closeouts as well as strong rip currents, making it best for experienced surfers only.

All levels of surfing are catered to, though, by going south to Kari Kari, a beach break with nice left and right bar-rels and a good soft wall. By going north to the Muriwai Beach, a sand-bottomed left- and right-hand break awaits surfers looking for additional options. Muriwai Beach is good for all surfers, having a slow wave ideal for beginners on the smaller days, and nice for bodyboards, longboards, and intermediate shortboards on a 3-foot-plus day.

Piha is backed by the Waitakere Range, protected park-land of subtropical forest, accessible only through numerous bush tracks. The Waitakere Range was formed around twenty million years ago by a violent volcanic upheaval be-neath the sea. The Waitakeres are home to a few well-known formations such as the pillow lavas at Maori Bay, cliffs as high as 300 feet at Mercer Bay, and Lion Rock of Piha.

The best camping is at the Piha Mota camp, which is ideally placed for surfing, walking, climbing, and fishing, and is close to the 90-foot-tall Kitkite Falls. At the bottom of the waterfall are tranquil pools of blues and greens. Journey to the mystical land of Piha Canyon and explore the historic logging dams of a hundred years ago. Piha is a thriving, albeit small beach community. The lifestyle is sim-ple and laid back, allowing surfers to enjoy the waves with-out the hassle of large crowds.

Photo D. Sumpter

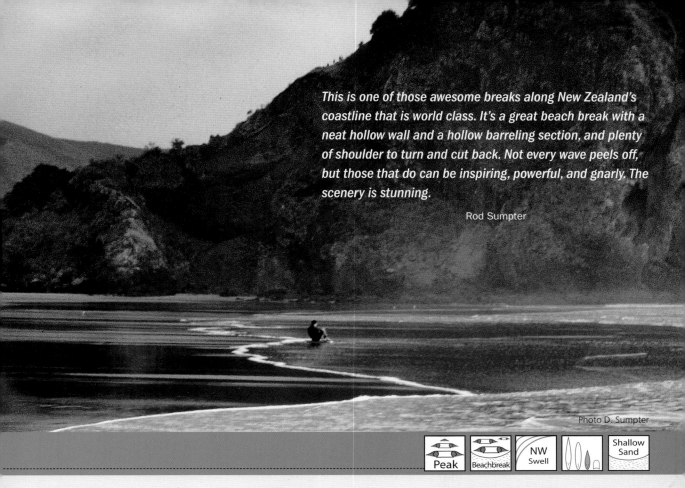

This is one of those awesome breaks along New Zealand's coastline that is world class. It's a great beach break with a neat hollow wall and a hollow barreling section, and plenty of shoulder to turn and cut back. Not every wave peels off, but those that do can be inspiring, powerful, and gnarly. The scenery is stunning.

Rod Sumpter

Photo D. Sumpter

Peak	Beachbreak	NW Swell		Shallow Sand

Break: Beach break

Skill Level: Expert

Commitment: 8–10

Best Boards: Shortboard

Lifeguard: In season, October to Easter

Hazards: Dangerous rip currents, shallow bottom, rocky outcrops, big waves. Black sand and murky water make this a tough surf spot.

Currency: New Zealand dollar.

Going There: Visa required except by Australian and New Zealand citizens. Vaccinations required except by Australian and New Zealand citizens—tetanus. Check with your doctor, health clinic, and embassy for up-to-date info.

Where to Stay: Piha Beach Valley Cabin, +64 (0)2 196 9924. Devonport Sea Cottage, +64 (0)9 445 7117. Kiwi Accommodation, +64 (0)9 812 8403. Piha Seaview Hideaway, +64 (0)9 812 8105. Piha Lodge, +64 (0)9 812 8595. Piha Camping, +64 (0)9 812 8815

Finding the Break: From the airport take the motorway toward Auckland City (Route 20). Turn left along Hillsborough Road (Route 15). Travel through Green Bay village. At the top of the hill you will come to a T-intersection. Turn right onto Titirangi Road. Once you pass through Titirangi Village shops, you will come to a roundabout with a PIHA SCENIC ROUTE sign posted. Park next to the beach.

Keep in Mind: Rarely crowded.

Months	JF	MA	MJ	JA	SO	ND
Average Swell (feet)	3	4	5–6	5–6	3–4	2–3
Air Temp (C/F)	24/75	20/68	13/57	15/60	17/63	20/69
Water Temp (C/F)	18/64	17/62	16/60	11/52	12/54	15/59
Wetsuit	full	full	full	full	full	full
Average Sunshine p/d (hours)	6	4–5	4	5	5	7
Average Rain p/m (inches)	8	11	13	15	12	9
Average Surfable Days p/m	10	14	18	22	19	16

94. RAGLAN
North Island, New Zealand

With a Maori warrior's face you launch into the towering inferno of a boiling Raglan wave. There's only seconds between you and dry rock. These waves have a habit of eating surfers alive and spreading their bodies and boards on the reef, like a pod of beached whales.

Situated 30 miles west of Hamilton and 1 mile east of Indicators (Spot 92), Raglan is a classic series of left-hand reef breaks. The breaks—Indicators, Whale Bay, Manu Bay, and Wainui Beach—all form the area known as Raglan. The coastal town has a population of 3,200 in winter, a number that swells enormously during the summer months as this popular resort town welcomes vacationers and beach lovers. Surfers here in Raglan are treated with plenty of health food restaurants and all the respect they deserve, including one place with tables made from broken surfboards.

Point Manu has got to be Raglan's most surfed wave—a left point break made famous in the film *Endless Summer* for having waves so long, "You surf all day and almost fall asleep while riding." It's an easy, lazy wave, at times caressing you back to the beach. But don't be fooled. At times it's also a pumping handful, a steaming, grinding 6-to-8-foot-plus barreling beast. There's a tight section called the Ledge, often with twelve lines to a set and a 0.5-mile ride as the norm. The beach break of Wainui Beach is also excellent in the right swell for all grades of surfers, at times somewhat fickle but good with a light southeast offshore wind, giving a left and right peak. This is the first beach you view as you travel out to the breaks from Raglan Harbor.

Raglan is a small, friendly town bustling with tourists, lots of places to stay, and nearby camping. With lots of surf shops and plenty of restaurants, Raglan is a haven for surfing backpackers. The surroundings are lush and green, and the coastline picturesque.

The written record of Raglan's history goes back to 1841, when the area was named for Lord Raglan, who led the charge of the Light Brigade in the Crimean War. But Raglan's history can go back 1,000 years, all the way to the Maori people known as the Moa hunters. The Maoris traveled far and wide throughout the Pacific, and they probably surfed the waves as the early Hawaiians did. Raglan is ideal for all beginners and intermediates on the right day, but it's mostly the experts' surf destination.

Photo D. Sumpter

Raglan is my favorite wave in the Southern Hemisphere. It's an unbelievable wave, a mega surf area for waves, a serious surf spot. It's an honor to surf here with such nice people and scenery.

Rod Sumpter

Photo D. Sumpter

L.Point | NW Swell | Shallow Reef

Break: Left-hand point break

Skill Level: Intermediate to expert

Commitment: 5–10

Best Boards: Shortboard

Lifeguard: None

Hazards: Rips and currents. Rocks litter the surf lineup. Waves peel off into shallow platform ledge at takeoff and make for a dangerous drop-in. The wall spreads out wider past the rocky point as you ride.

Currency: New Zealand dollar.

Going There: Visa required except by Australian and New Zealand citizens. Vaccinations required except by Australian and New Zealand citizens—tetanus. Check with your doctor, health clinic, and embassy for up-to-date info.

Where to Stay: Raglan Cottages and Cabins, +64 (0)7 825 6892. Magic Mountain Farm Lodge, +64 (0)7 825 6892. Waters Edge B&B, +64 (0)7 825 0567. Solscape Backpackers Raglan, +64 (0)7 825 8268. Campsites Raglan, +64 (0)7 866 0072. Raglan Information Center +64 (0)7 825 0556

Finding the Break: Raglan is situated in Waikato, on the North Island of New Zealand, and is approximately 20 miles west from Hamilton and 40 miles from Auckland International Airport. From Raglan's town center take Wainui Road 1.5 miles to the Raglan parking area

Surf School: Raglan Surfing School, +64 (0)7 825 7873.

Keep in Mind: Crowded when the word gets out there's surf over 6 feet.

Months	JF	MA	MJ	JA	SO	ND
Average Swell (feet)	2	4	5–6	5–6	3–4	2–3
Air Temp (C/F)	24/75	20/68	13/57	15/60	17/63	20/69
Water Temp (C/F)	18/64	17/62	16/60	11/52	12/54	15/59
Wetsuit	full	full	full	full	full	full
Average Sunshine p/d (hours)	6	4–5	4	5	5	7
Average Rain p/m (inches)	8	11	13	15	12	9
Average Surfable Days p/m	7	10	14	16	15	10

95. TAVARUA ISLAND
Fiji

Through the early-morning mist you can hear the barrels and feel the motion as your guide pulls alongside another boat. A big barrel zooms by in the distance and you hear a savage roar like a beast from hell, a *hiss-bang* sound as it crashes the inside reef. The mist begins to lift, and the sound of the sea becomes louder as flume-filled funnels hiss and bear down on the tiny craft. Your pulse races as pipelines of waves blow and whistle. With a little paddle, you're out to the takeoff area and off on the smoothest rides on the cleanest waves in the world. No doubt, a little *"Yahoo!"* is in order when your feet retouch the board, the spray engulfs your space. On your umpteenth wave you make it, once again, to the channel alive.

Situated approximately 20 miles southwest of Fiji's international airport in Nadi, Tavarua and myriad of other islands make up what is called Fiji. There are more than 800 islands in all—100 of them uninhabited—with hundreds of places to surf.

Of all of Fiji's offshore coral reefs and islands, the main island of Viti Levu is the best place to get started. The king of the surf spots, however, is quite possibly Tavarua Island, a resort surf break containing the fabulous breaks of Restaurants and Cloudbreak. Both classic left-hand breaks contain pure power from the Pacific Ocean's deep blue water. Their perfectly shaped waves run down the coral reefs one after another. Both breaks work best in swells from 4 to 12 feet and bigger.

Tavarua Island Resort is expensive, but many say it's worth the $200-a-day tab for perfect waves with guides, boats, and everything else a surfer may need for an ideal vacation. There are plenty of less expensive hotels on Fiji, but discovering your own break with your own guide and a boat packed with lunch can be a lot of fun.

Even though you might be entranced by the thunderous barrels at Tavarua, there's always this nagging suspicion that just around the corner at another nearby island another coral reef may be breaking better. This area heralds a fantastic variety of quality waves of all shapes and sizes, and your suspicions may be right. The uniqueness in the strength and speed of Fiji's waves is the direct result of swells engaging steeply sloping coral reefs and then dispersing quickly.

While most of the well-known breaks are on or near the large island of Viti Levu, access often requires a boat—or a very long paddle out (as much as 5 miles!). Boat trips are from the Pacific Harbor on Viti Levu, and take you 5 miles out to sea with a guide. Once you've made the trip out here, you will come upon the legendary near shore. Frigate Pass, known locally as one of the best waves in Fiji, is just 0.5 miles from shore. This is a long left-hander with barrel sections for 300 yards, as it wraps around the reef with perfectly uniform waves. An exciting adrenaline feast even before you paddle out.

To find a beach break on Viti Levu, you must head west along Queens Highway from Nadi until you reach Sigatoka, home of the largest sand dunes in the South Pacific. This is Fiji's only consistent beach break. At the mouth of the Sigatoka River, sandbars form waves that break as well-lined-up peaks on small days. When the swell gets into the 6-to-8-foot range, all the peaks straighten out, creating a single left and right.

The south side of Viti Levu is called the Coral Coast as well as the Soft Coral Capital of the World because of the huge number and variety of corals that live here. They attract a host of tropical fish, including some thirty-five species of angelfish. Snorkling and diving are therefore very popular, and scuba diving schools abound. For about $50 a day, you can dive or surf the Frigate Pass, leaving from the Batiluva Beach Resort. This resort is just one of many nestled among the palm trees at the foot of the mountains.

Off the south coast of Viti Levu is the island of Nagagia, which has excellent reef surf at Cape Washington. One of the best breaks here is called King Kong Left after the 1935 movie that was made here, at nearby Mount Nabukelevuira.

Photo © ASP Tostee

Tavarua Island is supersick. I like Restaurants, one of my favorite waves. It's probably one of the most perfect waves in the world. Just wave for wave, every wave is exactly the same. I call it in the top three surf spots in the world

Andy Irons,
2002–2003 World Surfing
Champion

Photo © ASP Tostee

L.Point | SW Swell | Shallow Reef

Break: Left-hand reef break
Skill Level: Expert
Commitment: 7–10
Best Boards: Shortboard to 8-foot, 11-inch gun
Lifeguard: None; boats for support only
Hazards: Reefs and boats make dangerous conditions when surf is double overhead.
Currency: Fijian dollar
Getting There: Visa not required by U.S., Canadian, Australian, British, and Japanese citizens. EU citizens require visas. Vaccinations required: Hepatitis A, typhoid, tetanus, polio. Check with your doctor, health clinic, and embassy for latest info.
Where to Stay: Tavarua Island Resort, +679 6706 513. Surfing Fiji Adventures, +679 923 230. Namotu Island Blue Water Sports Resort, +679 706 439. Penners Surf Camp, +679 3450 801. Marlin Bay Resort, +679 3304 042. Club Masa Surf Camp, +679 925 717. Surfing Fiji, +679 9923 230. Sea Cove, Momi Bay, +679 706 100. Magic Island-Tavarua Tours, +679 723 883. Yanuca Island Surf Camp, +679 9924 368. Mothership Charter Company, surf trips on a 58-foot ketch, +679 651 136. The Surf & Dive Rendezvous, +679 651 057. Rendezvous Resort, surf boat trips daily with lifeguard, +679 6510 571; cell +679 9933 065.
Finding the Break: From the Nadi airport take public transport to Tavarua or a surf tour to include it. Tavarua Island is approximately twenty minutes by ferryboat from the nearest boat landing at Uciwai. Travel times to the landing are approximately twenty minutes from Nadi and two hours from Suva by road.
Contest: Quicksilver Pro (WCT), June.
Keep in Mind: Crowded during June and July.

Months	JF	MA	MJ	JA	SO	ND
Average Swell (feet)	4	5	6	7	6	4–5
Air Temp (C/F)	31/89	30/87	29/85	28/84	29/85	31/88
Water Temp (C/F)	28/82	28/82	27/81	26/79	25/77	27/81
Wetsuit	none	none	none	none	none	none
Average Sunshine p/d (hours)	7	6	7	7	7	7
Average Rain p/m (inches)	3	2	3	2	2	3
Average Surfable Days p/m	5	6	20	23	12	7

96. TEAHUPOO
Tahiti

The mother of all tubes. The heaviest waves on the planet. These are just a couple of phrases that not only will make your pulse race, but are frequently used to describe this Pacific gem. Even the champions get scared of this place, so awesome are its waves, so thick is its lip. The sets seem to boil on the horizon line, the reef sucks dry, and you're in a boat with a guide who's saying a prayer.

Situated slap-bang in the middle of the Pacific Ocean, Teahupoo (pronounced *cho-pu*) is an unspoiled village on the small peninsula of the island of Tahiti, also known as Tahiti-Iti, meaning "little Tahiti." Tahiti is shaped like a figure-eight, and Teahupoo is on the northwest tip of the lower bulge, 20 miles south of Faa'a International Airport.

Tahiti is part of French Polynesia, the name given to the group of islands that includes Bora Bora, Taha'a, and others numbering more than 116 islands and atolls in all. The island of Tahiti is the largest. Set deep in the South Pacific, this is an ideal surfing spot with internationally renowned waves of the Havae Pass at Teahupoo. This gives perfect lefts off a reef that runs into the Havae Pass channel. This ultrafantastic break is a long walling wave with a steep drop-in and a U-shaped wave face that makes it unique. It starts off as a hair-raising speed wall and ends in a giant barrel. Surfers brave enough to take on these waves need to tuck under the lip and out onto a shoulder for the safety of the channel if they hope to survive.

It's a fifteen- to twenty-minute paddle out from land, or an easy paddle out if dropped off by boat in the Havae Passage. Surfing here is a matter of size; its danger varies depending on the height of its waves. The bigger it gets, the thicker and heavier its lip, and the scarier it is to surf. There

is a smaller beach break near the town of Pueu, which is good for beginners visiting Tahiti for the first time and hoping to go home alive. Other surf spots include, traveling clockwise around the island, Vairao, a left break off a coral reef; and Papara, a right and left beach break where local surf championships are held annually. There's Maraa, a left coral reef break; Sapinus, which is both reef and beach breaks; and Taapuna, a left off a coral reef. Papeete Harbor has a right and left off coral reefs, and Papeete is where most surf shops are to be found. La Fayatte is a right and left beach break, while Papenoo has a right and left off a river mouth and a beach break. All of these breaks aside, however, Teahupoo is simply a must-see surf spot, ideal for the advanced surfer to big wave rider and for the beginner to stand aside and watch.

The picture-perfect tropical island of Tahiti is the surfing definition of paradise. The town of Papeete is at the foot of Mount Aora, the highest peak on Tahiti, at 6,800 feet.

The excellent waves must have been noticed by Captain James Cook, when, upon his return from an earlier trip to the islands in 1777, he described how a Tahitian caught waves with an outrigger canoe just for the fun of it. "On walking one day about Matavai Point, where our tents were erected, I saw a man paddling in a small canoe so quickly and looking about him with such eagerness on each side, as to command all my attention. He went out from the shore till he was near the place where the swell begins to take its rise and, watching its first motion very attentively, paddled before it with great quickness, till he found it overtook him, and had acquired sufficient force to carry his canoe before it without passing underneath. He then sat motionless and was carried along at the same swift rate as the wave, till it landed him upon the beach. Then he started out, emptied his canoe, and went in search of another swell. I could not help but conclude that this man felt the most supreme pleasure while he was driven on so fast and so smoothly by the sea."

Captain Cook first came to the islands in 1769 and made special note of the "Timorodee dance" performed for him by the Tahitians, a dance still enjoyed today by the island's many tourists. Others come to buy the cultured black pearls that French Polynesia is famous for. These islands are the largest producers of these pearls in the world. Visitors can see them grown in the lagoons at Tuamoto.

Photo Harper Maddox

*Some of the heaviest and biggest South Pacific waves break
here. It may look like a barrel of fun, but it's shallow, and
thick-crunching-lips-onto-the-reef is the order of the day.*

Rod Sumpter

Photo © ASP Tostee

Lefts | L.Point | SW Swell | Shallow Reef

Break: Reef break

Skill Level: Expert

Commitment: 10–10

Best Boards: Shortboard; up to 11-foot gun

Lifeguard: None

Hazards: On small days, up to head high, there is enough face to work running over a shallow reef, but as the swell gets bigger the waves get thicker and Teahupoo becomes a place to fulfill your surfing death wish. Extreme double-up waves drying out off flat coral ledges cause dramatic tubes in four to six times overhead waves.

Currency: French Pacific franc.

Going There: Visa required by all except British and Irish passport holders and bona fide foreign tourists for stays of less than twenty-one days. Check your embassy for up-to-date info. Vaccinations required—polio, tetanus, typhoid, hepatitis A. Check with your doctor, health clinic, and embassy.

Where to Stay: Outrigger Hotel Tahiti, Papeete, reservation@outrigger.pf. Relais Fenua Tahiti, maroto@mail.pf. Tahiti Beachcomber Parkroyal, Papeete airport, tahiti@parkroyal.pf. Le Meridien Tahiti, sales@lemeridien-tahiti.com. Taaroa Lodge Tahiti, taaroalodge@hotmail.com. Moana Surf Tours, moanasurftours@mail.pf

Finding the Break: From Tahiti's Faa'a International Airport near Papeete to Tahiti-Iti takes ninety minutes of drive time. The largest town you pass through is Taravao. The south coast road ends at the town of Teahupoo.

Contest: Billabong Championships (WCT), May.

Keep in Mind: Crowds in May. The best waves are during the dry season, May through October. There are basically two surf seasons in Tahiti: From October through March, the summer swell is from the north; from April through September, swell from the south in winter.

Months	JF	MA	MJ	JA	SO	ND
Average Swell (feet)	4	5	6	7	6	4-5
Air Temp (C/F)	31/87	31/87	29/85	28/84	29/83	29/85
Water Temp (C/F)	28/82	28/82	27/81	26/79	25/77	26/79
Wetsuit	none	none	none	none	none	none
Average Sunshine p/d (hours)	7	6	7	8	8	7
Average Rain p/m (inches)	12	6	4	2	2	8
Average Surfable Days p/m	4	5	21	19	14	6

97. NIIJIMA ISLAND
Japan

Big slabs of sea break like thunder, echoing the thud of sumo wrestlers, huge and powerful, naked and raw. Surfers scream across the waves, etching the shape of the samurai sword in their wake. This is the land of the rising sun, and a place where you'll offer your head to some of the heaviest beach breaks in the world.

Situated 100 miles south of the main island of Japan are the five islands known as the Izu Islands. Niijima is the second largest in the chain and is just eight hours by ferry from Tokyo. Measuring 9 miles long and 3 miles wide, Niijima has the relaxed atmosphere of a secluded resort with friendly people and many wonderful places to stay. This is wave riders' destination of choice for getting away from the busy Tokyo scene.

Niijima's surf is primarily on its east and west coasts. Its east coast has long white sand beaches that produce some of the best barrels in Japan, attracting surfers from all over the world to compete. The waves are powerful, and the point surf can be demanding. But the beach breaks usually have nice sandbars from February to May, making this the best time of year to visit. The point surf can be amazing, big and powerful, but only for experts. On the island's west

One of the first surfers to explore and ride the four corners of Japan's waves was Dougie Osaka, using American boards from "Bing" imported from California. In 1965 he rode Kanagawa reefs and developed a unique surfing style, similar to what Bruce Lee was doing with martial arts—a crouching stance to tube-ride and a flexible arching back to trim, with hand and arm held rigid between poses. Japan's culture has given Japanese surfers an awareness and knowledge of the surfer's best positioning. It almost seems natural for them to surf instantly with style.

coast there are also some popular surf spots, such as Herishita. Unfortunately, with the swell being much smaller here, long flat spells are possible.

Surfers have discovered a number of great Japanese surf locations since Western surfers introduced the sport to the land of the rising sun in the early 1960s; Shizuoka, Shonan, and Chiba are very popular today. These surf spots are just 20 miles south from Tokyo center, on the Chiba peninsula; they are best at low tide, and have a 6-foot tidal change. These dark sandy beaches have some good beach breaks all around the peninsula. They can be flat a lot of the time, especially in summer, so the springtime is the best for consistent waves and warmish water. In winter when the water temperature is cold enough for boots and gloves, there is the chance of a typhoon tracking past in the right path, and the swell will pump heavy waves and barrels onto the beaches. At other times the predominant winter swell will be an average of 4 to 5 feet, usually formed from low-pressure systems generating strong winds in January and February. Another good break is Kanagawa, which is ten miles southwest of Tokyo with some good beach breaks and reef points, which pick up frequent glassy 4-foot swells, being protected in the bay from onshore winds, and peel off nicely. Niijima is an ideal get-away-from-it-all surfing destination for the intermediate to expert surfer.

Photo R. Sumpter

A beauty spot with big cliffs, very unusual, nice clear water, white sands, overhead barrels and short sections, a high-performance wave.

John Sumpter,
1997 Ligger Bay Surfing Champion

Photo R. Sumpter

Peak	Beachbreak	S Swell	SW Swell		Shallow Sand

Break: Beach break, left- and right-hand point breaks

Skill Level: Beginner to expert

Commitment: 5–10

Best Boards: Shortboard

Lifeguard: None

Hazards: Sand bottom. Waves punch deep so duck diving is no escape from the impact zone. Surf double overhead becomes almost unsurfable due to the boiling break zone.

Currency: Yen.

Going There: Visa required by U.S., Canadian, Australian, EU citizens, and all others, except Austria, Germany, Ireland, UK, Mexico, Liechtenstein, and Switzerland. Vaccinations required. Check with your doctor, health clinic, and embassy for up-to-date info.

Where to Stay: Call the Niijima Tourist Association +81 (0)4 9925 0048) to make a reservation. Niijima Hotel has *fujiya ryokan,* or Japanese-style rooms. Call +81 (0)4 9925 0174 or +81 (0)4 9925 1338. Japan Youth Hostels, www.jyh.or.jp/english/index.html

Finding the Break: Direct ferry from Tokyo during July and August, a distance of 200 miles, taking eight hours' sailing time, into Niijimi harbor.

Keep in Mind: Rarely crowded.

For More Information: Japan Travel/Sport Information, +81(0)8 822 4800 (toll free).

Months	JF	MA	MJ	JA	SO	ND
Average Swell (feet)	2	3–4	5	6	3–4	2–3
Air Temp (C/F)	26/80	21/70	18/65	19/66	20/68	16/79
Water Temp (C/F)	21/70	19/68	17/62	16/61	17/62	18/68
Wetsuit	none	shorty	spring	spring	shorty	none
Average Sunshine p/d (hours)	5–6	5	6	4	6	4–5
Average Rain p/m (inches)	2	3	5	5	8	3
Average Surfable Days p/m	16	17	18	20	15	14

98. ULUWATU
Bali, Indonesia

When you're paddling out through early-morning mist, you can just see those green-eyed demons on the outer reef. Another set breaks, the oncoming monsters roar past, and you're paddling hard, breaking the glass. In the distant haze the swell is rising and falling, the spirits of the sea surface and dive, sending you some of the best pumping barrels in the world.

Bali's volcanic reef-fringed coastline has made this island one of the great surfing meccas of the world. Bali is situated east of the island of Java. Uluwatu is 8 miles south of Bali's resort town of Kuta and 13 miles south of the capital city of Denpasar. Located on the western side of the Bukit peninsula, it is blessed with perfect surf conditions on both shorelines from April to October when the southeast trade winds blow. From November to March the winds blow from the northwest, so Sanur and Nusa Dua are still surfable.

Uluwatu is just a twenty-minute drive south from Bali's Ngurah Rai International Airport. To actually get to the waves from the roadside at Uluwatu involves a fifteen-minute walk down winding tropical paths, past monuments, T-shirt sellers, monkeys, insects, and very steep steps. You follow the path through thick vegetation and on to the hilltop. And then, there it is—a panoramic view of the perfect left below. To the surf you go, down through alleyways of coral and out through a cave to a coral lagoon. Then, in front of a cliff, a lovely 4-to-8-foot left-hand wave peels off just yards away from the cave entry point. Once out, the wave has a hollow walling section. Surfing past cliff faces and jagged pinnacles, carving turns and speeding through the sections is amazing, a long ride on a good day.

There are many famous surfing breaks along this stretch

> *Segara* means "the god of the sea," and the Island of the Gods means Bali. What a classic surf zone it is.

of coast, including Kuta Reefs, Dreamland, Impossible, and Padang Padang. This is simply the best coast for surfing. But let's not forget the east coast breaks of Nusa Dua, Sanur, and Lembongan. Remember that the coral is sharp and dangerous, and nearly all the breaks are reefs that are best surfed by experts only. With other islands nearby, this is an uncharted area for potential surf that can only be tapped and explored by speedboat or yacht. Other known breaks to head for include G-Land, Desert Point, Lombok, Scar Reef, and Medewi, a classic left in the northwest of Bali. Charter boats can be hired from Benar Harbor, Bali.

American Bob Koke, cofounder of one of Kuta's first hotels, is said to have started the surfing craze in 1936. He learned to surf in Hawaii then taught his staff here. He then began to build his own boards. The late 1960s saw the first boom in Australian surfers, and in 1980 the first international pro surf contest was held here.

Bali is a mix of tourist towns, nightclubs, and bars, all living alongside a culture steeped in the Hindu religion. The cheerful locals, warm weather, and good surf make for throngs of happy backpackers. Accommodations range from cheap hostels to huge spa resorts set in lush semi-jungle.

Photo D. Sumpter

I went out and just surfed for about half an hour by myself. I came in and the captain of the boat said, "It's the first time anyone ever surfed it." So he gave me the pleasure of naming it. I called it Road Rules.

Joel Parkinson,
2001 World Junior
Surfing Champion

Photo D. Sumpter

L.Point | SW Swell | Shallow Reef

Break: Left-hand reef break

Skill Level: Intermediate to expert

Commitment: 7–10

Best Boards: Shortboard

Lifeguard: None

Hazards: Sweep undertow and currents. Lagoon paddle over razor sharp coral to a heavy power house grinding left, which will flatten anyone in its path when double overhead. Steep path through coral to bays, rock pools, gullies, caves, and cliffs.

Currency: Rupiahs (RP).

Going There: No visa is required by U.S., Canadian, Australian, British, and Japanese citizens. EU citizens require a visa. Vaccinations required—hepatitis A, typhoid, tetanus, polio, malaria,

tuberculosis (children only). Check with your doctor, health clinic, and embassy for up-to-date info.

Where to Stay: Warning: since the Kuta, Bali bombing of October 2002, peace and paradise have been shattered. Check with your embassy for the latest advice before traveling. Neither the publisher nor the author accept any responsibility for accident, injury, or death from the information within this book. Bali Hyatt, +62 361 288271. The Grand Bali Beach, +62 361 288511, or fax +62 361 287917. Diwangkara Beach Hotel, +62 361 288577, or fax +62 361 288894. Intercontinental Resort, +62 361 701888. Kuta Bungalow Hotel, +62

361 08123 914438. Easy Rider Tours Bali, +62 361 289 023; +62 361 286 008. For cheaper family-run accommodations search the following Web sites and then e-mail questions directly to the owners: www.balicheap accommodation.com, www.Bootssn All.com, www.holidaycity.com, or e-mail wigman@xs4all.nl

Finding the Break: Your first real taste of Bali begins the moment you venture out through the Denpasar airport doors and become quickly bombarded by drivers yelling "Transport!" (Taxis are cheap.) Twenty minutes north from the airport is the extremely touristy town of Kuta with no fewer than twenty surf shops. If you head south down to the Bukit peninsula, you'll end up at Uluwatu and some of the best surf breaks on Bali. The trip is over bumpy sealed roads, forty minutes from Kuta.

Keep in Mind: Crowds during the dry season, June to September

Surf Schools: Cheyne Horan School of Surfing, 0361 735858. Bali Adventure Tour Lessons, 0361 721480.

Months	JF	MA	MJ	JA	SO	ND
Average Swell (feet)	4	6	7	6–8	5–6	5
Air Temp (C/F)	30/86	29/84	31/88	31/88	30/86	29/84
Water Temp (C/F)	29/84	28/82	28/82	27/81	27/81	29/84
Wetsuit	none	none	none	none	none	none
Average Sunshine p/d (hours)	5	7	8	9	10	7
Average Rain p/m (inches)	9	5	2	0	1	6
Average Surfable Days p/m	9	10	21	24	18	10